fun with the family

Virginia

Praise for the *Fun with the Family* series

"Enables parents to turn family travel into an exploration."
—Alexandra Kennedy, Editor, *Family Fun*

"Bound to lead you and your kids to fun-filled days, those times
that help compose the memories of childhood."
—Dorothy Jordon, *Family Travel Times*

Help Us Keep This Guide Up to Date

We would love to hear from you concerning your experiences with this guide and how you feel it could be improved and kept up to date. Please send your comments and suggestions to:

editorial@GlobePequot.com

Thanks for your input, and happy travels!

fun with the family

Virginia

hundreds of ideas for day trips with the kids

Eighth Edition

Candyce H. Stapen

gpp®

travel

Guilford, Connecticut

All the information in this guidebook is subject to change. We recommend that you call ahead to obtain current information before traveling.

To buy books in quantity for corporate use or incentives, call **(800) 962-0973** or e-mail **premiums@GlobePequot.com**.

Editor: Amy Lyons
Project Editor: Lynn Zelem
Layout: Joanna Beyer
Text Design: Nancy Freeborn and Linda R. Loiewski
Maps: Rusty Nelson © Morris Book Publishing, LLC
Spot photography throughout © Photodisc and © RubberBall Productions

ISSN 1540-4366
ISBN 978-0-7627-5725-1

Printed in the United States of America
10 9 8 7 6 5 4 3 2 1

Contents

About the Author

Candyce H. Stapen has written more than 2,200 articles on family travel. She is a contributing editor to Family Vacation Critic.com and the Adventure Living travel editor for BellaOnline.com. Her articles appear in many outlets, including *Continental* magazine, FamilyVacationCritic.com, Away.com, *Caribbean Travel and Life,* the *Miami Herald,* the *New York Post, National Geographic Traveler,* and many other publications. The award-winning travel journalist has written 29 books, including two for *National Geographic Guide,* as well as a series of family trip apps for iPhones: FamilyiTrips. Her Web site is www.gfvac.com.

Dedication

To my favorite traveling companions, Alissa, Matt, and David.

Acknowledgments

I want to thank Virginia Myers and Anna-Siân Eigen for their valuable assistance in updating this volume.

Introduction

Virginia has much to offer families. Historic towns, plantations, battlefields, scenic drives through softly curving mountains, bustling beaches, quiet wildlife sanctuaries, luxurious resorts, and wild roller coasters are just some of Virginia's charms.

To get the most out of this book, use it to help plan explorations for your family. First, select a region of the state that appeals to you. Then thumb through the corresponding section of the book to find attractions that match your interests. Next chart your itinerary, including only the stops you choose. You can splurge on an upscale resort that features children's programs and golf or travel on a more conservative budget by lodging at family-friendly bed-and-breakfast inns and moderately priced motels. Be sure to underplan to allow time for serendipitous discoveries and to take advantage of Virginia's numerous parks and open spaces. Plan to revisit a region you enjoy to follow different fancies and explore new sites.

Each region of the state has its own allure. The Shenandoah Valley stretches for some 200 miles between the Blue Ridge and Allegheny mountain ranges and offers some of the state's most spectacular countryside made of craggy mountain peaks and rolling farmland. The underground wonderland known as Luray Caverns offers the chance to see fantastical formations of stalactites and stalagmites.

The Shenandoah region is rich in history. At Washington and Lee University in Lexington you can see Robert E. Lee's office just as it was on the day he died. At Staunton's Museum of the American Frontier, the farmsteads reveal the customs of the area's early immigrant pioneers. Lexington also gives you a taste for one of Virginia's other passions: horses. If your kids love *Black Beauty* and dream of riding like the wind, take them to see the thoroughbreds at the multimillion-dollar Virginia Horse Center.

Tidewater Virginia takes you back to 1607 and the days of Jamestown's first settlers. The plantations along the James River reflect the pomp and the pleasures that came with life in the prosperous New World. Colonial Williamsburg affords a more detailed glimpse of our nation's fledgling years. Walk along the cobbled streets and you can almost feel the presence of George Washington and hear the fiery words of Patrick Henry.

Hampton offers the saga of different kinds of American pioneers. The Virginia Air and Space Center details the history of the astronauts and the American space program. The Mariner's Museum in Newport News displays ship models, figureheads, and a small craft collection that runs the gamut from a gondola to a Chinese sampan. In Norfolk you can tour the naval base and experience hands-on high-tech naval encounters at Norfolk's Nauticus. Be sure to stop over in Virginia Beach, a bustling ocean town.

In Alexandria, Northern Virginia's historic and once bustling seaport, visit the Torpedo Factory, a renovated World War II plant that once assembled torpedoes but now houses the studios of some of the region's noted potters, jewelers, weavers, and photographers.

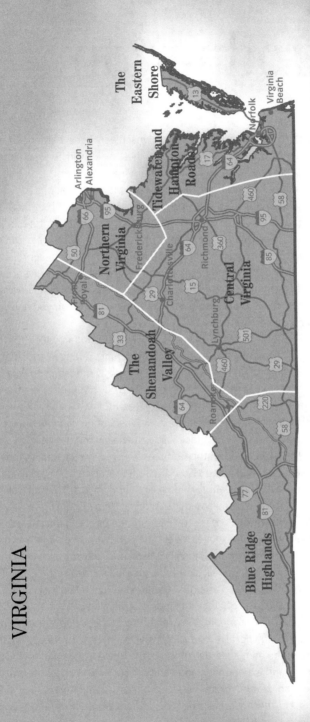

Arlington National Cemetery, resting place of John F. Kennedy and the Unknown Soldier, is not far from Alexandria. Civil War buffs won't want to miss the battlefields of Fredericksburg, Chancelorsville, and Manassas. If you are in the area on a clear summer night, pack a picnic and head for Wolf Trap National Park for the Performing Arts. Kids enjoy exploring the grounds and listening to outdoor concerts.

Virginia's Eastern Shore, a popular getaway for Washingtonians, offers a relaxing escape. A hike along Assateague Island National Seashore treats you to a wild beach, a loblolly pine forest, and marshes. You might see white-tailed deer, snow geese, and the island's famous wild ponies. Towns like Onancock continue a fishing tradition that dates from the 17th century.

Central Virginia offers families a wide variety of attractions. In Charlottesville you can tour Monticello, Thomas Jefferson's home. You sense his revolutionary vision and his love of the Piedmont's rolling hills. Richmond glitters with a large collection of Fabergé jewels housed at the Virginia Museum of Fine Arts. For pure escapist pleasure head to the movie-themed fun of Kings Dominion. Older kids get their thrills on roller coasters, while younger tots play with such favorite pals as Yogi Bear and Fred Flintstone at Hanna–Barbera Land.

The Blue Ridge Highlands serve up down-to-earth simplicity. As you drive backcountry roads, take time to hike to a waterfall, skip rocks in the streams, walk through the pine groves of Cumberland Gap National Historic Park, and fish for pike in the 108-acre lake of Hungry Mother State Park.

Whatever your changing fancy, Virginia offers great family vacations. Enjoy the pleasure of each other's company as you embark on these family adventures.

INFORMATION CENTERS AND RESOURCES

Information centers and resources that apply to just one region are included within the pertinent chapter. Here are some additional resources that are helpful in planning:

Virginia Tourism Corporation: (804) 786-2051; www.vatc.org or www.virginia.org.

Virginia Disabilities Guide, Virginia Tourism Corporation: (804) 633-6752 or (804) 786-2051; www.virginia.org.

Virginia State Park Reservation system for cabins and campgrounds: (800) 933-7275.

Virginia State Parks Web site: www.dcr.virginia.gov.

Skiing information: (800) THE-SNOW; www.virginia.org.

Virginia Department of Game and Inland Fisheries: 4010 West Broad St., Richmond, VA 23230-1104; (804) 367-1000; www.dgif.state.va.us. Provides information on where to find what kinds of fish. Helpful for anglers and snorkelers.

RATES USED IN THIS GUIDE

Rates for places to stay and eat, as well as attraction admission prices, are represented with dollar signs and offer a sense of the price ranges at press time.

Rates for Accommodations

$	up to $100
$$	$101 to $150
$$$	$151 to $249
$$$$	$250 and up

Rates for Attractions

$	up to $10 adult
$$	$11 to $25 adult
$$$	$26 and up adult

Rates for Restaurants

$	most entrees under $12
$$	most $12 to $18
$$$	most $19 to $29
$$$$	most $30 or more

Attractions Key

The following is a key to the icons found throughout the text.

SWIMMING		**FOOD**	
BOATING/BOAT TOUR		**LODGING**	
HISTORIC SITE		**CAMPING**	
HIKING/WALKING		**MUSEUM**	
FISHING		**PERFORMING ARTS**	
BIKING		**SPORTS/ATHLETICS**	
AMUSEMENT PARK		**PICNICKING**	
HORSEBACK RIDING		**PLAYGROUND**	
SKIING/WINTER SPORTS		**SHOPPING**	
PARK		**PLANTS/GARDENS/NATURE TRAILS**	
ANIMAL VIEWING		**FARM**	

The Shenandoah Valley

The Shenandoah Valley stretches for some 200 miles between the Blue Ridge and Allegheny mountain ranges in northwest Virginia. The scenic mountains and valleys make this region one of the most beautiful in the East. In the valley towns, visitors can enjoy an array of country culture as down-home and as lively as apple blossom festivals, bluegrass concerts, and square dances and as unique as Staunton's presidential museum and historic farmsteads.

The Shenandoah Valley boasts another ingredient vital for a family vacation destination: an abundance of recreational opportunities. Hike along park trails where tree branches form lush canopies. Go underground to explore the eerie and awesome formations found in water-carved limestone caverns. Enjoy the pastoral views of ridges and valleys offered by the 105-mile Skyline Drive, which runs along the mountains' crests the entire length of Shenandoah National Park. Both this and the Blue Ridge Parkway offer splendid vistas; in fall they turn into glorious, although crowded, leaf-peeping routes.

This trip through the Shenandoah Valley begins about 18 miles north of the beginning of Skyline Drive in Winchester and leads through Middletown to Front Royal, a gateway for the Shenandoah National Park. Towns near Skyline Drive include Luray, New Market, Staunton, Lexington, and Roanoke. Strasburg and Natural Bridge are nearby and make for

TopPicks in the Shenandoah Valley Area

1. **Shenandoah National Park**

2. **Skyline Drive**

3. **Skyline Caverns**, Front Royal; and **Luray Caverns**, Luray

4. **The Frontier Culture Museum**, Staunton

5. **The Homestead Resort**, Hot Springs

THE SHENANDOAH VALLEY

Winchester

Middletown
Strasburg

Front Royal

522

50

81

259

New Market

Luray

340

George Washington
National Forest

33

George Washington
National Forest

250

81

340

Blue Ridge Parkway

220

Staunton

11

64

39

Bath
County

64

Lexington

60

Jefferson
National Forest

Natural
Bridge

501

George Washington
National Forest

220

81

460

Roanoke

convenient day trips. For information on Culpeper and Lynchburg, also in the Shenandoah Valley region, see the Northern Virginia and Central Virginia chapters.

Front Royal

The town of Front Royal is the gateway to the Shenandoah National Park and Skyline Drive. Skyline Drive starts here at Front Royal and continues for 105.4 miles until it ends at Rockfish Gap where the Blue Ridge Parkway begins. Front Royal is worth a pre- or post-park visit for several reasons. The town is a good place to eat or to stay after a Shenandoah National Park visit. Nearby Skyline Caverns features interesting formations, and George Washington National Forest, another popular place for hikers, is 5 miles west of Front Royal. Also, the town dubs itself "the official canoe capital of Virginia." That's because at Front Royal the north and south forks of the Shenandoah River join to form the main stem of this mighty waterway.

Skyline Caverns (ages 5 and up)

10344 Stonewall Jackson Hwy., 1 mile south of Front Royal on US 340 (just beyond the entrance to Shenandoah National Park); (540) 635-4545 or (800) 296-4545; www.skyline caverns.com. Open daily year-round. $–$$.

Although the region features several caverns, Skyline Caverns is notable for being one of the few caverns reputedly in the world that exhibits clusters of shimmering white calcium carbonate crystals called anthodites. These rare formations, nicknamed "the orchids of the mineral kingdom," are also slow growing, gaining only 1 inch every 7,000 years, compared to the 120 to 125 years required for similar growth in stalagmites and stalactites.

On the guided one-hour tour, the twelve stairs going down and the forty-eight going up are "doable" for younger kids. Just don't attempt this single-handedly before a tot's naptime because carrying a child up the steps can be hard, slippery work. Kids like Rainbow Falls, which plunges more than 37 feet from one of three underground streams that flow through the caverns, as well as the 1-mile miniature-train ride around the grounds. A special delight for wee tots, the ten-minute ride on the miniature Skyline Arrow train is offered daily, weather permitting. There's a snack bar, and the gift shop has lots of trinkets. Remember, the temperature in the caverns is a cool 54 degrees F, so bring jackets. Discount coupons are available on the Web site.

Front Royal Canoe Company (ages 8 and up)

8567 Stonewall Jackson Hwy., Front Royal; (540) 635-5440 or (800) 270-8808; www.front royalcanoe.com. Open Apr through Oct. $$–$$$

Paddle down the Shenandoah River on a guided outing or rent canoes, kayaks, rafts, and tubes. Also available are guided Full Moon Floats at night. Indian Hollow Stables offers guided horseback trail rides. Trail rides and river trips can be combined. Midweek discounts.

Front Royal Canoe/Shenandoah River Trips (ages 8 and up)

8567 Stonewall Jackson Hwy., Front Royal (mail: P.O. Box 473, Front Royal, VA 22630); (800) RAPIDS-1 or (540) 635-5050; www.shenandoah.cc. Open daily Apr through Sept; only Sun in Oct. Rates vary.

Offers affordable family rafting trips on the Shenandoah River with professional, certified staff. Also rents canoes, kayaks, rafts, and tubes. Midweek and group discounts.

Where to Eat

China Jade, 213 East South St.; (540) 635-9161. Buffet lunches and takeout. $–$$

The Main Street Mill, 500 East Main St. (next to the Front Royal Visitor Center); (540) 636-3123. Enjoy the atmosphere of a remodeled 1800s feed mill with chestnut beams and hand-painted murals. The restaurant specializes in pasta, steak, seafood, and desserts. $–$$

Skyland, Shenandoah National Park, Skyline Drive Mile Post 41.7; (800) 999-2211; www.visitshenandoah.com. Located along Skyline Drive, Skyland serves breakfast, lunch, and dinner. Open spring through fall. $

Skyline Restaurant, 915 North Royal Ave.; (540) 635-6615. Open daily for lunch and dinner. Enjoy a wide selection of seafood, pastas, steaks, and pizza. Children's menu available. $–$$

Where to Stay

Hampton Inn, 9800 Winchester Rd., (540) 635-1882 or (800) HAMPTON. The hotel has seventy rooms as well as a restaurant. $$–$$$

Quality Inn–Skyline Drive, 10 Commerce Ave.; (540) 635-3161 or (800) 821-4488. Moderately priced lodging with an outdoor pool and an on-site restaurant. $$$

Super 8, 111 South St.; (540) 636-4888 or (800) 800-8000. A complimentary breakfast is included in the room rates. $$

For More Information

Front Royal–Warren County Visitor Center/Chamber of Commerce, 414 East Main St., Main Street Station, Front Royal, VA 22630; (800) 338-2576; www.ci.front-royal.va.us. Stock up on regional brochures at this renovated-train-depot visitor center.

Shenandoah National Park

"Shenandoah" is believed to mean either "daughter of the stars" or "river of high mountains" in a Native American language. Whatever the real meaning, the area's beauty is legendary and best preserved in Shenandoah National Park with its 197,438 acres of forests, mountains, and streams. The park is unofficially divided into three main sections: The northern area, just 72 miles from Washington, D.C., has a campground, a counter serving breakfast and lunch, a gift shop, the tallest waterfall in the park and a National Park Visitor Center. The central section features the park's main overnight lodging, two campgrounds, food service, stables, and a gift shop. The southern section has gorgeous backcountry, plus a visitor information center with a lunch counter and gift shop and also a campground.

Prime Leaf-Peeping

During autumn the mountainsides blazing with red, yellow, and gold leaves draw crowds. The park is beautiful but crowded. If you visit during leaf-peeping season, prepare to go slow and have patience. Call ahead to these "hotlines" for the latest update on foliage:

Skyline Drive/Shenandoah National Park, (540) 999-3500

Virginia portion of the Blue Ridge, (276) 619-5003

Shenandoah National Park (all ages)

Park Superintendent at 3655 US 211 East, Luray. General information (540) 999-3500 or (800) 999-4714; www.visitshenandoah.com (concession information); www.nps.gov/shen (park information). Shenandoah National Park is one of the 150 national parks that does charge an entry fee. Eighty percent of the fees are returned to the park for specific projects. $–$$ (depending on the season and on the number of people).

Most facilities in the park are open mid-May through late Oct, and some areas are also open Apr, May, and Nov. From Dec through late Mar, it's best to call ahead to find out what's available: (540) 999-3500. Count on getting food, gas, and lodging outside the park during the winter months.

The famous scenic two-lane route, **Skyline Drive,** stretching 105 miles from Front Royal to Rockfish Gap, cuts through the park and can be accessed from all four park entrances. Once on this road, use the mile markers on the west side of the drive to find your locale, as well as the nearest facilities, services, and areas of interest.

The countdown for the mile markers starts after the Front Royal Entrance Station in the north, at milepost 1 and ends at the Rockfish Gap Entrance Station in the south just after milepost 105. The northern park entrance is easily reached; it's just south of Front Royal, close to the junction of I-81 and I-66, and accessible via US 340 and US 55. Other entrances to Skyline Drive are at Thornton Gap (mile 31.5, accessible via US 211), and at Swift Run Gap (mile 65.5, accessible via US 33). In this section the mile markers are listed along with the sites and trails to make them easy to find when you are traveling along Skyline Drive.

Shenandoah Travel Tips

Skyline Drive remains open year-round except in the event of ice or snowstorms, so visitors who don't mind a little cold may find it easier to commune with nature when there are fewer crowds. With snow or mud on the ground, it's easier to track animals. If there's snow—or even mud—is the best time to look for animal tracks.

Amazing
Shenandoah Facts

- **Elevation** in the park ranges from 600 feet at the north entrance to 4,050 feet at the summit of Hawksbill Peak, among the highest points in northern Virginia.

- **Appalachian Trail:** About 101 miles of the Appalachian Trail, which stretches 2,160 miles from Maine to Georgia, is located within Shenandoah National Park.

Ranger programs, hikes, and walks explore the natural beauty and cultural history of the park. Most kids' programs are designed for ages 7 and older. In summer at the visitor centers and gift shops, pick up a Junior Ranger Explorer Notebook. After kids complete the activities (two of which may include attending a ranger-led program), the kids receive an official Junior Ranger badge or patch, which makes a nice reward and a worthwhile keepsake.

Shenandoah National Park offers families wonders literally as big as all outdoors plus various ways to enjoy them. Remember that Skyline Drive comes with many curves and a 35-mile-per-hour speed limit, as well as crowds and many cars in leaf-peeping season. As a result, plan ahead and allow more time than usual when calculating driving distances. If you only have one day to spend in the park, officials recommend driving along Skyline Drive, admiring the scenery and scouting for animals (maybe even a bear). But be sure to get out of your car to stroll a trail or two. Check the park brochures to see which of the short trails are nearby. You can also try a segment of the Appalachian Trail, 101 miles of which cut through the park. Along the park's trail you can rest awhile at one of the five shelters for day use. These come with a table, fireplace, and pit toilet.

Be aware that while swimming is permitted in all the park streams, it is also done at your own risk.

When conditions are right, the park allows cross-country skiing and snowshoeing, but bring your own gear—the park has no rental facilities. (Remember, winter storms often close Skyline Drive for safety reasons.)

Fishing enthusiasts can also try their luck year-round. The park's many streams offer great angling opportunities. Anyone 16 or older must have a valid Virginia fishing license and use only artificial lures with a single hook. A temporary five-day license can be purchased at Big Meadows Wayside, Loft Mountain Wayside, or at local sporting-goods stores.

Bird-watching and wildlife-viewing opportunities abound throughout the park. Best hours for viewing are usually in the early morning or early evening.

Hiking Trails

The first five of these popular trails are easy enough for families with young, energetic kids. Doyles River Falls is more difficult and best suited to older grade-schoolers who like hiking.

Little Stony Man (mile 39.1): 0.9 miles with a 270-foot elevation gain to a far-reaching westward view. Allow one hour round-trip.

Blackrock Summit (mile 84.8): 1 milelong round-trip hike with a 175-foot elevation gain to a 360-degree view. Allow one hour round-trip.

Fox Hollow Trail (mile 4.6): 1.2-mile circuit hike near Dickey Ridge Visitor Center with a 310-foot elevation gain. Allow about one and a quarter hours. This trail leads past ruins of old farm fences and a cemetery, one of the many remnants of the home sites of the mountaineers who lived here decades ago.

The Story of the Forest Families Trail (milepost 51): near Byrd Visitor Center, a 1.8-mile route with a 290-foot elevation gain. Allow about one and a half hours. The trail gives visitors a sense of the natural and cultural history of the forest and swamp. You may see deer, chipmunks, and birds along the way.

Dark Hollow Falls (mile 50.7): near the Byrd Visitor Center, a 1.4-milelong round-trip hike with a 440-foot climb back to the start. Allow one and a half hours. This popular trail leads to a beautiful cascading waterfall, the nearest waterfall to Skyline Drive.

Doyles River Falls (mile 81.1): near Loft Mountain Information Center, a 2.7-mile round-trip trail with an 850-foot change in elevation. Allow at least three hours. The trail leads to a waterfall surrounded by trees. Some places are steep. Pack a picnic lunch and linger.

Skyland Stables (mile 41.7)
Located near Skyland Lodge; P.O. Box 727, Luray, VA 22835; (540) 999-2210. Open May through Nov. $$–$$$.

A great way to enjoy the trails is from atop a horse. This stable offers one-hour guided trail rides for adults and children at least 4 feet 10 inches tall, Apr through Nov. Your best bet is to reserve ahead, either through the lodge or by calling the stables. Riders may also bring their own horses and enjoy the more than 150 miles of horse trails in the park.

Overlooks: **Great Views**

The park delights visitors with 75 scenic overlooks. Here are some top spots.

Shenandoah Valley Overlook (mile 2.8): From here you can see Signal Knob on Massanutten Mountain, used by the Confederate troops in the Civil War to convey semaphore signals.

Range View Overlook (mile 17.1): Located at 2,800 feet, this overlook offers panoramic views—among the best in the park's northern region—of the ridgetops of the Blue Ridge, Massanutten, and Allegheny mountains.

Stony Man Overlook (mile 38.6): Enjoy sweeping views of cliffs and the Shenandoah Valley.

Thoroughfare Mountain Overlook (mile 40.5): One of the highest overlooks at nearly 3600-feet, this one offers views of several mountains to the east and northeast.

Big Run Overlook (mile 81.2): From an elevation of 2,860 feet, this spot offers one of the park's most beautiful overlooks, taking in the Big Run watershed (part of the park's wilderness area) as well as views of mountains.

Where to Eat

Within Shenandoah National Park, there are several restaurants as well as snack bars. Still, the easiest way to eat in the park is alfresco; pack your own picnic and pause where you like to enjoy the food and the scenery. There are seven picnic grounds.

Big Meadows Lodge Dining Room (mile 51.3, 1 mile off Skyline Drive), open from early May through late fall. Local specialties such as fried chicken and mountain trout as well as burgers are served. See if your kids want the special dessert: blackberry ice-cream pie topped with blackberry syrup. $–$$$

Elkwallow Wayside (mile 24.1), open Apr through Oct. Breakfast selections, plus sandwiches and grilled items for lunch and dinner. $–$$

Loft Mountain Wayside (mile 79.5), open May through Oct. Dining room with counter service and picnic tables. A variety of breakfast selections, sandwiches, and grilled items. $–$$

Skyland Resort Dining Room (mile 41.7), usually open from late Mar through Nov. Offers the same fare as Big Meadows Lodge Dining Room. $$–$$$

Where to Stay

Park lodges don't charge for cribs or for children under 16 who share a room with parents. Reserve far ahead (nine months to one year depending upon the season) for the following park lodgings. Call (800) 999-4714 or (540) 743-5108 to make your reservation; www.visitshenandoah.com.

All campsites are near a section of the Appalachian Trail and are reached from Skyline Drive. Campsites are available on a first-come basis, except Big Meadows and Dundo. Call (800) 365-CAMP or use the Web site www.nps.gov/shen. All except Mathews Arm have showers, laundry, and a camp store. No campground has hookups for water, electricity, or sewage, but Mathews Arm, Big Meadows, and Loft Mountain have dump stations.

Big Meadows Campground (mile 51.2). There are 217 tent or trailer sites, flush toilets, showers, and laundry facilities. Reservations required from Memorial Day weekend through Nov. $$

Big Meadows Lodge (mile 51.3), open from late Apr through Oct 1. A historic park lodge, Big Meadows offers views of the Shenandoah Valley and frequent glimpses of deer, particularly in the evening and early morning. Accommodations range from twenty-five rooms in the main lodge to seventy-two rustic cabins and multiunits with modern suites. The facility has a playground, televisions in some rooms, a restaurant, a gift shop, and nightly entertainment. $$–$$$

Dundo Group Campground (mile 83.7), open Apr through early Nov. A primitive campground open to groups with a minimum of eight campers and a maximum of twenty. Facilities include seven large group sites, pit toilets, and water. One site has a wheelchair-accessible picnic table and a raised fire grate. $

Lewis Mountain (mile 57.5). The campground has thirty-two tent sites, flush toilets, and showers. It is open May to Nov. $

Lewis Mountain Cabins (mile 57.5), open early May through Oct. Features semirustic cabins with private baths and heat; linens are provided. Cooking facilities include a fireplace, grills, and picnic tables in the connecting outdoor area. It has a coin-operated laundromat and showers at the camp store. $$

Loft Mountain Campground (mile 79.5), open May through Oct. The largest campground in the park, it sits atop Big Flat Mountain and offers outstanding views east and west. Campers can use 219 tent or trailer sites, flush toilets, and showers. $

Loft Mountain Wayside (mile 79.5), open late spring through late fall. Breakfast, lunch and snack foods, souvenirs, camper store. $

Mathews Arm Campground (mile 22.1), open May through Oct. There are 179 tent or trailer sites, flush toilets, no showers. Next to a nature trail and the trail to Overall Run Falls, the tallest waterfall in the park. $

Skyland (mile 41.7), open from the end of Mar usually to late Nov. Established in the late 1880s, Skyland offers 179 guest units, including modern rooms and rustic cabins. Facilities include a restaurant, gift shop, naturalist programs, horseback activities, playground, television in some rooms, and nightly entertainment. $$–$$$

Accommodations are also available in neighboring communities (see the Luray section).

Annual Events

The *Shenandoah Overlook* lists information about seasonal special events. Aramark, the park's main concessionaire, produces an annual calendar of events at www.visit shenandoah.com.

MAY

Wildflower Weekend in Shenandoah National Park, generally the second weekend in May. Special walks and exhibits highlight the park's spring flowers.

Shenandoah Apple Blossom Festival, 135 North Cameron St., Winchester; (540) 662-3863; www.thebloom.com. More than thirty events over one weekend, including dances, parades, a 10K run, a circus, food, and fun.

SUMMER

Shenandoah Valley Music Festival, held on select weekends between Memorial Day and Labor Day; (800) 459-3396; www .musicfest.org. Admission charged. The last two weekends in July are the symphonic weekends and are held at the Orkney Springs Hotel in Orkney Springs, with juried arts and crafts shows. On Sat afternoons of both weekends, cross-cultural events are held for children to teach them about different cultures' music.

JULY

New Market Fourth of July celebration; (540) 740-3132. The celebration is held in the town park with activities for kids such as face painting and pony rides. There are also picnics, food concessions, live music, and great fireworks.

AUGUST–SEPTEMBER

Shenandoah County Fair, Woodstock; (540) 459-3867. For more than eighty years, this county fair has had it all: midway rides, greased-pig contests, prize livestock, country music concerts, harness races, and bubble gum contests.

SEPTEMBER

Apple Harvest Festival, every Sept in Mount Jackson; (540) 477-3275.

OCTOBER

New Market also has a **Heritage Days Fall Festival** in late Oct every year, with food, crafts, and games. For information, call (540) 740-3132.

For More Information

The Dickey Ridge Visitor Center (mile 4.6), near the Front Royal Entrance Station. Open daily (later hours during the summer season), but closed from Nov through the end of Mar. An exhibit and a film introduce visitors to the park. Maps, books, and other items for sale.

The Byrd Visitor Center (mile 51), open daily (later hours during the summer season) from Apr through Oct. This center has interpretive exhibits, plus a good selection of books, maps, trail guides, and park-related items.

Loft Mountain Information Center (mile 79.5), open end of May through Oct on holidays and weekends only. The center provides visitor orientation information and has publications for sale.

Park Entrance Stations sell passes and provide visitors with a park map and, in season, a copy of the *Shenandoah Overlook,* the visitor guide. Check out the numerous ranger-led activities for adults and kids, most of which take place in and around visitor centers and campgrounds, in the park's *Overlook.*

For recorded park information, call (540) 999-3500.

The Blue Ridge Parkway

The Blue Ridge Parkway, stretches for 469 miles, connecting the southern portion of Shenandoah National Park's Skyline Drive to the Great Smoky Mountains National Park.

The Blue Ridge Parkway begins at Rockfish Gap near Waynesboro, Virginia, where Skyline Drive ends, and continues through North Carolina, crossing the North Carolina border at mile 218 and ending at Cherokee, NC, mile 469. The Blue Ridge Parkway straddles mountain peaks and dips into scenic valleys, twisting by overlooks and dappled hillsides. Because of the winding roads and reduced speeds, you may want to alternate travel between the Blue Ridge Parkway and I-81 which runs parallel to the parkway in many places and also traverses scenic areas.

Blue Ridge Parkway Association

P.O. Box 2136, Asheville, NC 28802; (828) 298-0398; 2551 Mountain View Rd., Vinton; www .blueridgeparkway.org in Virginia, (800) VISIT-VA or (540) 999-3500 and www.nps.gov. Free.

For a complete list of the trails and their difficulty levels, as well as attractions, obtain the *Blue Ridge Parkway Information Guide* from the visitor center. Although the parkway is open all year, winter may bring icy conditions that temporarily close the roads, so call ahead.

Like Skyline Drive, this toll-free, 469-milelong, noncommercialized mountain route offers a great scenic drive. With a speed limit of 45 mph on meandering mountain roads, the drive is slow; many cars stop at the scenic overlooks to gaze out across the valleys. Allow plenty of time. The most popular and crowded times are spring through summer and fall. The road also offers a number of hiking trails, some of them easy enough for young children.

You can find lodging, gas stations, and restaurants along the parkway.

There are several visitor centers (www.nps.gov) along the parkway in Virginia, each providing information on area activities and facilities. Highlights and visitor centers include:

Rockfish Gap Tourist Information (milepost 0), US 250 at the parkway's access; (540) 943-5187. Gather information here and get oriented to the parkway at this information center.

Humpback Rocks (mile 5.8) has a small museum with an exhibit on late- 19th and early-20th-century life. A U.S. Forest Service campground is located 4 miles south of the center off the parkway, and a ninety-one-site picnic area is located at mile 8.5. The center maintains a reconstructed pioneer mountain farmstead accessible via an easy, quarter-mile, self-guided trail. During the summer, costumed rangers demonstrate mountain crafts and skills.

James River (mile 63.7) has picnic tables located downhill from the center. Otter Creek (mile 60.8) has a campground with sites for forty-two tents and twenty-six trailers and a restaurant. From the center, hike the half-mile Trail of Trees and the easy James River Trail that leads to the restored Kanawha Canal Lock. In the summer there are guided lock tours, as well as the James River Batteau Festival. This area is not wheelchair accessible.

Peaks of Otter (mileposts 86) is famed for its scenic view of mountains ringing a valley. The visitor center is open May through Oct. The Fallingwater Cascades trail, a 1.6-mile loop, rewards you with a view of a waterfall. Nearby is the sixty-two-room Peaks of Otter Lodge (540-586-1081) and restaurant, open year-round. Also nearby is the Johnson Farm, a living-history farm where kids can play period games and help work the garden.

Virginia's Explore Park (mile 115.1). See Roanoke Valley section for a full description.

Roanoke Mountain Overlook (mile 120.4) is a 4-mile, one-way loop road (no trailers allowed) that affords beautiful views of Roanoke Valley and Mill Mountain and is adjacent to a campground (mile 120.4) with sites for seventy-four tents and thirty-one trailers. (Three sites are wheelchair accessible.) There are evening country music programs during the summer.

Rocky Knob (milepost 167–169), with 4,800 acres, features 15 miles of hiking trails, including the Rock Castle Gorge National Recreational Trail. It has a campground with sites for eighty-one tents and twenty-eight trailers, with a 150-capacity campfire circle where interpretive programs are given on summer weekends. There are also demonstrations of crafts, blacksmithing, spinning, and weaving.

There are a variety of programs for your family to enjoy here on weekends from June through Oct. Campfire talks, history demonstrations, music programs, nature walks, and other presentations are given by rangers and volunteers. Schedules are posted at visitor centers, campground entrances, and parkway concessions.

Mabry Mill (mile 176.1), a picturesque early-20th-century mill, is the parkway's most photographed site. When the mill and nearby blacksmith shop and Matthews Cabin are open (May through Oct), interpreters, on certain days, demonstrate 19th-century skills. On Sunday afternoons in summer and fall, come for the old-time and bluegrass music concerts at the Blue Ridge Music Center at milepost 213. Check with parkway information for the schedule of events.

Luray

Luray is located 9 miles west of Skyline Drive on US 211.

Luray Caverns (ages 4 and up)

9 miles west of Skyline Drive on US 211 West; (540) 743-6551; www.luraycaverns.com. Open daily year-round. Call for reservations for the motel accommodations on property. $–$$.

Luray Caverns is the largest cavern in Virginia and the most popular in the East. Remember to bring along a sweater; no matter how hot the surface temperature, the underground rooms remain cool. The subterranean chambers range from 30 to 140 feet high

Skiing at Massanutten

In winter ski at Massanutten Resort in McGaheysville (540-289-9441 or 800-207-6277; www.massresort.com). Virginia skiing isn't like skiing out West, but Massanutten is much closer to home. Massanutten offers Slope Sliders classes for ages 4 to 12 and snowboarding group instruction for ages 9 to 14. The mountain has seventy skiable acres and a vertical drop of 1,110 feet. The ski resort features six hotels and 2000 condominiums. Child-care programs are available for children ages 3 to 12. In summer, you can also horseback ride and mountain bike.

and feature thousands of colored formations. Even the most blasé of teens will turn off the headphones to listen to chords played on the **Great Stalacpipe Organ,** billed as the world's largest natural musical instrument. The tunes resonate throughout the chamber when plungers tap the stalactites. One-hour cavern tours begin every twenty minutes, and the admission fee also includes a self-guided tour of the on-premises **Car and Carriage Caravan** of Luray Caverns. More than 140 vehicles include such finds as an 1892 Mercedes Benz, a Rolls Royce Silver Ghost, and other vehicles and costumes dating back to 1725. There's also a one-acre **Garden Maze** in which to get lost (and found) among 8-foot-high trees enveloped in mist. Across from the caverns is the **Luray Singing Tower,** a 117-foot-high carillon that provides music throughout the spring, summer, and fall. Three shops sell kid-pleasing trinkets. The caverns complex also has a food court.

Shenandoah River Outfitters (ages 6 and up)

6502 South Page Valley Rd.; (540) 743-4159 or (800) 6-CANOE2; www.shenandoahriver.com. Open from Apr through mid-Nov. $$–$$$.

Paddle the river with this company's canoeing, kayaking, and tubing trips on the Shenandoah River. Typically, the outfitter offers a midweek special from April until the end of October, with a discount rate for an 8-mile canoe trip. On some trips, spend the night in a river side cabin.

Luray Zoo (all ages)

1087 US 211 West; (540) 743-4113; www.lurayzoo.com. Open daily year-round except when icy, then open only on weekends. $.

For slithery things, visit this park whose residents include huge pythons, alligators, rattlesnakes, and cobras. These will either elicit an "awesome" or an "aggh" shriek. The zoo also features owls, hawks, and other raptors. Younger children can pet African pygmy goats and deer at the petting zoo and enjoy live animal shows daily.

Horseback Riding in
George Washington National Forest

Fort Valley Stable (540-933-6633 or 888-754-5771; www.fortvalleystable.com) offers guided trail rides through 80 miles of George Washington National Forest trails, providing views from some of the highest ridges in the Massanutten Mountains. Riders must be 7 years of age or older. All skill levels are accommodated; no previous riding experience required. Trail guides lead one- and one-and-a-half-hour rides, or half-day and full-day trips with a trail lunch. The stable is located at 299 South Fort Valley Rd. in Fort Valley.

Where to Eat

A Moment to Remember, 55 E. Main St.; (540) 743-1121; www.a-moment2remember .com. Open Mon through Wed 9 a.m. to 5 p.m., Thurs through Sat 9 a.m. to 9 p.m. This former hardware store turned cafe offers such traditional German fare as sausages and Schnitzel as well as fish, chicken, salads, and sandwiches. $–$$

Brookside Restaurant and Gift Shop, 2978 US 211 East; (540) 743-5698. Open daily for breakfast, lunch, and dinner; closed from mid-Dec through mid-Jan. This home-style restaurant features such entrees as pork barbecue, Virginia ham steak, and catfish, as well as a large salad bar and daily buffets. Brookside bakes its own bread and desserts. $–$$

Artisan's Grill, 2 East Main St.; (540) 743-7030. Open Wed through Mon for lunch and dinner. The gallery exhibits art by local and nationally-known artists and serves beef, chicken, and game as well as sandwiches. $$$

Where to Stay

Best Western Intown of Luray, 410 West Main St.; (540) 743-6511 or (800) 528-1234; www.bestwesternluray.com. This motel has an outdoor pool and a restaurant on premises plus a swing set and a grassy play area. $$–$$$

Days Inn at Shenandoah National Park, 138 Whispering Hill Rd.; (540) 743-4521; www.daysinn-luray.com. The property has comfortable rooms, allows pets, and has a restaurant. $$

Page County is known for the 250 privately owned cabins that vary from primitive to upmarket. For more information, visit www .cabincapital.com. For more lodging, check out www.luraypage.com.

Annual Events

MAY
Festival of Spring on Main Street, an annual spring festival with crafts, games, activities, and antiques vendors.

OCTOBER
Heritage Festival, a Blue Ridge tradition commemorating the mountain history of Page Valley with crafts, food, and entertainment.

DECEMBER
Christmas Bird Count in Shenandoah National Park. Volunteers call (540) 999-3500.

For More Information

Luray–Page County Chamber of Com-merce, 18 Campbell St., Luray, VA 22835;

(540) 743-3915 or (888) 743-3915; www.luray page.com.

New Market

New Market is just off I-81, 12 miles west of Luray on US 211.

New Market Battlefield State Historical Park

(ages 7 and up)

Off Route 305 (George Collins Parkway); (540) 740-3101; www2.vmi.edu/museum/nm. Open daily; closed major holidays. $.

Older grade-schoolers interested in the Civil War connect with this park because it commemorates the corps of 257 Virginia Military Institute (VMI) students, some as young as 15 (although the average age was 18), who were called to active duty. Although the cadets were supposed to be kept in reserve until needed to fill a gap in the advancing line of badly outnumbered Confederate troops, these schoolboys were accidentally put on the front lines to face the Union soldiers. The cadets managed to hold the line for thirty minutes, forcing the Union troops to retreat. Ten VMI students were killed. The park honors the troop's heroism. The Hall of Valor Civil War Museum shows a film about the battle and another about Stonewall Jackson's Shenandoah campaign. Also, models and dioramas describe the Civil War, and you can drive along one-mile of the battlefield. Guided tours are offered in the summer. A reenactment of the battle takes place here every May, the weekend following Mother's Day. Inside the museum, look for Camp Discovery, an interactive learning area, and ask about the scavenger hunts for children throughout the museum. For kids 7 to 12, Civil War Day Camps are held on Wed in July and Aug. Kids learn what war was like for the average soldier. (Reservations required for the camp, call (540) 740-3101.

Rebel Park

9418 John Sevier Rd.; (540) 740-3432; www.newmarketvirginia.com/parks.htm. Open daily from 7 a.m. to 11 p.m. Free for ages 5 and younger, but $$$ for others.

The community-owned park has baseball diamonds, jungle gyms with swings, a gravel walking/jogging path, picnic shelters, and a barbecue pit, as well as a soccer field, tennis courts, basketball courts, and a community pool. Rebel Park is also home to the Valley League New Market Rebels Baseball Team.

Endless Caverns (ages 3 and up)

Take exit 264 off I-81, then travel 3 miles south on US 11, New Market; (540) 896-2283 or (800) 544-2283; www.endlesscaverns.com. Open every day except Christmas. $–$$.

Discovered by accident in 1879 when two boys were rabbit hunting, these caverns have now been mapped to stretch more than 5 miles, and there's no end in sight. Guided tours take approximately 75 minutes.

Where to Eat

Johnny Appleseed Restaurant and Applecore Village Gift Shop, I-81, exit 264, New Market; (540) 740-3141. Open for breakfast, lunch, and dinner. Restaurant offers fried chicken, country-fried steak, biscuits-and-gravy, and apple fritters for dessert. Children's menu. The store sells a large assortment of Virginia specialty foods. $–$$

Southern Kitchen, US 11, 3 blocks south of US 211; (540) 740-3514. Open for breakfast, lunch, and dinner. Steaks, Virginia ham, seafood, Lloyd's Virginia fried chicken, peanut soup, plus carryout. $$

Where to Stay

Apple Blossom Inn Bed and Breakfast; 9317 Congress St.; (540) 740-3747; http:// appleblossominn.net. This inn originally built in 1806, is a small bed and breakfast house. Guests rent the entire inn, a property with two bedrooms, a kitchen, parlor, and living area. Children age 9 years and older are welcome. The Inn is home to New Market Walking Tours. You can sign-up for several walks—including one on Boys and Bugles, and one on women in New Market—before, during, and after the Civil War. $$

Crossroads Inn Bed and Breakfast; 9222 John Sevier Rd.; (540) 740-4157; www.cross roadsinnva.com. The 6-room Inn is near the Civil War "Battle of New Market." Children can visit the goats, watch the fish in the nearby pond, or play on the playground. Children 5 and under are **free.** $–$$

Blue Ridge Inn, US 11, 1 mile north of New Market; (540) 740-4136 or (800) 545-8776; www.blueridgeinn.com. Cozy, country-decor rooms, children stay **free.** Playground, basketball, horseshoes, barbecue, and picnic area. In-room coffeemakers, refrigerators, and cable. $$–$$$

Days Inn New Market Battlefield, 9360 George Collins Parkway; (540) 740-4100; www.daysinn.com. The hotel offers serviceable and clean rooms. $–$$

Quality Inn–Shenandoah Valley, I-81 at exit 264, New Market; (540) 740-3141 or (800) 228-5151. In-room coffeemakers, outdoor pool, sauna, and minigolf. Johnny Appleseed Restaurant and Applecore Village Gift Shop on-site. $$–$$$

Shenvalee Golf Resort, 1 mile south of I-81, exit on US 11; (540) 740-3181 or (888) 339-3181; www.shenvalee.com. The resort has a twenty-seven-hole golf course (package plans available), tennis courts, outdoor pool, and restaurant. $$$

Jacob Swartz House, 574 Jiggady Rd.; (540) 740-9208; http://jacobswartz.com. Open Feb through Dec. Visitors have this converted cobbler's shop guest house all to themselves. The guesthouse has two bedrooms, a full kitchen, living area, dining area, a cozy wood-burning stove, and a screened-in porch. Wireless Internet available. A full breakfast is served. Infants and toddlers are **free.** $$

For More Information

Shenandoah Valley Visitor Center and Travel Association, 277 West Old Cross Rd., New Market, VA 22844; (540) 740-3132 or (877) VISIT-SV; www.shenandoah.org.

New Market Chamber of Commerce, 9184 John Sevier Rd., New Market, VA 22844; (540) 740-3212.

Staunton

Staunton (pronounced *Stan*-ton), 42 miles south of New Market and 11 miles west of the southern end of Skyline Drive at Waynesboro, is the birthplace of Woodrow Wilson and one of the oldest cities west of the Blue Ridge Mountains. As Staunton survived the Civil War intact, the town has some splendid 19th-century buildings. Walking-tour maps are available weekdays from the Chamber of Commerce.

The Woodrow Wilson Presidential Library (ages 7 and up)

18–24 North Coalter St.; (888) 496-6376 or (540) 885-0897; www.woodrowwilson.org. Open daily year-round; closed major holidays. Free admission on December 28, Wilson's birthday. $.

The 12-room house has been restored to look the way it did when the former president was born here in 1856. The facility features memorabilia of the Wilson family, including Wilson's crib. His father was a Presbyterian minister and the family moved when Wilson was 2. At the museum building, which contains seven galleries, school-age kids learn about Wilson's life and career and American history during his presidency, 1913 to 1921, including the United States's entry into World War I. Kids particularly enjoy a glimpse of the presidential limousine in the garage: it's a 1919 Pierce–Arrow. There's even a 19th-century mousetrap on view. Children touring the museum are given a clipboard and a list of questions about objects in the museum and Wilson's life and career. Those who answer all the questions correctly win a counterfeit $100,000 bill printed with Wilson's face.

Frontier Culture Museum (all ages)

I-81, US 250, 1290 Richmond Rd.; (540) 332-7850; www.frontiermuseum.org. Open daily; closed Thanksgiving, Christmas, and New Year's Day. $.

A living-history museum, the facility pays tribute to the pioneers who came to the region in the 17th, 18th, and 19th centuries. The permanent exhibits consist of six villages of period buildings from West Africa, England, Ireland, Germany, and from America in the 1740s, 1820s, and 1850s. Plan to spend at least several hours here, if not a full day.

Although while touring this complex you can still hear the traffic on the nearby highway, the 17th-, 18th-, and 19th-century homes transport you to a preindustrial time. In the buildings costumed interpreters illustrate the hopes and the customs that the hardy immigrants brought with them and planted in the fertile Virginia soil. The interpretive guides and the hands-on history lessons make learning fun for all. A bonneted matron at the 18th-century German home sits in the Stube (the family room) carding wool. She carefully teaches kids to pick the straw and hay from the fibers. Outside, another Hausfrau knits fingerless gloves, which kept workers' hands warm while still enabling them to toss grain to the animals. The stone fence, thatched roof, and Prudence the pig rooting in the mud endear the Scotch–Irish farm to city kids. In this proverbial cottage of yore dating to the mid-19th century, pull up a "creepie stool" (because you crept closer to the fire as the night wore on) and learn how to cook Donegal pie in the open-hearth fireplace. At the 17th-century English farm in a poor man's one-room abode with a cattail roof and mud cob walls, you can practice your darning. At the log American house with its double-pen log barn, you can flail wheat on the central threshing floor, then try your hand at the "new-fangled" fanning mill, which cleaned a bushel a minute. As you look into the sunset, imagine women cooking a country supper, and the folks readying for a barn dance to celebrate the harvest.

The museum offers more than fifty programs a year, many of them geared to the seasons. In May, Wool Days have costumed staff members shearing sheep by hand, cleaning the fleeces, and spinning the wool. Autumn hosts a special celebration of fall and a music festival in Sept. A Halloween tour takes visitors to the Scotch–Irish farm to hear ghost stories and folktales. Special programs for children are also held throughout the year. In July programs for 4- to 10-year-olds include a variety of crafts, farm visits, and recreation, and there is a Children's Holiday Party in Dec. Reservations (made at least two weeks in advance) are necessary for the children's programs; call (540) 332-7850, ext. 159.

American **Shakespeare Center**

Even kids who have never heard of Shakespeare (and those who think it's all boring) will enjoy the American Shakespeare Center's theater company. This is MTV-generation Shakespeare, but with respect for the work and contagious enthusiasm. Experience the Bard as Renaissance audiences did: a simple stage, minimal sets in the Elizabethan Blackfriars Playhouse (a re-creation of Shakespeare's indoor theater), and with the lights up on the audience as well as the stage. Plays are performed without intermission and kept under two hours long.

American Shakespeare Center, 11 East Beverly St.; (540) 885-5588. Administrative offices: 13 West Beverley St., fourth floor; (540) 885-5588. Box office: Blackfriars Playhouse, 10 South Market St.; (540) 851-1733 or (877) MUCH-ADO; www.americanshakespearecenter.com. Check the schedule for summer day camps for children ages 9 to 12.

Gypsy Hill Park

Intersection of Churchville Avenue and Thornrose Avenue (Rt. 250); (540) 332-3945: www
.virginia.org. Open daily 4 a.m. to 11 p.m. **Free.**

Gypsy Hill Park is a 214-acre multi-use recreational facility located in the heart of Staunton.
The Park includes a public golf course, football and baseball stadiums, a gymnasium, a
lake, an armory, two playgrounds, three youth baseball fields, a public swimming pool,
volleyball court, horseshoe pits, the Gypsy Express mini-train, and the famous Duck Pond.
A 1.3-mile circular roadway through the center of Park is suitable for walkers, bicyclists,
and Rollerbladers.

Shops and Stops

Staunton Antique Market, 19 West
Beverly St.; (540) 886-7277. Open daily,
hours vary. Forty dealers display a variety of
antiques and collectibles.

The Staunton Fire Department (500
North Augusta St.; 540-332-3885) displays a
1911 Jumbo Antique Fire Engine, the only sur-
viving fire engine of its type in the world.

Staunton Trains & Hobbies (331 N. Central Ave.; 540-885-6750) sells Lionel trains,
including Thomas the Tank Engine.

Where to Eat

Baja Bean Co. Restaurant & Cantina, 9
West Beverley St.; (540) 885-9988. Open daily
for lunch and dinner. The standard Mexican
fare includes tacos, chimichangas, and enchiladas. Charbroiled chicken, steak, and shrimp
are also served. Children's menu available.
$–$$

The Beverley Restaurant, 12 East Beverley St.; (540) 886-4317. Open Mon through
Sat for breakfast, lunch, and dinner, closed
Sun. Home-cooked meals are made fresh
daily. Leave room for the pie. $–$$

The Depot Grille, 42 Middlebrook Ave.;
(540) 885-7332. Open daily for lunch and dinner. Located in the old freight depot of the
Staunton Train Station, the restaurant serves
seafood and steaks and offers a children's
menu. $$

Shenandoah Pizza, 19 E. Beverly St.: (540)
213-0008; www.shenandoahpizza.com. Open
Tues through Sat 11:30 a.m to 10 p.m, Sun
12 p.m to 8 p.m. Serves pizza, calzones, subs/
sandwiches, and salads. $–$$

The Split Banana, 7 West Beverly St.; (866)
492-3668; www.thesplitbanana.com. Open
Daily 11 a.m. to 11 p.m. This ice cream and
gelato shop makes their own homemade
gelato and sorbet, 18 flavors. $

Where to Stay

Best Western, US 250; (800) 752-9471;
www.dominionlodging.com. Comfortable
rooms come with cable TV and in-room coffeemaker. The property has an indoor pool
and rates include a continental breakfast.
$$$

**Stonewall Jackson Hotel & Conference
Center,** 24 South Market St.; (540) 885-
4848 or (866) 880-0024. This renovated his-
toric downtown hotel originally opened in
1924. Now the property offers 120 rooms,
each with cable TV, Internet access, and
in-room coffeemaker. Kids like the indoor
pool. $$$$

Annual Events

Unless otherwise noted, information about
these events can be obtained from the
**Staunton Convention and Visitors
Bureau** at (540) 332-3865.

APRIL–NOVEMBER

The Staunton–Augusta Farmers' Market in Staunton. Seasonal fruits and vegetables, baked goods, and other locally grown products are available.Sat from 7 a.m. until noon at the Wharf Parking Lot, Johnson Street and Central Avenue. Visit www.safarmers market.com for more information.

JUNE–OCTOBER

Guided walking tours of historic Staunton, Sat 10 a.m., leaving from the Woodrow Wilson Birthplace and Museum; (540) 885-7676. **Free.**

JULY–AUGUST

Jazz in the Park, Thurs nights at the Gypsy Hill Park; (540) 332-3972. **Free.**

Shenandoah Valley Music Festival, selected weeks in July, Aug, and Sept (800) 459-3396, www.musicfest.org.

SEPTEMBER

Annual African–American Heritage Festival with live music and dance performances, arts and crafts, and historic exhibits; (540) 332-3972.

For More Information

Staunton–Augusta Travel Information Center, exit 222 off I-81, 1290 Richmond Rd., Staunton, VA 24401; (540) 332-3972 or (800) 332-5219; www.staunton.va.us. Open daily.

Staunton Visitor Center, 35 South New St., Staunton, VA 24401; (540) 332-3971 or (800) 342-7942.

Lexington

Lexington, 35 miles south of Staunton, is a college town with two venerable institutions located next to one another: the Virginia Military Institute (VMI) and Washington and Lee University. The lively college atmosphere and the Civil War history make this area an appealing place to visit with kids, but maybe not for too long. Judge your kids' patience with historic settings and war lore.

Virginia Military Institute (VMI) (ages 7 and up)

Located at the intersection of I-64 and I-81. VMI Visitor Center; (540) 464-7806 (except in the summer) or (540) 464-7230 (general information); www.vmi.edu. Free.

Founded in 1839, VMI lays claim to being the nation's first state-supported military college. Stonewall Jackson taught here for ten years before the Civil War, which may have been part of the reason Union forces shelled and burned this institute. Another possible contributing factor was the cadets who fought in the Battle of New Market (see New Market section). Every May 15 a solemn New Market Day Ceremony (**free** and open to the public) honors the cadets who died in that battle.

   The VMI Museum displays artifacts of Stonewall Jackson's such as his military uniform and his warhorse Little Sorrel. Children can try on uniforms and play in a replica of a cadet's barracks room. During the academic year, take the cadet-led guided tour, which begins from the VMI Museum. The cadets in uniform and the full-dress parades appeal to kids. (No parades in the summer.)

Lee Chapel and Museum (ages 10 and up)

On the campus of Washington and Lee University, off I-64 or I-81; (540) 458-8768; http://leechapel.wlu.edu. The chapel is open daily except Thanksgiving and the day after, Christmas Eve and Christmas Day, and New Year's Day. $.

The chapel, now used for concerts and other special events, was built in 1867 under the supervision of General Robert E. Lee, president of the college from the end of the Civil War until his death in 1870 (when the name of the college was changed to include his name). The brick chapel contains Lee's office, Lee family memorabilia, and a famous portrait of George Washington by Charles Wilson Peale. A white marble sculpture of the recumbent Lee by Edward Valentine is in the memorial chamber, a solemn but impressive sight. Lee and his family are buried beneath the chapel on the museum level. Lee's beloved horse, Traveller, is interred in a marked plot outside Lee's office. The museum is wheelchair accessible.

Stonewall Jackson House (ages 9 and up)

8 East Washington St.; (540) 463-2552; www.stonewalljackson.org. Open daily except Easter Sunday, Thanksgiving, Christmas Day, and New Year's Day. $.

This was the home of the general from 1859 until he went to war in 1861 (he died in 1863). Just 5 blocks from the Virginia Military Institute campus where he taught, the house contains period furnishings and a reproduction of Jackson's vegetable garden. Youngsters are given a small slate listing household items to find, such as the upright desk where Jackson stood to prepare his lessons or his razor resting on the bedroom bureau. There's also a museum shop.

Horse-Drawn Carriage Tours of Historic Lexington (all ages)

Headquartered across from the Lexington Visitor Center, 106 East Washington St.; (540) 463-5647; www.lexcarriage.com. Open daily Apr through Oct, weather permitting. $$.

Children who don't have the attention span or don't like to walk through houses may brighten up at the prospect of a narrated ride on a horse-drawn carriage. The tour passes by the Jackson House, the restored historic downtown district, Washington and Lee University, Lee Chapel, the historic residential district, and the Stonewall Jackson Memorial Cemetery.

Haunting Tales of Lexington (all ages)

Leaves from the visitor center, 106 East Washington St.; (540) 464-2250. Tours run from late May through Oct. $.

Experience the eerie transformation of the charming city of Lexington after the sun goes down. This guided candlelit walking tour lasts 90 minutes and begins at 8:30 p.m. Reservations advised.

Virginia Horse Center (all ages)

On Highway 39 West near the intersection of I-64 and I-81; (540) 464-2950; www.horsecenter.org. Open year-round, shows on selected dates. Most shows are free of charge.

Call ahead to see if there's anything special going on during your visit. This nearly 660-acre center presents horse shows throughout the year and also offers English and Western riding demonstrations, rodeos, and drill team exhibitions, as well as miniature-horse shows and pony club shows.

Hull's Drive-In Movie Theater (all ages)

2367 North Lee Highway, Lexington; (540) 463-2621; www.hullsdrivein.com. Open Fri through Sun from Apr to Oct. $.

Enjoy an evening out at this old-fashioned drive-in movie theater, the only non-profit, community owned drive-in in the country. Kids ages 11 and under admitted **free.** A double feature is shown each Fri and Sat at dusk with the movies shown in reverse order on Sun evenings.

Where to Eat

Country Café, 1476 West Faulkner Hwy., Natural Bridge Station; (540) 291-2843. Breakfast, lunch, and dinner daily. Sandwich and full dinner menu, homemade biscuits, salads, desserts, 1950s soda fountain, and children's menu. No credit cards. $–$$

A Joyful Spirit Café, 26 South Main St.; (540) 463-4191. Open daily for breakfast and lunch and early dinners. Good vegetarian meals plus chicken, turkey, and tuna for everyone else. $

Franks for the Memories, 2117 Magnolia Ave., Buena Vista; (540) 261-5533. Open Mon through Sat. This sidewalk cafe serves hotdogs with more than 40 available toppings, as well as sandwiches and smoothies. $

Sweet Things Ice Cream Shoppe, 106 West Washington St.; (540) 463-6055. Open daily. Take a milkshake, sundae, or frozen yogurt break at this dessert haven where the ice cream and cones are homemade. $

Where to Stay

Country Inn and Suites, 875 North Lee Hwy.; (540) 464-9000 or (800) 456-4000. Offers complimentary continental breakfast, indoor pool, exercise room, in-room refrigerator, and coffeemaker. $$$

Lavender Hill Farm Bed & Breakfast, 1374 Big Spring Dr.; (540) 464-5877 or (800) 446-4240. Country charm and good food on a 1780s working sheep farm, 7 miles from the Lexington Visitor Center. Fishing, biking, hiking, and riding, too. $$$$

Howard Johnson Hotel, 2836 N. Lee Hwy., Lexington; (540) 463-9181. Recently renovated hotel with outdoor pool, 18-hole minigolf, gym, and complimentary breakfast. $$$

Annual Events

APRIL

Scott–Irish Heritage Festival, Lexington; (540) 464 6545. Traditional food, music, games, and crafts.

Easter egg hunt and kite contest, Glen Maury Park; (540) 261-7321. **Free.** Community event for kids.

JUNE–JULY

Rockbridge Rapids Baseball Games, Smith Field; (540) 463-3686. Top national collegiate players compete in a family atmosphere. Kids ages 10 and under admitted **free.**

JUNE–AUGUST

Friday's Alive Concert, Davidson Park; (540) 463-3777. **Free** summer concert series.

JULY

Lexington Hot Air Balloon Rally and Fourth of July Celebration, at the VMI parade grounds; (540) 463-3777. Enjoy hot-air-balloon rides, tethered balloon rides, food, games, and entertainment. Fireworks on the Fourth cap off the two-day event.

Rockbridge Regional Fair, mid-July at the Virginia Horse Center; (540) 463-6263. This festival has lumberjacks, horses, art, a rodeo, and an antique car show, as well as food and music.

AUGUST

Rockbridge Community Festival, late August, downtown Lexington; (540) 463-3777. The community gathers together in the streets of Lexington to celebrate and enjoy the summer with crafts, food, and entertainment.

SEPTEMBER

Annual Labor Day Festival, Buena Vista; (540) 463-3777. Parade, music, and activities.

Annual Rockbridge Mountain Music and Dance Festival, Glen Maury Park; (540) 463-3777.

OCTOBER

Mountain Day Celebration, Buena Vista; (540) 261-9463. Traditional craft demonstrations for kids, music, games, and vendors.

DECEMBER

Downtown Lexington Holiday Parade; (540) 463-3777.

Living Nativity, Buena Vista; (540) 463-3777. Entire village complete with living actors, zoo animals, and a 45-minute tour.

For More Information

Lexington Visitor Center, 106 East Washington St., Lexington, VA 22450; (540) 463-3777; www.lexingtonvirginia.com. Open daily. The center has a walking tour, hiking trails, and art tour brochures.

Bath County

The drive to Bath County, some 40 miles from Lexington along Highway 39, includes the former stagecoach route into Lexington, whose scenic highlight is the 3-milelong Goshen Pass. This pleasant drive winds through the mountains along the Maury River. There are no incorporated towns and no traffic lights in Bath County, but there are several small communities. For centuries visitors—especially the socially prominent and ambitious—have ventured to Warm Springs for the thermal waters sheltered in 18th-century bathhouses. Urbanites are still coming for relaxation. The Homestead, an upscale resort, offers fine dining and family activities.

The Homestead Resort (all ages)

US 220, Hot Springs; (540) 839-1766 or (800) 838-1766; www.thehomestead.com. $$$–$$$$.

Soaking, supping, or simply relaxing is easy here. This year-round resort, long favored by the rich, the politically influential (including presidents), and the famous, offers families lots of recreational possibilities, including a winter snowboard park. Most activities cost extra, so a stay here can get pricey, especially for an active family. Adults can reenergize at the spa, a facility employing the county's famed healing waters in a variety of tub and rub combinations. The KidSpa makes this grande dame resort in the Allegheny Mountains especially appealing to preteens and teens. This hard-to-please group can now indulge in facials designed for them, try Swedish massages (clothes on), sign up for personalized makeup lessons, and luxuriate in treatments that soak their toes in a rich chocolate milk-like mix and their fingers in strawberries and cream. In season, families enjoy golf, tennis, falconry, mountain biking, fishing, horseback riding and pony riding (for smaller children), hiking, bowling, snowboarding, snow tubing, ice-skating, and snowshoeing.

The Homestead KidsClub, for ages 3 to 12, operates year-round, with half-day and full-day supervised play centered around a theme. Kids' Night Out is offered on Sat evenings in the summer and winter. Activities include computer games, arts and crafts, science projects, kite flying, pottery making, swimming, pole fishing at the Children's Pond and hiking. In the winter kids can enjoy ice-skating and hot cocoa.

Homestead Ski Area

US 220, Hot Springs; (540) 839-1766 or (800) 838-1766; www.thehomestead.com. $–$$$.

The Homestead Resort's Ski Area offers manageable terrain that's good for beginners. Playland Terrain Park is for snowboarders.

Lake Moomaw (all ages)

George Washington National Park, Covington; (540) 839-2521; www.bathcountyva.org/recreation/GWNF.htm. $$.

Lake Moomaw is a 2,530 acre lake surrounded by the George Washington National Forest. The lake is 19 miles north of Covington. Lake Moomaw provides a variety of outdoor activities such boating, swimming, hiking, fishing, as well as camping.

Douthat State Park (all ages)

14239 Douthat State Park Rd., Millboro; (540) 862-8100; www.dcr.virginia.gov/state_parks/dou.shtml. The park straddles Bath and Alleghany counties. $–$$.

Douthat State Park, listed on the Register of Historic Places, was one of the original six Virginia State Parks that opened June 15, 1936. A 50-acre lake offers swimming, boating, and seasonal trout fishing. Other activities include hiking and cycling along bike trails. From mid-June through Sept and on weekends in Apr, May, Sept, and Oct, the park offers guided hikes, canoe tours, children's programs, and lectures.

Natural Bridge

Take exit 175 or exit 180 from I-81 to get to Natural Bridge, which is located on US 11; (540) 291-2121 or (800) 533-1410; www.naturalbridgeva.com. $–$$$.

Natural Bridge, a pleasant day trip from the Homestead Resort or a half-day trip from Lexington makes a good stop on the way to Roanoke. The bridge is a limestone arch, 215 feet high and 90 feet wide, carved by Cedar Creek. The bridge contains 450,000 cubic feet of rock and likely weighs about 36,000 tons. Like almost everything else in Virginia, the Natural Bridge has a historic past. George Washington surveyed it for Lord Fairfax (you can see where he was believed to have carved his initials), and Thomas Jefferson, so taken by its beauty, bought the arch and the surrounding land.

The arch is the centerpiece for a complex of attractions. Natural Bridge of Virginia puts on *The Drama of Creation,* a nightly light show. The Wax Museum (540) 291-2121 or (800) 533-1410) exhibits 150 lifelike replicas of historic people in Virginia history. At the **Toy Museum,** advertised as the largest collection of childhood memorabilia in the world, you can view 45,000 items, including toys, games, and dolls, dating from 1740 to the present.

At the **Monacan Indian Living History Village,** reached by a nature trail, children can participate in canoe building, shelter construction, hide tanning, and mat and rope weaving. The Monacans, one of Virginia's oldest Native American tribes, welcome the opportunity to explain and demonstrate their culture to visitors. At the Fall Festival every year, visitors learn songs and dances and sample Monacan vegetables grown at the village.

The Natural Bridge Caverns (all ages)

US 11; (800) 533-1410 or (540) 291-2121. Open daily, closed mid-Dec through mid-Mar. $$.

On the forty-five-minute guided tour, you see one of the largest flowstone formations on the East Coast. Legend has it that the caverns are haunted. The temperature is 54 degrees F year-round, so bring a light sweater or jacket. Discount coupons are available on the Natural Bridge Web site. Buy a ticket for any combination of the bridge, caverns, wax museum, and toy museum.

Garth Newel Music Center (all ages)

Route 220, half-way between Hot Springs and Warm Springs; (540) 839-5018; end of Apr to the end of Oct; www.garthnewel.org. $$$.

The Garth Newel Music Center offers musical concerts and food in a scenic setting. The facility is home to the Virginia Blues and Jazz Festival each June.

Virginia Safari Park (all ages)

229 Safari Lane, Natural Bridge; (540) 291-3205; www.virginiasafaripark.com. Open daily mid-Mar through Nov. $.

Drive through the 180 acres to view free-roaming elk, bison, zebra, antelope, and ostrich. Little ones enjoy the petting zoo and the guided tractor-driven wagon ride on weekends (daily during the summer).

The Wilderness Canoe Company (ages 14 and up)

US 11 and Highway 130, Natural Bridge; (540) 291-2295; http://wildernesscanoe.com. $$–$$$.

Rent a canoe for a self-guided trip or sign-on for a guided expedition on the Upper James River along the foothills of the Allegheny Mountains and the Blue Ridge. Overnight trips use a fifty-acre base camp from which you hike and canoe. Dogs are welcome.

For More Information
Bath County Chamber of Commerce, US 220, P.O. Box 718, Hot Springs, VA 24445;   (540) 839-5409 or (800) 628-8091; www.bath countyva.org.

Roanoke Valley

Roanoke, 54 miles south of Lexington offers recreational and educational attractions.

Science Museum of Western Virginia (all ages)
Center in the Square, corner of Campbell and Market Streets, Levels 4 and 5; (540) 342-5710; www.smwv.org. Open Tues through Sun; closed Easter, Memorial Day, Labor Day, Thanksgiving, Christmas Day, and New Year's Day. $.

Hands-on explorations range from broadcasting weather on closed-circuit television to fingering critters in the Hardbottom Reel Tank, a 750-gallon marine aquarium. In the Geology Gallery, kids can unearth clues about the Earth's age, and in Body Tech they can explore the body's circulatory system. The Light and Sound Arcade is an interactive exploration of color, sound, and light. The Illusion's Gallery offers interactive computer puzzles and distorted illusions. Treasures displays minerals and crystals from all over the world. The Watershed Gallery features a 42-footlong river model with five habitats (and live residents) representing those habitats natural to the local area as the river flows from the mountains to the sea.

Check out the changing exhibits on the fifth floor and the live animal demonstrations on Sat afternoon. Three- and five-day science camps are held every summer for preschoolers through ninth-graders.

Watch the stars at the William B. Hopkins Planetarium, part of the Science Museum. In addition, you can watch movies on the MegaDome, a 40-foot dome-shaped screen with surround sound.

Taubman Museum of Art (ages 5 and up)
110 Salem Ave. SE, Levels 1 and 2; (540) 342-5760; www.taubmanmuseum.org. Open Tues through Sun. $.

The Taubman Museum of Art showcases American, modern and contemporary art as well as design and decorative folk art. Tours, gallery talks, musical performances, films, family days, classes, camps, and special events are part of the museum's offerings.

Art Venture, the museum's interactive gallery and art center for children, features nine stations designed to engage kids through hands-on activities.

Family-friendly weekend activities include weekly Sunday Afternoon Music by regional musicians, and a monthly Arts in Concert Family Series of performances by members of the Roanoke Symphony orchestra.

History Museum of Western Virginia (ages 5 and up)
Center in the Square, Level 3; (540) 342-5770; www.history-museum.org. Open Tues through Sun. $.

This museum tells the area's natural and cultural heritage. Peruse prehistoric artifacts, Native American relics, colonial costumes, and a 1890s dry-goods store. Exhibits feature a Native American wigwam, a land grant deed signed by Thomas Jefferson, Civil War surgical implements and sabers, a Victorian parlor, and a 1925 Marshall & Wendell baby grand player piano. Fantasyland, held each year from Thanksgiving to Christmas, brings memories to life with displays of characters from area department stores' Christmas decorations from past eras. Santa also tells stories, sings songs, and plays piano and guitar. The museum's store, the History Shop, sells old-fashioned toys, historical maps, and books.

Virginia Museum of Transportation (ages 3 to 9)
303 Norfolk Ave.; (540) 342-5670; www.vmt.org. Open daily. $.

This museum is a great place for kids to learn about all kinds of transportation. The collection includes examples from railroad's golden past such as steam, diesel, and vintage electric locomotives, cabooses, a railway postal car, and business car. Although the museum is primarily devoted to rail, other eye-catchers include automotive and aviation exhibits, as well as horse-drawn buggies and a trolley bus. The Star Station Transportation Playground has child-sized helicopters, cars, and trains, and a rocket for kids to play in and on. Don't miss the model-trains exhibit, a star with six tracks, multiple viewing levels, and a model of a Barnum and Bailey Circus. The museum store is a great source of hard-to-find transportation-related toys and gifts. After your visit, stroll along the David R. and Susan S. Goode Railwalk toward the Farmers' Market to watch more trains.

Roanoke Star/Overlook (all ages)
Off the Blue Ridge Parkway at mile 120; or from downtown follow Jefferson Street to Walnut Avenue.

The city's most visible attraction since 1949, the 100-foot-tall illuminated star made out of steel, concrete, and 2,000 feet of neon tubing shines from the top of Mill Mountain, less than a ten-minute drive from downtown.

Mill Mountain Zoo (all ages)
Off US 220 South, mile 120 on the Blue Ridge Parkway; (540) 343-3241; www.mmzoo.org. Open daily from 10 a.m. to 5 p.m. except Thanksgiving, Christmas, and New Year's Day. $.

Along with its great view of the valley, the zoo exhibits 50 species of exotic and native animals, such as red pandas, a Siberian tiger, hawks, snow leopards, and reptiles. The ZooChoo train is fun for smaller children. Picnic facilities are available. In summer, check the schedule of live programs in the amphitheater.

Arts Council of the Blue Ridge

20 East Church Ave., Level 1; (540) 342-5790; www.theartscouncil.org. Open Tues through Fri.

Use this resource center to see if anything special is going on during your visit. Regular programs include the Roanoke City Art Show, the High School Art Exhibition, and Art A La Carte. A toll-free Culture Hot Line helps out-of-town visitors plan their trip; call (877) SWV-TODO; locally (540) 224-1248.

Dixie Caverns and Pottery Shop (ages 4 and up)

5753 West Main St., Salem; (540) 380-2085; www.dixiecaverns.com. Open daily year-round. $.

Dixie Caverns is located at exit 132 off I-81 South. On the forty-five-minute tour, see the Cathedral Room (the main area), as well as the Wedding Bell and Turkey Wing named after key formations. The temperature is a constant 56 degrees F, so grab the sweaters. The gift shop has a good selection of rocks and minerals.

Booker T. Washington National Monument (ages 7 and up)

On Highway 122, 6 miles east of Burnt Chimney; (540) 721-2094; www.nps.gov/bowa. Open daily except Thanksgiving, Christmas, and New Year's Day. Free.

Booker T. Washington was born into slavery in the kitchen of this 19th-century tobacco plantation. He lived here until the age of 9, when he was freed by the Emancipation Proclamation. Later Washington became a respected educator and founder of the Tuskegee Institute in Alabama, as well as an adviser to presidents. Start at the visitor center with a fourteen-minute video on Washington's life. The historic 0.25-milelong Plantation Trail loops through this 207-acre restored plantation and leads to several reconstructed buildings, which include a kitchen cabin (showing what the kitchen looked like when Washington was born) and the tobacco barn (the cash crop during Washington's days). During the summer a variety of programs are offered for children. Kids can also participate in the Junior Ranger program.

Harrison Museum of African-American Culture (all ages)

523 Harrison Ave.; (540) 345-4818; www.harrisonmuseum.com. Open Tues through Sun. Free.

Located on the ground level of the 1916 Harrison School, the first high school for African Americans in southwestern Virginia, this museum celebrates African-American culture through both local and regional historical exhibitions, art displays, and special events throughout the year, including the Henry Street Festival the last Sat in Sept.

Salem Red Sox Baseball (all ages)

P.O. Box 842, Salem, VA 24153; (540) 389-3333; www.salemavalanche.com. $.

The Boston Red Sox's top Class A Minor League Baseball team plays ball Apr through Labor Day at the Lewis–Gale field adjacent to the Salem Civic Center at 1004 Texas St.

Where to Eat

Carlos Brazilian International Cuisine, 4167 Electric Rd.; (540) 776-1117. Lunch and dinner, Mon through Sat. If you're in the mood for something a little different, like paella Valenciana (seafood, chicken, pork, and sausage with rice and herbs), this might be the place. Kids will enjoy trying guarana, a popular Brazilian soft drink. $$–$$$

Homeplace, 4968 Catawba Dr. in Catawba; (540) 384-7252. Open Thurs through Sat for dinner and Sun for lunch and dinner. The family-style meals feature fried chicken, hot biscuits, and mashed potatoes and gravy. $

Market Building, 32 Market Sq.; (540) 774-1641. This historic building, once the city's meat market, now sports an international food court serving kids' favorites such as tacos, burgers, and pizza. $

Where to Stay

AmeriSuites/Hyatt Place, 5040 Valley View Blvd., Roanoke; (540) 366-4700 or (800) 833-1516. Complimentary continental breakfast; **free** wireless Internet, large indoor pool, and a fitness center. Guest rooms have a small refrigerator, microwave, and coffeemaker in rooms. Located at the Valley View Mall, with shopping and food court. $$$–$$$$

Baymont Inn/LaQuinta, 140 Sheraton Dr., Salem; (540) 562-2717 or (877) BAYMONT; www.LQ.com. Newly remodeled the inn offers complimentary breakfast including hot waffles. There are micro-fridges in all rooms, **free** cable, and satellite movies. $$$

Best Western Inn at Valley View, I-81 to I-581, exit 3E, 5050 Valley View Blvd., Roanoke; (540) 363-2400 or (800) 362-2410. Continental breakfast and an indoor pool. $$$–$$$$

Comfort Suites, The Inn at Ridgewood Farm, 2898 Keagy Rd., Salem; (540)

375-4800 or (800) 628-1922. Outdoor pool; exercise room; refrigerator and microwave in room. $$$–$$$$

Dixie Caverns Campground, 5753 West Main St., Salem; (540) 380-2085. Open year-round. Hookups include electricity, water, cable TV; showers and dump station. $

Annual Events

APRIL

Kite Festival, Green Hill Park, (540) 387-0267. The festival held yearly the third Sat of Apr involves amateur to professional kite-flying with plenty of fun and activities.

MAY

Annual Sidewalk Art Show, (540) 342-5760. Works by hundreds of regional artists displayed in downtown Roanoke, sponsored by the Taubman Museum of Art.

Roanoke Festival in the Park, around Memorial Day; (540) 342-2640; www.roanokefestival.org. Features music, a crafts show, and many children's activities.

Salem Fair & Exposition; (540) 375-3004; www.salemfair.com. Rides, games, food, and music.

JULY

Commonwealth Games of Virginia, mid-July; (540) 343-0987. An amateur sports festival for all ages. Recognized by the U.S. Olympic Committee and National Congress of State Games, these are Virginia's Olympics. In the past, over 10,000 athletes have competed in forty-five sports. Gold, silver, and bronze medals are awarded.

AUGUST

Annual Vinton Old-Time Bluegrass Festival and Competition, mid-Aug; (540) 983-0613. Features four days of bluegrass, vendors, crafts, kiddie rides, and more.

Virginia Mountain Peach Festival, first Fri and Sat of Aug. Peach shakes, sundaes, cobbler, and shortcakes, accompanied by live entertainment.

SEPTEMBER
Appalachian Folk Festival, at Virginia's Explore Park; (540) 427-1800. Dedicated to celebrating traditional Appalachian music and folkways, with Native American storytelling, stone tool making, cattail and gourd crafts, quilting, and children's games.

DECEMBER
Fantasyland, Thanksgiving to Christmas. Visit Santa who tells stories, sings songs, plays piano and guitar, and teaches children of all ages the meaning of giving all year long. At the History Museum of Western Virginia.

For More Information
The Roanoke Valley Convention and Visitors Bureau Visitor Information, 101 Shenandoah Ave., Northeast, Roanoke, VA 24016; (540) 342-6025 or (800) 635-5535; www.visitroanokeva.com. Open daily year-round.

Winchester

Located 140 miles northwest of Richmond and 18 miles north of the start of Skyline Drive, Winchester is a good starting point for exploring the Shenandoah Valley and the Virginia highlands. This city played a significant role in both the French and Indian and Civil Wars. During the latter the town changed hands more than seventy times, including thirteen times in one day. If your family comes in the spring, you'll be treated to the heavenly sight of apple blossoms at the Shenandoah Apple Blossom Festival, whose parade includes marching bands, floats, and the Fire Fighter's Parade, one of the nation's largest displays of firefighting equipment.

Stonewall Jackson's Headquarters Museum (ages 10 and up)
415 Braddock St.; (540) 667-3242; www.winchesterhistory.org. **Open daily Apr through Oct. $.**

This house looks much as it did when General Thomas J. "Stonewall" Jackson coordinated his valley campaign here from November 1861 to March 1862. On display are maps, memorabilia, photos, and artifacts of Jackson and other Civil War soldiers, including the table Jackson used as a desk and his prayer table, which was taken into the field with him. A small shop sells coloring books, Confederate hats, and children's books about the Civil War. Fans of classic television shows might be interested to know that this building was originally owned by Colonel Lewis T. Moore, great-grandfather of actress Mary Tyler Moore; the colonel invited Jackson to use it while he was headquartered in Winchester.

George Washington's Office Museum (ages 10 and up)
32 West Cork St., on the corner of Cork and Braddock; (540) 662-4412; www.winchester history.org. **Open daily Apr through Oct. $.**

This small log cabin served as Washington's office from September 1755 to December 1756 while he built Fort Loudon to defend the 300-mile frontier of Virginia during the

French and Indian War. Memorabilia, including some rare surveying tools, are on display, but kids will probably be more interested in the detailed table model of the city of Winchester in the 1750s, plus the two authentic cannons. One is from Fort Loudon and the other was used by the British general Edward Braddock in the French and Indian War. (Legend has it that Braddock's cannon was fished out of the Potomac River, where his soldiers had tossed it.) An exhibit called *George Washington and the West* demonstrates that the frontiers of Virginia were where Washington gained his military experience.

Jim Barnett Park (all ages)
Adjoins the visitor center and Abram's Delight; (540) 662-4946. Open year-round, dawn to dusk. Free.

The city's major recreation area with 174 acres, this park gives you and your kids a chance to play and picnic. Try the fitness trail, swim in the indoor or outdoor pools, play tennis, basketball, horseshoes, and miniature golf. There is also a fitness room and a racquetball court. Admission to the park is **free,** but there is a fee for some of the activities.

Horseback Riding
See the countryside from horseback at two area ranches:

Rocking S Ranch (suggested ages 8 and up)
564 Glazie Orchard Rd., Winchester; (540) 678-8501; www.therockingsranch.com. $$$.

Ride through the same Shenandoah Valley foothills ridden by the Confederate and Union forces.

Amazing Winchester Facts

- **George Washingto**n slept in Winchester. He began his surveying career here in 1748. Later he helped build Fort Loudon and was headquartered in town as commander of the Virginia frontier.

- **Patsy Cline,** country music's sweetheart of the 1960s, was born in Winchester. US 522 has been named the Patsy Cline Memorial Highway in her honor. Plans are under way to raise money to buy Cline's home and restore it to the way it was when Patsy lived there to honor the artist and her talent.

- **George Washington** left another legacy in Winchester: As a landlord, he required each tenant to plant four acres of apples. As a result, ample apple orchards surround the town.

Wagon Wheel Ranch (suggested ages 8 and up)

5522 Cedar Creek Grade, Winchester; http://thewagonwheelranch.org. $$$.

Ride alongside cattle and through rolling hills.

The State Arboretum of Virginia (ages 5 and up)

400 Blandy Farm Lane, Boyce. 10 miles east of Winchester; (540) 837-1758; www.virginia .edu/~blandy. Open year-round, dawn to dusk. Free.

Also called the Orland E. White Arboretum, the State Arboretum of Virginia consists of 170 acres of trees and meadows that are part of the 700-acre Blandy Experimental Farm, a University of Virginia research facility. The arboretum offers families a tranquil place to unwind and affords children a chance to experience nature up close. At Lake Georgette there are more than one hundred painted turtles for kids to see and at least that many bluebird boxes among the trees. Every spring a pair of barn swallows returns to nest in the Information Pavilion, adjacent to the parking area. Using binoculars, kids can view the swallows and their young. Walking and driving trails are available, and there's a 5-mile bridle trail for horses (bring your own horse). Family concerts are held throughout the summer at the Margaret Byrd Stimpson Amphitheater, and the gift shop has a very good selection of nature and gardening books written for children. A 3-mile loop road takes visitors to the arboretum's more remote areas.

Shenandoah Valley Discovery Museum (ages 2 to 7)

54 South Loudon St., between Boscawen and Cork Streets, Winchester; (540) 722-2020; www.discoverymuseum.net. Open daily year-round. $.

Although a small facility, this museum appeals to young children by offering hands-on activities in art, science, and natural history. The climbing wall is popular, as are the Hospital Emergency Room and the Mirrors attractions. Kids love the paleontology exhibit, where a staff member works on a dinosaur skull, preparing it for display, and answers questions about how the work is done and what the skull tells paleontologists about the dinosaur. Throughout the year, the museum offers special programs and workshops. Classes have covered the steps of dissecting a brain and Mayan archaeology, as well as readings offered by a well-known author of children's books. The Visiting Artist Series (second weekend of each month; free with admission; no reservations needed) offers families the chance to work on art projects together. The museum's Web site has interesting interactive experiments and puzzles.

Museum of the Shenandoah Valley (all ages)

901 Amherst St., Winchester; (540) 662-1473 or (888) 556-5799. Museum open year-round. The house and gardens are open Mar through Nov. Facilities open Tues through Sun. $–$$.

The complex features a six-acre garden, the Glen Burnie Historic House, plus the four-gallery, 50,000-square-foot Museum of the Shenandoah Valley. Take kids straight to the Miniature Gallery, a display of miniature houses furnished with artisan-crafted tiny silverware, hand-woven rugs, and even crystal chandeliers. The Shenandoah Valley Gallery

Follow the Apple Trail (all ages)

Drive past Winchester's orchards by following a 45-mile scenic route. An audio CD keeps you informed. Pick the CD or tape up at the Visitor Center, 1400 South Pleasant Valley Rd., Winchester; (540) 542-1326. $

details how and why people settled in the region, and the Shenandoah Valley Decorative Arts Gallery displays quilts, furniture, and other folk art.

Virginia Farm Market (all ages)

US 522, 1 mile north of Winchester, 1881 North Frederick Pike; (540) 665-8000. Open daily Apr through mid-Dec. **Free.**

In the summer, fresh fruits, such as peaches and cantaloupes, and vegetables from Shenandoah Valley and nearby areas are for sale, along with pies, muffins, and cookies baked fresh daily. In the fall enjoy the Pumpkin Patch, with a maze, photo area, a 40-foot-long toy train for kids to play in, and pumpkins galore. Fresh cider and hot apple pie, too.

Old Court House Civil War Museum (all ages)

20 North Loudon St., in Winchester's Old Town Walking Mall; (540) 542-1145; www.civilwar museum.org. Open Wed through Sun; closed Thanksgiving Day, Christmas Eve, Christmas Day, and New Year's Day. $.

Housed in the historic Winchester–Frederick Court House, this museum focuses on the life of common soldiers, especially those who were prisoners of war. Winchester changed hands more than seventy times during the war, and prisoners from both sides were housed in this building. Graffiti on the walls testifies to their presence and their thoughts on the war. (On the south wall is a strongly worded curse aimed at Jefferson Davis, president of the Confederacy.) There are also armaments and other relics of the war. Kids will enjoy ringing the courthouse bell, and the gift shop has an excellent selection of children's books, stickers, and games.

Shenandoah Summer Music Theatre (ages 4 and up)

1460 University Dr., Winchester; (540) 665-4569 or (877) 580-8025; http://shenandoahsummer musictheatre.com. Open June through Aug. $$–$$$.

Broadway musical productions with a full live orchestra for the whole family.

Where to Eat

Brewbakers Restaurant, 168 North Loudon St.; (540) 535-0111. Open Tues through Sat for lunch and dinner. On sunny days, sit outside and enjoy a bountiful barbecued sandwich, plus other standard fare. $$ Children's menu. $

CiCi's Pizza, 2059 South Pleasant Valley Rd.; (540) 535-0002. Open daily. Kids like the tasty pizza. $

Cork Street Tavern, 8 West Cork St.; (540) 667-3777. Open Tues through Sat for lunch and dinner. For more than twenty years, the Cork Street Tavern has been known for its ribs. Steaks, seafood, and sandwiches are also on the menu. In warm weather enjoy dining on the patio. $–$$

Snow White Grill, 159 North Loudon St., Winchester; (540) 662-5955. Open Mon through Fri for lunch and dinner. This restaurant is another blast from the past, with a 1949 soda fountain, counter, and stools. The shakes, ice cream, and silver-dollar-size burgers appeal to kids. $

Triangle Diner, 27 West Gerrard St., Winchester; (866) 529-6065; www.mikestriangle diner.com. The diner, undergoing extensive renovations, hopes to open in spring 2010.

Venice Italian Restaurant, US 522 North; (540) 722-0992. This family restaurant serves lunch and dinner, both Italian food and hamburgers. $–$$

Where to Stay

Country Inn and Suites, 141 Kernstown Commons Blvd. (intersection of I-81, exit 310, Route 11, and I-37); (800) 201-1746; www .countryinns.com/winchesterva. All rooms include complimentary breakfast, Internet access, and coffeemakers. There is an indoor pool. The nearby Outback Steakhouse delivers. $$–$$$

Courtyard by Marriott, 300 Marriott Dr., Winchester; (540) 678-8822 or (800) 321-2211; www.marriott.com. The property offers such conveniences for families as a 24-hour market, a cafe, and indoor pool, as well as complimentary newspaper and high-speed Internet. $$–$$$

The Cove Campground, 980 Cove Rd., Gore (12 miles west of Winchester); (540) 858-2882; www.vvalley.com/cove. This facility has more than one hundred campsites and cabins on its 3,000 mountain acres. In season you can fish and swim in the three lakes, bike, go snow tubing (they have tubes for rent), or cross-country ski. There is electricity for campsites and a small store selling supplies. $

Hampton Inn, 1655 Apple Blossom Dr.; (540) 667-8011 or (800) HAMPTON; www .hampton-inn.com. Convenient to restaurants and historic sites. Room rates include a continental breakfast and **free** HBO, plus in-room Super Nintendo. Adjacent to the Apple Blossom Mall, which has eighty-five stores and a food court. There's an outdoor pool. $$

Holiday Inn Express & Suites, 142 Fox Ridge Lane; (540) 667-7050; www.hiexpress .com. Rates include **free** breakfast, and the property has an indoor pool and high-speed Internet access. $$$

Annual Events
MAY
Shenandoah Apple Blossom Festival. Crafts, a carnival, fireworks, and what is reputed to be the world's largest firefighters' parade are part of the festivities. Call (540) 662-3863 or visit www.thebloom.com.

SEPTEMBER
Apple Harvest Arts & Crafts Festival, one of the area's largest annual events, with arts, crafts, music, apple-butter making, square dancing, and lots more. Usually held the third weekend in Sept in Jim Barnett Park. Call (540) 662-3996.

OCTOBER
Battle of Cedar Creek Reenactment, Route 11, Middletown. Relive the October 19, 1864, Civil War Battle of Cedar Creek on the original grounds as cavalry, artillery, and infantry meet in combat. Browse Civil War

merchants' stalls, listen to period music, and go on a candlelit tour of the camps. Held the third weekend in Oct. Call (540) 869-2064 or visit www.cedarcreekbattlefield.org.

Shenandoah Valley Hot Air Balloon and Wine Festival, with more than thirty hot-air-balloon launches, powered parachutes, wine tastings, antique fire engines, children's amphitheater, and crafts. Call (540) 837-1856 or (888) 558-5567.

For More Information

Winchester–Frederick County Convention and Visitors Bureau, 1400 South Pleasant Valley Rd., Winchester, VA 22601; (540) 542-1326 or (877) 871-1326; www.visit winchesterva.com. Open daily year-round except major holidays. The eighteen-minute film *Welcome to the Top* offers background on the city and the surrounding area at the visitor center. A **free** tourist information packet is also available.

Middletown

Middletown, a small town 13 miles south of Winchester, sports two attractions for families: the historic Belle Grove Plantation and performances at the Wayside Theatre.

Belle Grove Plantation (ages 6 and up)

336 Belle Grove Rd.; (540) 869-2028; www.bellegrove.org/about.html. Open daily from Apr through Oct; only weekends in Nov. Special holiday tours at Thanksgiving and in Dec. $.

This native limestone mansion was built in the late 1700s by Major Isaac Hite for his bride, Nelly Madison, sister of President James Madison. The president honeymooned here with his wife, Dolley. Thomas Jefferson played an active role in the design of Belle Grove after Madison requested his advice.

The house, restored in 1930, suffered damage during the Civil War Battle of Cedar Creek. Union General Philip Sheridan's troops occupied the plantation and Confederate forces attacked. The early-19th-century forge and icehouse are particularly interesting, and if you're lucky enough to be here when groups are touring, be sure to see the working demonstrations.

In July there's the Old-Fashioned Ice Cream Social, with ice-cream sundaes and early American music. Each Oct the plantation hosts a Civil War Battle reenactment, complete with encampments, and in Nov there is a Living History Weekend with craftspeople in period costume giving demonstrations and selling their wares. The grounds are spectacular, with sweeping views of the Shenandoah Valley and surrounding Blue Ridge and Allegheny Mountains.

Wayside Theatre (all ages)

7853 Main St., on the corner of Second and Main Streets; (540) 869-1776 or (800) 951-1776; www.waysidetheatre.org. Open Feb through Dec. $$–$$$.

For more than forty-five years the stage performances at the Wayside Theatre have entertained the townsfolk and launched the careers of many well-known actors and dramatists such as Susan Sarandon, Jill Eikenberry, and Peter Boyle. In general, several plays a season are suited to families. In the spring there are special shows for children. Upcoming shows are posted on the Web site.

Where to Eat

Civil Cricket Café, 7868 Main St.; (540) 868-0919; www.civilcricket.com. Open daily for breakfast and lunch Tues through Sat. Dinner on Fri and Sat. Brunch on Sun. The casual cafe offers big country breakfasts, homemade sandwiches, soups, quiche, and chili. The weekend menu may include pan seared salmon and honey roasted chicken. $$

Where to Stay

Wayside Inn, 7783 Main St.; (540) 869-1797; www.alongthewayside.com. This historical inn has been serving the public for over 200 years, and has 22 guest rooms and suites. American cuisine is available year-round and is served in seven dining rooms by servers in colonial costumes. $$–$$$

Strasburg

Strasburg is about 5 miles south from Middletown on US 11. *Note:* Ask about the special three-for-one package when visiting the Museum of American Presidents, Stonewall Jackson Museum at Hupp's Hill, and Crystal Caverns at Hupp's Hill.

Stonewall Jackson Museum at Hupp's Hill
(ages 7 and up)

33229 Old Valley Pike (Route 11, just south of I-81 exit 208); (540) 465-5884; www.waysideofva.com. Open daily. $.

This museum portrays Stonewall Jackson's military career through exhibits. Kids see a soldier's wool jacket, swords, and other military items. A highlight for younger kids is the hands-on Civil War camp complete with tents, tin cups, muskets, kid-size soldier's clothing, and wooden horses with authentic cavalry saddles and bridles. Older kids will enjoy using "discovery boxes" to explore a historic topic through games, puzzles, and artifacts. There is also a Haversack Tour for kids that features haversacks hung from the ceiling from which kids can pull out an item related to a nearby exhibit.

Crystal Caverns at Hupp's Hill (ages 3 and up)

33231 Old Valley Pike (US 11), just north of Strasburg; (540) 465-8660; www.waysideofva.com. Open daily. $.

Discovered in 1775, Crystal Caverns is the oldest cave open to the public. Its 0.25-mile trail includes unusual crystal formations and an interpretive museum with exhibits on the cave's geology, paleontology, and history. Native Americans, local settlers, and Civil War soldiers have used the cave. Lantern Light Living History tours with guides in period costumes are available by reservation.

Strasburg and the Civil War

Strasburg played a strategic role in both Stonewall Jackson's Valley Campaign of 1862 as well as in Federal General Philip Sheridan's Shenandoah Valley Campaign of 1864. From Strasburg you can visit such nearby Civil War battlefields as Cedar Creek, Toms Brook, Fisher's Hill, and Hupp's Hill.

Hiking (all ages)

There are many hiking trails near Strasburg in the George Washington and Jefferson National Forests. The Pig Iron Interpretive Trail, a 2.5-mile loop, winds past the Elizabeth Furnace and details the area's 19th-century pig-iron industry.

Where to Eat

Hotel Strasburg, 213 South Holiday St., Strasburg, about 5 miles from Middletown; (540) 465-9191 or (800) 348-8327; www.hotelstrasburg.com. Open daily for dinner, Sun for lunch and dinner, and weekends for breakfast. Converted from a hospital to an Edwardian hotel in 1915, the restaurant serves local specialties (split-pea soup, butter-pecan chicken, and Smithfield ham in apple brandy) in a dining room accented with antiques and collectibles. $$–$$$

Where to Stay

The Ramada Inn, 21 Signal Dr. (I-81 exit 298); (540) 465-2444. One of Strasburg's newer hotels, the Ramada offers eighty-nine rooms. $$–$$$

Super 8–Middletown, 2120 Reliance Rd., on I-81, exit 302; (540) 868-1800 or (877) 9-SUPERS. Complimentary continental breakfast, plus HBO and an indoor pool. $$

The Wayside Inn, 7783 Main St.; (540) 869-1797 or (877) 869-1797; www.waysideofva.com. This rambling inn dates back to 1797. Each of the twenty-four air-conditioned rooms (including several suites) are individually decorated with antiques and collectibles (a television is in each room). A visit here can be somewhat intimidating if your kids are young and restless. Well-behaved, older children are welcome, however. Some teens especially appreciate the setting. Extra attraction: Visitors have reported seeing the ghosts of Civil War soldiers wandering through the lobby. The inn was converted into a hospital during the conflict. $$–$$$

Additional lodging is available in nearby Winchester.

For More Information

Shenandoah County Tourism, 600 North Main St., Woodstock, VA 22664; (540) 459-6227 or (888) 367-3965; www.shenandoahtravel.org.

Tidewater and Hampton Roads

A s Washingtonians, we have been escaping to Virginia for years. My family's favorite let's-have-fun foray takes us through Tidewater, an area that combines the earliest history of the American colonies with such hands-on high-tech fun as a nautical center and such sure-to-please vacation spots as Virginia Beach.

Colonial Williamsburg, Jamestown, and Yorktown, known collectively as Virginia's historic triangle, are connected by the Colonial Parkway. As you tour the area, you and your children will see the progression of American history from the first colonial settlement at Jamestown to the flowering of colonial culture and the beginnings of a revolution at Williamsburg to the final triumph over the British at Yorktown.

From here the route leads to Newport News, Hampton, and Norfolk before ending at the sandy shores of Virginia Beach. The region's abundance of family attractions, including Busch Gardens Williamsburg and its sister theme park, Water Country USA, has led this area to be dubbed Virginia's "kids' corner." A long weekend or, better yet, a week in this area is how we like our colonial history, sprinkled with science and salted with sea spray, and in summer spiced by roller coasters and cooled by water parks.

TopPicks in the Tidewater Region

1. **Colonial Williamsburg**

2. **Busch Gardens Williamsburg**

3. **Nauticus, the National Maritime Center,** Norfolk

4. **Virginia Beach**

TIDEWATER AND HAMPTON ROADS

Colonial Williamsburg

Colonial Williamsburg is about 150 miles south of Washington, D.C., approximately mid-way between Richmond and Norfolk on I-64.

Colonial Williamsburg is certainly among America's most well-known living-history museums. The area served as the capital of Virginia, England's oldest, largest, most populous, and richest colony from 1699 to 1776. How Williamsburg's leading citizens felt made a great deal of difference in the struggle toward independence. This former Virginia capital bred independent politics and drew revolutionaries such as Thomas Jefferson and Patrick Henry. Colonial Williamsburg re-creates life in Virginia as it existed in the 1770s, just before the Revolutionary War. Williamsburg, once the political and cultural center of the new world, has more than 500 buildings on its 173 acres, of which 88 homes, shops, public buildings, and taverns are original and the others are re-creations. Two on-site museums provide glimpses into the arts and crafts of the era, and the Peyton Randolph and the reconstructed Great Hopes Plantation provide insight into the lives of owners and slaves alike in 18th-century Virginia.

Historic Williamsburg lets you see life as the colonists did. By visiting the powder magazine, courthouse, wig maker, milliner, apothecary, shoemaker, and other trade shops, you get a sense of the realities of 18th-century life. Most historic buildings and exhibits are open from 9 a.m. to 5 p.m. The best way to make the most of a visit and to see beyond the area's commercialism is to take part in several special programs. During these you get to interact with "a person of the past" or learn from an interpreter of the past. The clash between the characters' 18th-century world and ours makes for lively time travel. Check the *Visitor's Companion,* available at any Colonial Williamsburg ticket outlet, for program times. Favorite programs of ours include Order in the Court, trials at the courthouse; the military encampment, "Welcome, Little Stranger," an interactive talk about colonial clothing for kids at the Milliner, and "In Their Own Words," a walking tour about slaves and free blacks in Colonial Williamsburg.

Children's and Special Programs (ages 5 to adult)

Special children's programs allow kids to experience Colonial Williamsburg as children of that era by providing interactive fun. During the day kids can help the colonial fire brigade put out a fire or march in musket drills. Evenings bring a pirate trial, candlelit tours (the only ones that take you inside homes and trade shops), or ghost stories. These programs are open to children ages 5 to 12 but are likely to be best appreciated by kids between 5 and 10. Some may require advance reservations, and all require additional fees. Inquire at the visitor center.

Colonial Apprentice Program. This daylong program, offered in the summer, gives families a chance to take an in-depth look at 18th-century trades, such as silversmithing, blacksmithing, wig making, and gunsmithing.

Kids' Summer Program. These daylong programs change each summer and may include an in-depth look at revolutions in science and technology that occurred during the colonial period, finding out what women did to help prepare for the Revolution, or learning about the lives of Williamsburg's rich and famous.

Spinning Stories/Spanning Time. This fall event brings nationally acclaimed story-tellers to Williamsburg for a weekend of stories from the 18th to the 21st centuries.

Remember Me. Children spend the evening with the slave Paris, an old man recalling his life in Africa, his enslavement, and how he's managed his cultural and spiritual survival.

The Military Encampment. For physically active children, a chance to "enlist" and experience 18th-century military life, with marching, musket drills, and a chance to learn how a cannon is fired, all in an authentic Revolutionary War campsite.

Papa Said, Mama Said. Adult slaves recall how they learned about their culture and its values from the stories of their people's past.

Colonial Kids on Parade. An evening program with a puppet show, 18th-century dancing, a fencing lesson, and African-American music and storytelling.

Cry Witch. This dramatic reenactment of the 1706 witchcraft trial of Grace Sherwood fascinates older children. Sherwood is accused of killing a baby through the use of the

Williamsburg Travel Tips

Colonial Williamsburg is the kind of place you can visit many times because what you do depends on the season and the age and interests of your children.

- **Check the Web site.** Before coming to Colonial Williamsburg, check the "Meet the People" section at www.colonialwilliamsburg.org. Peruse the biographies of the residents and historic figures. The Web's Kids Zone has information as well as games and activities.

- **Colonial Taverns.** When you book your lodging, make reservations to dine at one of these popular places.

- **Rent kids' period clothing.** These outfits are available to rent for the day at the Visitor Center. Girls don a white dress with a sash and boys get a shirt and haversack. For an additional fee, you can top the costume off with either a girl's bonnet or a tri-corn hat, items you may keep.

- **Summer.** In summer Colonial Williamsburg often teams up with other area attractions to offer combined lodging and admission tickets at a reduced price.

"black arts." The audience, after listening to the evidence and questioning witnesses, must determine the guilt or innocence of the accused.

Revolutionary City. This street theater takes place along Duke of Gloucester Street at select times. Depending on the program, overhear townspeople argue about independence, watch the governor arrive, or encounter a housewife hawking fresh eggs. Arrive 15 minutes early for Get Revved, an informative session geared to kids that adds fun to the background by teaching kids to curtsy or put their best foot forward.

In Their Own Words. Find out what "freedom" meant to the enslaved people in Williamsburg on this walking tour. Learn about the hardships and the sheer determination of some African-Americans such as Matthew Ashby, a free black man who worked hard and eventually had enough money to purchase his wife and children. To our surprise, we decided that as a slave we would have signed up with the British since they offered freedom for those slaves who fought with them. Some facts are hard to hear so the walk is recommended for ages 12 and older.

Duke of Gloucester Street (all ages)

A stroll along this main street conveys the ambience of this bustling town. Pause to peek into the stores, chat with costumed interpreters, and—a kid favorite—shop for keepsakes from clay wig curlers to quill pens. Mass here along with the locals for Revolutionary City.

The Courthouse (ages 8 and up)

With kids middle-school age or older, a good choice is the special program "Order in the Court." When the clerk at the courthouse calls out for jurors, if you are, as required by law, a man, over 21, Protestant, white, and a landowner, you can serve. Others can be plaintiffs, defendants, and witnesses. Cases vary. On one visit we observed a husband, whose tipsy wife sang a ditty belittling the king, receive a two-pound fine. The poor man, played by a visitor reading from cue cards, complained that such a fee is beyond his means. How then is justice served? The judge ordered the wife to be lashed to a stool and

Amazing
Williamsburg Facts

- **Declaration of Independence.** On July 25, 1776, a huge crowd gathered outside the courthouse to hear the reading of the Declaration of Independence. Cannons were fired to signal the crowd's approval.

- During colonial times the **average life expectancy** for a white male was 50 to 55 years; for a black male 40 to 45 years; and for a white or a black woman, 25 to 35 years.

dunked six times. "As you grow wet, may you grow wise," he intoned. As the guests filed out, a teenage girl in the audience wondered why the husband wasn't dunked instead.

The Powder Magazine (ages 4 and up)

Kids like touring this building, built in 1715, to see where shot, powder, and flints were stored.

The Guardhouse (ages 4 and up)

This reconstructed building was used in the colonial period to store military equipment such as tents.

The Shops (all ages)

A visit to the harness-and-saddle maker, apothecary, and shoemaker presents the everyday necessities of 18th-century life. Favorite stops of ours are:

The Greenhow Store. This store, we think, offers the most interesting assortment of allowance-affordable souvenir goodies reflecting the colonial era. Kids can buy items such as wax animals, scented soaps, chalk, ostrich plumes, initial seals, and clay wig curlers.

The Milliner. Along with providing hats for ladies, the milliner created clothes for women and children. On display are gowns, bonnets, bolts of cloth, and children's dresses (also worn by boys until they were about 4 or 5 years old and graduated to britches). Check the schedule so you can show up for *Welcome, Little Stranger,* a special program that's good fun and informative. When James Slate, a tailor at the Milliner's, discusses children's clothing, kids in the shop make those "I can't believe it" faces. Mothers (or servants) used "diapers," or linen cloths, to fold "clouts," what we think of as diapers, fastening them with straight pins. In reply to a visitor's question about safety pins, Mr. Slate, after a long perplexed look, says, "Indeed, they are safe, Madam, if fastened correctly." We also learn that toddlers put on "pudding caps," a kind of padded, open helmet, to protect their noggins from bumps, and that even tots wore "stays," those corsetlike contraptions.

Public Gaol (ages 4 and up)

For a look at another aspect of Williamsburg society, visit these small dark cells with their shackles and leg irons that once held pirates, runaway slaves, Indians, debtors, and the mentally ill. "Family Life at the Public Gaol" tells you about the lives of the gaoler and his family.

The Geddy House and Foundry (ages 9 and up)

Check out this site, which includes a silversmith shop, a home, and a foundry. There are hands-on activities in the yard, and at the foundry visitors can watch tradesmen craft brass, bronze, silver, and pewter castings.

Benjamin Powell House (ages 4 and up)

Open in summer only. Interpreters show kids how to play with colonial-era toys.

The Capitol (ages 5 and up)

The House of Burgesses met in the east wing. The landowners of each county elected two members to represent them, plus Jamestown, Williamsburg, Norfolk, and the College of William and Mary each had one representative. The Council, which met in the west wing, consisted of twelve leading colonists appointed for life by the king. This imposing building was the site for many of Patrick Henry's impassioned speeches for independence. Check the *Visitor's Companion* to see if Mr. Henry and his fiery revolutionaries are speaking during your visit.

Governor's Palace (ages 5 and up)

Decorated with bayonets, muskets, swords, and rifles to reinforce the sense of the Crown's power, the twenty-five-room palace is a highlight of any tour. The finery includes gilt mirrors, black-walnut paneling, marble floors, hand-tooled leather wall coverings, and mahogany and cherry furniture. Guides talk about the last governor, the Earl of Dunmore, and the life he, his wife, and six children led. The governor sent his family back to England after just two years in Williamsburg because of the brewing revolution. The tour ends in the ballroom. Thomas Jefferson once danced here and didn't leave, reports say, "until the sun came up in the garden." Be sure to allow time to walk through the palace garden. Kids especially like the holly maze. Families are encouraged to join in playing hoops, lawn bowling, pickup sticks, tops, checkers, and other colonial-era games.

Great Hopes Plantation (ages 5 and up)

Not originally at this site, the re-created middle-sized, colonial farm offers visitors a chance to see how ordinary folk lived, with slaves and their masters working side by side. There's a slave house and tobacco barn. At selected times, the plantation offers special programs about slaves and slavery.

The DeWitt Wallace Decorative Arts Museum (ages 8 and up)

325 Francis St., entrance through the Public Hospital at the corner of Francis and North Henry Streets, Williamsburg; (757) 220-7724. $.

This is home to Colonial Williamsburg's art masterworks. More than 8,000 17th-century through early-19th-century decorative delights, from silver and ceramics to linen and lace, are presented here. Although this facility may appeal more to older children, don't avoid it; instead, find something that will catch your child's interest. Go on a treasure hunt here: Let your kids follow their fancies through a door and see what they find. Does your child take music lessons? Then locate the case of 18th-century instruments. Is your fifth-grader learning about geography? Browse the gallery of hand-colored colonial maps where the pink for Virginia bleeds all the way past the Mississippi River, and Indian names mark the territory of Michigan. In the summer the gallery offers Wee Folk, which gives families a special tour of the exhibits followed by a hands-on activity session for kids. For older kids, ask for the Teen Takes: A New Angle on Art audio tour, available for **free** at the entrance desk. Narrated by teens, the tape directs listeners to seventeen objects, commenting about them as a typical teen would. For example, find out why the tall case clock by Thomas Tompian was the technological wonder of its day. The tape covers objects in this museum and in the Abby Aldrich Rockefeller Folk Art Museum.

Abby Aldrich Rockefeller Folk Art Museum (ages 5 and up)
307 South England St., across from the Williamsburg Lodge, Williamsburg; (757) 220-7698. $.

This facility houses one of the nation's finest collections of folk art. Kids are intrigued by folk art with its simple lines, bright colors, and easily recognizable figures. Paintings and objects from the 17th through 19th centuries are on display. My family's favorites are the whimsical hog and cow weather vanes, the old-fashioned toys, and the portraits of children with fat cats and flower baskets. Down on the Farm, geared to young kids, presents a display of ducks, cows, and other critters that illustrate a children's book. At the room's table, kids can use crayons and paper to draw their own farm scenes. The Folk Art Museum has a number of programs for families and kids, especially in the summer. From June through Aug, Abby's Art gives kids a chance to create their own masterpieces every Fri afternoon. Throughout the year on Wed and Fri mornings, kids can enjoy Wee Folk, a 45-minute tour and activity session for 3- to-7-year-olds. For older kids, ask for the Teen Takes: A New Angle on Art audio tour, available for **free** at the entrance desk. The tour, narrated by teens, covers items in this museum and in the DeWitt Wallace Museum.

Where to Eat

Colonial Taverns, within the historic area. Call to make reservations for all the Williamsburg taverns; (729) 229-1000. Dining at the colonial taverns is popular, so your best bet is to make these reservations when you make your lodging reservations. If you haven't, then reserve a table at the visitor center as soon as you arrive. Even though the entrees are more adequate than memorable, the wooden tables aglow in candlelight and the costumed staff help transport you back over 200 years. Such 18th-century Southern staples as spoon bread and Carolina fish muddle (a stew) help evoke the era. For the less adventuresome, kids' menus offer hamburgers, fried chicken, and other friendly fare. Each tavern's cuisine (described below) varies and each serves some colonial dishes. $$–$$$

Campbell's Tavern, 120 Waller St., features seafood and such noteworthy dishes as clam chowder, jambalaya, and muddle—a tomato-based stew of shrimp, scallops, and fish fillets. Be sure to sample the spoon bread. $$$

Chowning's Tavern, 100 East Duke of Gloucester St., specializes in meat (pork chops, prime rib, pork rib, and steak) and is best known for its Brunswick stew. An evening program for adults includes the 18th-century gambling game Hazards. $$$

The King's Arms Tavern, 409 East Duke of Gloucester St., tends toward Southern fare such as Virginia baked ham, fried chicken, and peanut soup. $$$

Shields Tavern, 417 East Duke of Gloucester St., serves seafood gumbo, buffalo stew, and vegetable wraps.

Additional area restaurants:

The Trellis, 403 Duke of Gloucester St.; (757) 229-8610. Award-winning chef Marcel Desaulniers is known for his creative cooking. At lunch a variety of affordable salads, sandwiches, and light fare are served. Dinner can be pricey, but the food is wonderful. Children will feel more comfortable at lunch, but the restaurant welcomes well-behaved children. Save room for the desserts, especially the chef's signature Death by Chocolate, a rich cakelike concoction that chocoholics "die for." $–$$$

Blue Talon Bistro, 420 Prince George St.; (757) 476-BLUE; www.bluetalonbistro.com. Chef David Everett calls his fare serious comfort food, especially the burgers, meatloaf, and mac & cheese, but you can also usually also order seafood and lamb shanks or other "grown-up" entrees.

Giuseppe's Italian Cafe, 5601 Richmond Rd.; (757) 565-1977. Locals voted this one of the best. Pasta, salads, homemade soups, tiramisu. Lunch and dinner daily. $

Pierce's Pitt Bar-B-Que, 447 East Rochambeau Dr.; (757) 565-2955. Lunch, and dinner. This eatery serves hickory smoked Tennessee style barbecue. $

The Whaling Company, 494 McLaws Circle; (757) 229-0275. Open for dinner. Discount for early diners and a children's menu available. Fresh seafood is the specialty, and the decor is New England fishing village. $$

Where to Stay

Williamsburg offers a variety of lodgings within the historic area as well as nearby. Call 800-HISTORY for reservations at the following lodgings operated by Colonial Williamsburg. Be sure to ask about special packages and discounts, and Colonial Williamsburg passes. Guests who lodge in a Colonial Williamsburg property, depending on the deal being offered, may receive discounted or complimentary admission to the Historic area as well as discounts on evening programs. Booking online—www.colonialwilliamsburg.org—may provide further discounts.

Colonial Houses. Within the historic area several properties serve as small inns, accommodating two to twelve people. A stay in one of these colonial houses adds to the fantasy of living in the historic era. Some, like the Chiswell–Bucktrout Tavern, have private gardens, a nice oasis after a day of touring. Renting a house would be fun for a family reunion. The rooms vary and so do the prices; some of these are the most expensive lodgings in the historic area. Some rooms are small and, despite the canopy beds, are more drab than charming.

Governor's Inn, 506 North Henry St.; (757) 229-1000, ext. 6000, or (800) 447-8679. This motel-type lodging just outside the historic area is the most economical choice for families. You can leave your car here and take one of Colonial Williamsburg's shuttle buses into the historic area. Guests at this inn can use the recreational activities at the Williamsburg Woodlands, including children's activities. $$$–$$$$

Kingsmill Resort, 1010 Kingsmill Rd.; (757) 253-1703 or (800) 832-5665; www.kingsmill.com. Located on the James River, this condominium property offers a nice oasis away from the historic area's hustle and bustle. The one- to three-bedroom condos give families the convenience of kitchens plus more room for the money. The on-site resort facilities include golf, tennis, a very nice spa, and a Sports Club featuring an indoor swimming pool, exercise equipment, racquetball, a recreation room with pool table and video games, and a restaurant. In summer the property offers a children's program for ages 5 and 12. $$$–$$$$

Williamsburg Inn, 136 East Francis St.; (757) 229-1000, ext. 3089, or (800) 447-8679. This five-star hotel exudes country elegance.

It's an upscale property with fine dining, swimming pool, lawn bowling, tennis courts, and golf. This is one of the most expensive properties on-site. Children are welcome, but the Inn requests that no more than three people occupy one room. With two kids, you would need a suite or two rooms. $$$$

Williamsburg Lodge, 310 South England St.; (757) 229-1000, ext. 4008, or (800) 447-8679. Family friendly, this lodge, renovated in 2007, offers 323 rooms in several buildings. In general, the rooms in the south wing are smaller than those in the north and east wings. $$$–$$$$

Williamsburg Woodlands Hotel & Suites is the most economical of the Colonial Williamsburg lodging options. This hotel's rooms are basic but comfortable. There are swimming pools, and in summer the Colonial Kids Club, an activities program, operates from this location. $$$

The Williamsburg area also has many chain motels and hotels. These include:

Embassy Suites, 3006 Mooretown Rd.; (757) 229-6800 or (800) 333-0924. Indoor pool, cable, in-room refrigerator and microwave. $$$

Great Wolf Lodge—Indoor Waterpark Resort, 555–559 East Rochambeau Dr.; (800) 551-9653. It will be hard to get your kids out of the pools of this resort, known for its 67,000-square-foot indoor waterpark with slides, wave pool, toddler splash area, and an interactive treehouse with sprays and water guns. In warm weather, the outdoor pool opens too. The resort also has a Cub Club, a supervised craft and play area for young kids, a GR8 Space for teens and a shop where kids can build a remote controlled race car. The 405 themed guest rooms come in several faux log cabin looks. Some have bunk beds for kids. $$$–$$$$

Hampton Inn Williamsburg Center, 201 Bypass Rd.; (757) 220-0880 or (800) 289-0880. Indoor pool, cable, complimentary continental breakfast. $$–$$$

AREA CAMPGROUNDS

Jamestown Beach Campsites, 2217 Jamestown Rd.; (757) 229-7609 or (800) 446-9228 (reservations only). Six hundred wooded campsites, fishing, boating, swimming, and a grocery store.

Williamsburg Resort KOA Kampground, 5210 Newman Rd.; (757) 565-2907 or (800) KOA-1733; www.koa.com. A complimentary shuttle service to Colonial Williamsburg is offered as well as an on-site pool and convenience store. There are 150 campsites, plus forty-three cabins with air-conditioning and heat.

Annual Events

JUNE

Reenactment of 1781, end of June. The British return and impose martial law on Colonial Williamsburg, reenacting the 1781 occupation. More than 250 military reenactors converge on the historic area to encamp and drill.

JUNE–AUGUST

Apprentice tours. Tradesmen and women in period attire provide interactive experiences for children. Extra fee.

JULY

Fourth of July. You and your family can celebrate the day with all the fervor of a newly independent nation. Enjoy an 18th-century garden party and a fireworks display.

JULY–AUGUST

Military Encampment, summer. This favorite event makes army folk out of tenderfoot visitors, kids included. After signing up with the Second Virginia Regiment, the new recruits practice drills, learn the bayonet lunge, present arms (using sticks instead of loaded muskets), and assist with cleaning and firing a cannon.

OCTOBER

Washington prepares for Yorktown.
The general and his staff use Williamsburg as their base of operations to plan the siege of Yorktown in the fall of 1781. More than 150 military reenactors encamp and drill, and General Washington talks about the war.

DECEMBER

Grand Illumination, early Dec. Winter not only brings fewer crowds than summer, but the colonial streets sport the festive decorations of the 18th century. It all starts when fireworks, music, and entertainment mark the beginning of Colonial Williamsburg's

Christmas season. Dance the minuet at a candlelit ball (book ahead for tickets), enjoy the carolers, and visit homes tastefully decorated with natural wreaths.

For More Information

Colonial Williamsburg's Visitor Center, Visitor Center Dr., Williamsburg, VA 23185; (757) 229-1000 or (800) HISTORY; www.colonialwilliamsburg.org. Obtain maps, guidebooks, and tickets for attractions and make reservations for lodging and meals if you haven't already. Also see the orientation film *Williamsburg—The Story of a Patriot.*

Williamsburg Area Convention and Visitors Bureau, 421 North Boundary St., Williamsburg, VA 23187 (mail: P.O. Box 3585, Williamsburg, VA 23187); (757) 253-0192; www.visitwilliamsburg.com, www.williamsburgcc.com.

Williamsburg–Area Theme Parks

Virginia's "kids' corner" isn't all history, hard facts, Redcoats, and revolution. Two in-season must-dos are Busch Gardens Williamsburg and Water Country USA. Check out the Web sites for each of these parks for an age-based itinerary and for combination packages.

Busch Gardens Williamsburg (ages 2 and up)

One Busch Gardens Blvd.; (800) 4-ADVENTURE; www.buschgardens.com. Busch Gardens is open daily from mid-May through Labor Day. In early Apr and from Labor Day to the end of Oct, the park is generally open Fri through Sun. Hours vary with the season, so be sure to check before you visit. $$$.

At this theme park you get twirled, tossed, drenched with torrents of water, scared by monsters, and still come away giggling for more. The park combines roller coasters and other fun rides with German, French, Italian, and Irish village themes. Griffon, billed as the world's first floorless and tallest dive coaster, takes the fearless up 205 feet, then plunges them down a gut-wrenching 90-degree angle at speeds up to 75 miles per hour. Curse of DarKastle . . . The Ride simulates a sleigh ride hurtling through the dark, ice-bound corridors of a deserted Bavarian castle at high speeds with lots of visual projections to explain that "curse" in the title. Alpengeist, one of the world's tallest, most-twisted inverted steel

Busch Gardens Travel Tips

- **Busch Gardens Williamsburg** is an exceptionally pretty park. For many years in a row the park has been voted "America's Most Beautiful Theme Park." A relaxing way to enjoy the scenery is to board the Rhine River Cruise for a scenic river foray.

- **Military Discounts:** Anheuser-Busch Adventure Parks have a long history of honoring the military through discount ticket programs for them and their families.

coasters, hurtles riders at top speeds of 67 mph, flipping them six times, and dropping them a dizzying 195 feet. The Big Big Bad Wolf is a bit more tame, although it's lots of fun. This coaster whizzes through an ersatz alpine village at a top clip of 50 mph before descending a stomach-wrenching—for us—99 feet. The thirteen-story-high Loch Ness Monster twirls riders through two serpentine loops at up to 60 mph. The Royal Preserve Petting Zoo, home to rare creatures such as baby cinnamon bears, is a nice stop for pre-schoolers. Busch Gardens Williamsburg adds thrills to the classic water ride with Escape from Pompeii. While traveling on a boat exploring an archaeological dig, you suddenly become caught in the eruption of Mount Vesuvius, complete with flames and a drastic plunge. Older kids and adults should love this; little kids may find the vivid special effects and the plunge a bit too much to handle.

To calm down after the coasters, and for a welcome break from walking, take in the shows and see the animals. Jack Hanna's Wild Reserve is a habitat for endangered and exotic animals such as gray wolves, who have an expanded habitat. At the lorikeet aviary, feed nectar to these colorful, tiny birds.

At Pirates, an interactive, audience-participation show, 4-D technology in the form of water sprays and air cannons surprise guests.

Sesame Street Forest of Fun, debuted in 2009. Since much of this attraction is water-based, it's a good idea to have your kids wear bathing suits and bring along a change of clothing. Kids romp through sprays and also get to meet Big Bird, Elmo, Cookie Monster, and other stars of the TV series after they sing and dance.

Each themed areas has inexpensive eateries and lots of gift shops.

Water Country USA (ages 2 and up)

176 Water Country Parkway (Highway 199); (757) 253-3350 or (800) 343-SWIM; www.water countryusa.com. Open daily from Memorial Day through Labor Day and select weekends in May and Sept. $$$.

Something else not to miss, especially when the Old Dominion's afternoons get particu-larly steamy, is Water Country USA, a forty-acre water park with rides, slides, pools, and shows. Hubba Hubba Highway covers three and a half acres and takes you through a lagoon to a winding quick-current course down a river of exploding geysers. Partner up with your older kids and slither through the Malibu Pipeline, a slippery chute with a partially enclosed tube. Aquazoid ups the thrills by adding a dark section to the slide that has laser light flashes and eerie howls plus "water curtains" that douse riders. The whole family can climb onto a giant inner tube and experience a river-rafting race through a 670-foot series of twists and turns on Big Daddy Falls. Cow-a-Bunga features a 4,500-square-foot heated, children's play pool with water slides, fountains, and water cannons. Young kids can splash through sprays and wiggle down at mini-slides at Kritter Koral.

Williamsburg–Area Shopping

We know you didn't come to the Williamsburg area to shop but, if you have time, two outlet malls and a pottery factory offer some good browsing:

Prime Outlets at Williamsburg (ages 9 and up)

I-64 to exit 234, US 60 West, 5715-62A Richmond Rd.; (757) 565-0702 or (800) 980-SHOP; www.primeoutlets.com. Open daily except Easter, Thanksgiving Day, and Christmas.

More than 120 outlet stores offer savings. Well-known names include Liz Claiborne, Osh-Kosh B'Gosh, Ann Taylor, Coach, Escada Lacoste, L. L. Bean, and others. If you have time for only one mall, this is the one.

Williamsburg Outlet Mall (ages 9 and up)

US 60 West in Lightfoot at 6401 Richmond Rd.; (757) 565-3378; www.williamsburgoutlet mall.com. Open daily except Easter, Thanksgiving, and Christmas.

This fully enclosed mall has more than forty outlet stores, including Lee/Wrangler, Leggs Hanes Totes, and Pendelton Woolen Mills.

Williamsburg Pottery Factory

6692 Richmond Rd., Lightfoot, US 60 West, just ten minutes west of Williamsburg; (757) 564-3326 or (800) POTTERY; www.williamsburgpottery.com. Open daily except Christmas.

This complex offers 200 acres of pottery, china, glassware, stemware, baskets, silk flower arrangements, toys, brass, and craft items at discount prices. The complex has a campground too.

Jamestown and Yorktown

From Williamsburg, the **Colonial Parkway** leads to Jamestown. The winding road cuts through groves of oaks and elms, winds over creeks, and travels past marshes thick with cattails and green reeds before opening to sweeping views of the James River. While it's only about a 10-mile drive, you "go back" to 1607 when the first permanent English settlement in the New World was established More than 400 years ago.

The 9,316-acre **Colonial National Historical Park** includes Historic Jamestown, the original site of the first permanent English settlement; Yorktown, the scene of the last major battle of the Revolutionary War; and the Colonial Parkway, a 23-mile roadway that connects Williamsburg, Jamestown, and Yorktown. For information on the Colonial National Historical Park, write P.O. Box 210, Yorktown, VA 23690; (757) 898-2410; www .nps.gov/colo.

Jamestown Settlement and Yorktown Victory Center are commercial living-history re-creations of Jamestown and of the events surrounding the Revolutionary War 170 years later. For information about these sites, contact the Jamestown–Yorktown Foundation, P.O. Box 1607, Williamsburg, VA 23187; (757) 253-4838 or (888) 593-4682; www.historyisfun.org.

Historic Jamestowne (ages 7 and up)
Located at the westernmost point of Colonial Parkway in Jamestown; (757) 229-9776; www .historicjamestowne.org. Open daily except Christmas Day. $.

Archeologists have unearthed pioneers—104 Englishmen and boys—who helped establish the 1607 Jamestown settlement, the first permanent English settlement in the New World, thirteen years before the Pilgrims landed in Massachusetts.

For Children Visiting Jamestown

- Beginning in mid-June and ending in mid-Aug each year, there are a number of National Park Service hands-on activities for children, such as the Pinch Pot Program, where they learn about the pottery making of the English and the Powhatan Indians and make a small pinch pot that they can take with them.

- Year-round Junior Ranger programs include answering written questions about the settlement, walking around the town site, and learning about the materials colonists would have found in the area, with "environmental bags" containing some of those same materials.

- The Young Soldiers Program (summers only) teams kids with a costumed interpreter to learn about life as a Revolutionary War soldier.

- In Oct, on the Sat of the Columbus Day holiday weekend, there are activities related to the process of archaeology, where kids try to earn a Junior Archaeologist Certificate by identifying "mystery artifacts" and how they were used.

- Also check out the NPS Web site, where there is excellent and detailed information about the settlement, its inhabitants (including African Americans), and the Native Americans living here at the time.

Ignore the obelisk memorial as well as the church, charming as it is, to concentrate on envisioning the settlement. The British flag flies over the fort—the colonists were British. Archeologists have found the post molds, discolorations in the earth that signal where the settlers placed wooden posts, for the old fort as well as what is likely the 1608 barracks. In summer, there may even be an active dig to watch.

The Visitor Center's multimedia screen presentation uses nine computers to show 3,000 images that introduce visitors to the community's personalities and its perils from plagues to near-starvation and Indian attacks. The Archaearium displays excavated artifacts. "Meet" one of the early settlers, believed to be a captain, by viewing his skeleton, and learn how real-life forensic techniques lead to assumptions about the identity of the bones. The three-dimensional representation of a 1620s well details how archaeologists unearthed suits of armor, wine bottles, and other 17th-century items. Among the interesting finds: a sheathed dagger, a surgically marked skull, and a silver ear picker, something well-bred gentlemen employed to scoop out wax from their ears.

As interesting as the new exhibits are, be sure to get beyond them to the undeveloped park. On the self-guided driving tour, you get a sense of the wilderness encountered by the stalwart pioneers. Sitting along the windblown riverbank, listening to the lapping gray waters, we find it easy to imagine the hopefuls who landed here and the hearty few who survived.

Jamestown Settlement (ages 5 and up)

Near Historic Jamestowne on Highway 31 South; (757) 253-4838 or (888) 593-4682; www .historyisfun.org. $–$$.

At Jamestown Settlement, a state-operated living-history museum near the historic site, the 1600s come alive. You meet interpreters (not actual characters who lived at Jamestown) attired in period clothing but speaking contemporary English.

At the **Powhatan Indian Village,** families can explore the Powhatan houses, called yehakins, and watch and even help prepare food, tan animal hides, and make pottery or tools from bones. Watching an interpreter dressed in buckskin weave storage bags from plant fibers, we wonder if Pocahontas, a Powhatan maiden, ever wove a similar sack.

The path from the village leads to the pier on the James River, where full-size replicas of the three ships that sailed to Jamestown are docked. Interpreters in period attire recount the four-and-a-half-month voyage, demonstrating piloting and navigational skills. Onboard the Susan Constant, visitors can explore a sailor's bunk, and try deducing latitude with an astrolabe, an early navigational tool. At the triangular James Fort, kids can defend the re-created 17th-century settlement of homes, church, storehouse, and guardhouse as well as try on armor and, at times, watch blacksmithing demonstrations and musket drills.

At the 30,000-square-foot exhibition space watch the film *1607: A Nation Takes Root,* chronicling 20 years of Jamestown's development. The galleries depict the interweaving in the New World soil of three cultures: Native American, English, and African. The first documented Africans arrived in Virginia in 1619. To compare the cultures, kids view a 17th-century London streetscape, a Native Indian village, and an Angolan settlement. Kids

Getting around **the Historic Triangle**

From mid-Mar through Oct, the Historic Triangle Shuttle bus takes visitors between Colonial Williamsburg, Jamestown, and Yorktown **free** of charge. From Jamestown, take the Jamestown Area Shuttle to the Jamestown Settlement. At Yorktown hop aboard the Yorktown Trolley to Yorktown Battlefield and the Yorktown Victory Center. The trolley also takes visitors on a tour of the town of Yorktown. (757) 898-2410; www.nps.gov/colo.

can also walk through a life-size planter's house, slave quarters, and a native home covered in bark.

Yorktown Victory Center (ages 7 and up)
Highway 238, the Colonial Parkway, Yorktown; (757) 253-4838 or (888) 593-4682; www.history isfun.org. $$.

At the other end of the Colonial Parkway, 23 miles away, is Yorktown, site of the last significant battle of the American Revolution, in 1781. Yorktown Victory Center makes effective use of timelines, exhibits, and outdoor living history to depict the lives of ordinary men and women during the Revolutionary War. The Witnesses to Revolution Gallery captures interest with its real war stories. While looking at the 3-D assemblage of mannequins, gun replicas, clothing, and cookery, viewers hear voices of early pioneers, soldiers, and women. Jeremiah Greenman, a continental soldier from Rhode Island, complains about the deep snow and the constant hunger while Tigoransera, a Mohawk chief, counsels his people to stay out of this white man's war. (Despite his neutrality, he was captured by the British and died in prison.)

An eighteen-minute film, *A Time of Revolution,* set in an encampment at night during the siege of Yorktown, continues the witnesses theme. Costumed interpreters depict 18th-century life in a wartime encampment, complete with musket drills, field medicine, and cooking demonstrations, as well as depicting life on a 1780s Tidewater farm, where kids can lend a hand weeding the garden, breaking flax into fiber for linen, and exploring the farmhouse, kitchen, and tobacco barn.

At the children's discovery room, kids learn about the Revolutionary era by trying on 18th-century clothing, copying from a hornbook, making rubbings of woodcuts, and playing the African game mancala.

Throughout the Victory Center, there are display panels at a child's eye level asking kids thought-provoking questions about their lives compared to the lives of colonial children. At the re-created encampment, children can ask the camp surgeon about 18th-century medical techniques, join a mock military drill, and watch the cannon being fired.

Special Events at **Jamestown and Yorktown**

The National Park Service regularly sponsors a number of special events throughout the year, including programs in Feb honoring African-American participation in the Jamestown settlement, Jamestown Day (May 11), Yorktown Civil War Weekend in May, Independence Day Celebration at Yorktown, Virginia Archaeological Celebration at Jamestown in Oct, and Yorktown Victory Weekend in Oct. Check out the NPS Web site for information: www.nps .gov/colo. Jamestown Settlement and Yorktown Victory Center also sponsor events on Jamestown Day and Yorktown Victory Day. Check out www.history isfun.org for information.

Yorktown Battlefield (ages 10 and up)

Located along the Colonial Parkway between Williamsburg and Yorktown; (757) 898-2410; www.nps.gov/colo. Open daily except Christmas. $.

This is the site of the finale of the American Revolution, October 1781. Administered by the National Park Service, the battlefield includes Washington's headquarters, the surrender field, and the Yorktown Victory Monument. Park rangers lead tours of the British inner defense line. At the Visitor Center see a fifteen-minute film on the siege of Yorktown as well as one of the tents used by George Washington during the Revolutionary War. The Children's Gallery has hands-on activities, and the Junior Ranger program is available for children up to the age of 12 for a nominal fee.

Yorktown—The Town (ages 10 and up)

Yorktown, the town, home to some 200 people, is nestled along the York River between the Yorktown Victory Center and the Yorktown Battlefield. A **free** pamphlet guides you on a walking tour of the historic town. Riverwalk Landing, the waterfront park, has shops, a few restaurants, and is the site of summer time concerts.

Day Trips

The James River Plantations

Several of Virginia's first plantations still thrive a short drive from Williamsburg along the James River. These plantations give a glimpse into the pomp and pleasures of a life grown prosperous in the new world. Two that may especially delight children are Shirley Plantation and Berkeley Plantation; both boast lawns that sweep to the river and ancestry traced back to England's Queen Elizabeth I.

Combination admission tickets are available for Shirley, Berkeley, Evelynton, and Sherwood Forest plantations.

Shirley Plantation (ages 9 and up)

35 miles west of Williamsburg on Highway 5, 501 Shirley Plantation Rd., Charles City; (804) 829-5121 or (800) 232-1613; www.shirleyplantation.com. Open daily except Thanksgiving and Christmas. $.

This is Virginia's oldest plantation and dates to 1613. The imposing brick Queen Anne-style manor house built in 1723 sits like a crown jewel, flanked by its dependencies. Shirley exudes a genteel hospitality and lived-in practicality and is still a working plantation, home to the ninth generation of Hill–Carters (Ann Hill Carter was the mother of Confederate General Robert E. Lee, whose scion may sometimes be seen dressed in blue jeans as he oversees farm chores). The tour highlights history, antique furniture, paintings, and silver. Kids who are bored with these won't be bored when they see the archaeological lab in the renovated barn. In June there's an American Revolution Encampment weekend and in Sept a Civil War reenactment and Living History Weekend.

Berkeley Plantation (ages 7 and up)

Two miles down the road from Shirley Plantation, Highway 5, 12602 Harrison Landing Rd., Charles City; (804) 829-6018 or (888) 466-6018; www.berkeleyplantation.com. Open daily except Thanksgiving and Christmas; reduced hours in Jan and Feb. $.

Discover the site of some unusual historic firsts. This brick Georgian manor house, built in 1726, is the birthplace of Benjamin Harrison, a signer of the Declaration of Independence, and William Henry Harrison, ninth president of the United States. It hosted the first "Thanksgiving" in 1619 and the composition of "Taps" during the Civil War encampment of Union General George McClellan and his 140,000 troops. Berkeley was bought in 1907 by Jon Jamieson, a drummer boy in McClellan's army. Today it's owned by Jamieson's great-grandson. In spring and summer Berkeley's gardens are especially nice. Although furnishings and antiques are emphasized, the site's firsts make this stop appealing to younger children.

Evelynton Plantation (ages 10 and up)

6701 John Tyler Hwy.; (800) 473-5075; www.jamesriverplantations.org. Open daily except Thanksgiving, Christmas, and New Year's Day. $.

Discovering **Pocahontas**

Pocahontas, the Walt Disney Company film that debuted in 1995, fired kids' curiosity about the real Pocahontas, the Indian maiden Captain John Smith credited with saving his life in 1607 by pleading with her father, Chief Powhatan. This is the region where the real Pocahontas lived 400 years ago.

Ferry **through History**

Aboard the ferries that cross the James River, it's easy to imagine the New World as the first colonists saw it. Car ferries leave from Jamestown and go to Surry County. It's a twenty-minute ride. **Chippoke's Plantation and State Park,** with its acres of greenery and fields of corn, peanuts, rye, and soybeans, plus an Olympic-size swimming pool, interpretive programs, and biking, hiking, and horse trails, makes for a great destination. For information, call 800-VA-FERRY.

If you are interested in other plantations, try this one. A Georgian-revival house with many antiques, the home is named after the daughter of the founder of Richmond, Virginia. The 2,500-acre farm is still family-owned and -operated. There's a Civil War reenactment every summer.

Sherwood Forest Plantation (ages 10 and up)

14501 John Tyler Hwy., Charles City; (804) 282-1441; www.sherwoodforest.org. Grounds open daily except Thanksgiving, Christmas, and New Year's Day. $.

This was the retirement home of President John Tyler, at more than 300 feet considered to be the longest frame house in the United States. Set on twenty-eight acres, the plantation still has its original twelve dependencies. The property, according to Tyler's descendants, is the only home of a former president still occupied by the family. The dependencies and the grounds, reputed to have America's oldest ginkgo tree, are open daily. The home is open by appointment. On March 29, President Tyler's birthday, there are special events and **free** birthday cake. Each May there is a reenactment of the first successful defense by the U.S. Colored (African-American) Troops on May 24, 1864.

Where to Eat

In Yorktown and its vicinity you can find several eateries, including the **Rivah Café**, and its sister restaurant, the **Riverwalk Dining Room**, 323 Water St., (757) 875-1522; www .riverwalkrestaurant.net. Enjoy river views with your seafood. Children's menus are available.

Hampton

This historic city is part of Hampton Roads, a southeastern section of Virginia that stretches from Williamsburg to Virginia Beach to the Chesapeake.

The Virginia Air and Space Center (ages 7 and up)
600 Settlers Landing Rd.; (757) 727-0800 or (800) 296-0800; www.vasc.org. Open daily year-round except Thanksgiving and Christmas. $$; IMAX movies cost extra.

More than 100 interactive exhibits engage adults and kids. In the exhibit Touch and Tornado, kids can watch a tornado form, then touch the funnel to make it change shape. Visitors can stand in front of the blue screen used by TV weather forecasters and see how they use "invisible" maps. Kids can try on a pair of wings and feel the lift in a wind tunnel, launch a rocket, or explore Mars. They can land a space shuttle, try out fighter pilot equipment, and use an old-fashioned ham radio.

There is also an IMAX theater, and an impressive array of historic aircraft are suspended—as if in midflight—in the atrium. Gaze on an F-4E Phantom II fighter used in the Vietnam War and a Corsair F-106B Delta Dart that was struck by lightning nearly 700 times as part of NASA research. The 15,000-square-foot Adventures in Flight gallery highlights commercial aviation in the Air Traffic Control section with a real-time electronic map of North America showing all aircraft in flight. Civil aviation is explored aboard an authentic DC-9, whose last commercial flight was in July 2002. With a 93-foot wingspan and a length nose to tail of 119 feet, this interactive exhibit helps kids understand the principles of flight. A B-24 motion simulator gives visitors a taste of what it was like in a World War II bomber. For younger children, the play area Little Wings is where they can build a plane, ride in a simulator, and climb into a cockpit. The center's science camps are outstanding opportunities for kids to explore the real fun of scientific discovery. Camps during the summer are weeklong and require prior registration. The one-day Saturday camps in the winter welcome walk-ins.

The first gallery of Space Quest: Exploring the Moon, Mars, & Beyond!, part of a three-phase opening to be completed in 2010, features giant planets floating overhead. Enter the gallery through a Mars Transport Module, a three-minute simulation of space travel that represents an eight-month trip to the red planet.

Hampton History Museum (ages 5 and up)
120 Hampton Lane; (757) 727-1610; www.hampton.va.us/history_museum. Open daily year-round except Thanksgiving, Christmas, and New Year's Day. $.

This two-story museum celebrates Hampton's heritage in galleries that trace the city's beginnings as a Native American settlement (the Kecoughtan tribe) to its settlement by Europeans, and through the Civil War years, industrialization, and its space program industry. Hands-on activities include touching deerskin and bone implements in the Native American Gallery, handling a Civil War musket, and touching the palisade of a fort and tobacco barrels in the 17th Century Gallery. Kids enjoy coming face-to-face with a reproduction of Blackbeard the Pirate's severed head. A Civil War exhibit re-creates the experience of walking through burned-out Hampton through the use of enlarged photographs taken at the time and re-created crumbling walls and charred brick. Modern times are also represented, with a video about the history of air power in Hampton. Half-day camps during the summer offer hands-on activities in calligraphy and archaeology. The gift shop has a nice selection of kid-friendly items.

Discover **Hampton's Parks**

Stroll or bike through **Grandview Nature Preserve** (757) 825-4657, on a trail that passes through a cordgrass salt marsh home to many birds. At the 500-acre preserve explore tidal creeks. **Sandy Bottom Nature Park** (757) 825-4657 has wooded and marshy wetlands with platforms for visitors to observe the migrating birds and the shorebirds who feed along the margins of a lake and the wetlands. Guided walks and other programs are offered. This park, once the site of a garbage dump, serves as a heartening reminder that natural resources can be reclaimed.

Fort Monroe and the Casemate Museum (ages 7 and up)

P.O. Box 51341, Fort Monroe; (757) 788-3391. Open daily except Thanksgiving, Christmas Day, and New Year's Day. Visitors to the fort must present a picture ID, car registration, and proof of car insurance. Free.

This portrays another view of Hampton's military history. Fort Monroe, the largest stone fort ever built in the United States, is currently the only moat-encircled fort still in active use. The fort now serves as the headquarters for the U.S. Army's Training and Doctrine Command. A tour of the fort includes the Chapel of the Centurion (named for the Roman centurion Cornelius), the Old Stockade, and Quarters Number One, the oldest residence on the post. In a network of caverns once filled with Fort Monroe's massive guns, the Casemate Museum traces the history of the Civil War and the U.S. Coast Artillery Corps. The museum includes the cell in which Confederate president Jefferson Davis was held after the war. A free brochure guides you on a walking tour of Fort Monroe.

Hampton Carousel (ages 2 and up)

602 Settlers Landing Rd., in a pavilion next to the Virginia Air and Space Center; (757) 727-0900; www.vasc.org. Call or check the Web site for seasonal hours. $.

While you're at the waterfront, take the kids to the restored 1920 merry-go-round with forty-eight prancing steeds and two chariots. Even if your video-age kids find riding this a bit tame, a spin will probably bring back great memories from your own childhood.

Air Power Park (ages 7 and up)

413 West Mercury Blvd.; (757) 727-1163; www.americasaviationadventure.com/airpower .htm. Open daily except Thanksgiving, Christmas Day, and New Year's Day. Free.

If your kids are crazy about airplanes, this fifteen-acre park and museum is the place to be. There are more than fifty indoor and outdoor exhibits, with fighter aircraft, missiles, and rockets, including the F-100D Super Sabre, the first Air Force fighter with supersonic performance, and a Nike surface-to-air missile. There's also a children's playground.

Bass Pro Shops® Outdoor World

In Coliseum Central in The Power Plant of Hampton Roads, I-64, exit 2 or exit 263A; (757) 262-5200; www.basspro.com. Open daily. Free.

This is more than just a store. Even if you're not into casting your line or eating by an open fire, you'll find a lot to see and do here. There's a 19,000-gallon freshwater aquarium, cascading waterfalls, rock-climbing walls, fly-casting spots, a shooting arcade, and an archery area. One Sat a month kids are invited to join in activities at the Kid's Club (no reservations necessary and no fee), where they can learn about fishing, camping, and other outdoor activities. Wander out into the Power Plant, Hampton's newest shopping/entertainment development, which faces an eight-acre lake and features a large selection of restaurants and retail shops.

Hampton University Museum (ages 7 and up)

In the Huntington Building, Frissell Avenue, Hampton University campus; (757) 727-5308; www.hamptonu.edu/museum/. Open Mon through Sat. Free.

Founded in 1868, this is one of Virginia's oldest museums and the oldest African-American museum in the United States. It houses more than 9,000 objects and pieces of art from around the world, including permanent exhibits such as African tribal art and Native American art. Included here are fine Native American basketry, gold jewelry from Ghana, a dress made of bark cloth from Hawaii, and the pen Abraham Lincoln used to sign the first legislation for the Emancipation Proclamation. Hampton University has an interesting and important history. Opened in 1868 as the Hampton Normal and Agricultural Institute, the school was dedicated to the education of the thousands of newly freed slaves, providing them with manual and agricultural skills. From 1878 to 1923, the school also educated Native Americans from more than sixty-five tribes who were brought here under a federal program geared at assimilation through education. Today the school has more than 5,000 students and 150 buildings. The museum offers a Discovery Room with hands-on activities for kids on Wed afternoons, but reservations are required.

Amazing Hampton Facts

- Hampton was the **first training ground for U.S. astronauts.**
- Hampton was the site of America's **first organized school for African Americans,** known now as Hampton University. The great black educator Booker T. Washington was a graduate of Hampton Institute.
- **Blackbeard's Point** on the Hampton River was named for the infamous pirate. Legend has it that this was where Blackbeard's head was displayed on a pike as a warning to would-be pirates.

On the **Water** ⬆

Want to spend some time out on the water? Check out these boating opportunities:

- Apr through Oct *Miss Hampton II* cruises the Hampton Roads Harbor, passing the world's largest naval installation at Norfolk and Fort Wool, a pre-Civil War island fortress. Catch the boat at 764 Settlers Landing Rd.; (757) 722-9113 or (888) 757-BOAT; www.misshamptoncruises.com. Departure times vary. "Ghost Fleet" cruises in the spring and fall.

- The gleam of sun on the water, the waves lapping against the boat, and the thrill of pulling your first trout out of the water are part of a trip on the *Ocean Eagle* (757-868-FISH; www.hamptonroadscharter.com), which offers five-hour fishing outings on the Chesapeake Bay. And for novices, the mates onboard will teach you fishing secrets and even bait your hook.

The American Theatre
125 East Mellen St.; (757) 722-2787; www.theamericantheatre.com. $–$$$.

Take a break from sea, sand, and museums and give your kids the gift of imagination. One Sat afternoon a month year-round, this theater presents child-oriented productions, ranging from classics like *The Ugly Duckling* to nontraditionals like *The Gizmo Guys* and *Toying with Science*.

Where to Eat

Captain George's Seafood Restaurant, 2710 West Mercury Blvd.; (757) 826-1435. Open daily for dinner, plus lunch on Sun. $$$

Marker, 21 East Queens Way; (757) 726-9410. Includes a wide variety of seafood. Outdoor dining. $–$$

Surf Rider, 1 Marina Rd.; (757) 723-9366. Delicious seafood, crab cakes, burgers, pasta and more. $$–$$$

Taphouse, 17 East Queens Way; (757) 224-5829. Includes local seafood and American fare. $–$$

Where to Stay

Courtyard by Marriott, 1917 Coliseum Dr.; (757) 838-3300 or (800) 321-2211. Offers a restaurant, **free** cable, and an outdoor pool. $$–$$$

Crowne Plaza Hampton Marina Hotel, 700 Settlers Landing Rd.; (757) 727-9700 or (866) 727-9900. Offers 172 newly renovated rooms and suites, many with waterfront views. Outdoor pool. Restaurant and lounge. $$–$$$

Embassy Suites, 1700 Coliseum Dr.; (757) 827-8200. Presenting 295 suites. Indoor pool, exercise facility, day spa. Restaurant and lounge. Full cooked-to-order breakfast included. Nightly manager's reception. $$–$$$

Hilton Garden Inn, 1999 Power Plant Parkway; (757) 310-6323 or (877) STAYHGI. The 149-room hotel offers Great American Grill restaurant serving breakfast, dinner, and room service. Fitness facility, indoor pool, and whirlpool. **Free** wireless high-speed Internet in guest rooms. $–$$$

Springhill Suites, 1997 Power Plant Parkway; (757) 310-6333. It has 124 guest rooms. Suites featuring pantry area with small refrigerator, sink, and microwave. Indoor pool and hot tub. **Free** continental breakfast. $$–$$$

Annual Events

For information about events, call the **Hampton Visitor Center** at (757) 727-1102 or (800) 800-2202.

APRIL

International Children's Festival, Mill Point Park; (757) 727-8314. A chance for kids to experience different cultures through song, dance, and food.

APRIL–AUGUST

Saturday Night Street Fest Series; (757) 727-0900. Block Party, downtown Hampton at the intersection of King and Queen's Way. Music, dancing, food, cold refreshments, and a children's area with rides and games.

APRIL–OCTOBER

NASCAR Whelen All-American Series Racing; (757) 865-7223. Late Model, Grand Stocks, Modifieds, Legends, Wolf Trucks, Super Trucks, UCARS, Super Street, Pro Wing Champ Karts, and Pro 6 Racing. Gates open noon, qualifying for all divisions, 4:30 p.m., with racing at 7 p.m. Langley Speedway.

LATE MAY–EARLY JUNE

Annual Blackbeard Festival, Mill Point Park, Queen's Way, Carousel Park, and along the Hampton River; (757) 727-1570; www .blackbeardpiratefestival.com. Join the city in celebrating the demise of Edward Teach, aka Blackbeard the Pirate. Pirate skirmishes, battle reenactments, a pirate ball, fireworks, food, costumes, and a children's activity area.

JUNE

Hampton Jazz Festival, Mill Point Park and the downtown waterfront; (757) 838-5650; www.hamptonjazzfestival.com. More than one hundred artists perform at this nationally acclaimed two-day celebration of jazz. Past artists have included Dizzy Gillespie, Aretha Franklin, and Roberta Flack.

AUGUST

Annual Hampton Cup Regatta, East Mercury Bridge at Fort Monroe; (757) 727-8311. North America's oldest continuously-run hydroplane boat race. Enjoy a children's area, food vendors, Bay Education, and environmental exhibits. Racing is noon to 5 p.m. daily.

SEPTEMBER

Hampton Bay Days, in downtown Hampton (757-727-1641); www.baydays.com. The city's largest annual festival, with live performances, arts and crafts, food, fireworks, and children's activities.

DECEMBER

Annual Lighted Boat Parade, Downtown Hampton Waterfront; (757) 727-1271 or (866) 556-9631. Experience the holiday season with more than 30 lighted power and sailboats as they pass along Hampton's waterfront. Sip hot cocoa and cider as Santa leads the parade up the Hampton River.

For More Information

Hampton Visitor Center, located within the Hampton History Museum, 120 Old Hampton Lane, Hampton, VA 23669; (757) 727-1102 or (800) 800-2202; www.hampton cvb.com. Pick up brochures and city information at this conveniently located center.

Check out the Web site for 360-degree virtual tours of the city and its attractions. Hampton has launched a series of iPod walking tours that interpret the city's historic past while helping visitors discover present gems. The tours mix history, actor-voice quotes, and commentary with period and relevant music.

The six routes take you through Hampton University Campus, Downtown Hampton, Virginia Air & Space Center, Fort Monroe, Phoebus, and Hampton's Historic Neighborhoods. Visit www.visithampton.com to download the tours.

Newport News

Located along the James River near Virginia Beach, Norfolk, and Williamsburg, Newport News is home to the world's largest and Virginia's second-largest employer, the Northrop Grumman Newport News.

The Mariners' Museum (ages 7 and up)
100 Museum Dr.; (757) 596-2222 or (800) 581-SAIL; www.marinersmuseum.org. Open daily except Thanksgiving and Christmas. $$.

This museum explores the sea's use for transportation, warfare, food, and pleasure. Perhaps the museum's most celebrated exhibit is the USS Monitor. After the Mariners' Museum and the National Oceanic and Atmospheric Administration recovered parts of the Civil War ironclad Monitor, a wreck that rested 16 miles off the coast of Cape Hatteras, North Carolina, at 240 feet below sea level, the museum opened the USS Monitor Center. The facility uses original documents, artifacts, and hands-on exhibits to detail the USS Monitor's history and importance as well as the conservation and science required to rescue the craft. Kids can maneuver a sailing frigate and experience aspects of the Battle of Hampton Roads at the "battle theater."

In other galleries, examine miniature and handcrafted ship models, carved figureheads, scrimshaw, maritime paintings, and working steam engines. Favorites with kids include the Age of Exploration Gallery with its hands-on replicas of early maps and navigational tools and its fifteen short videos; the Crabtree Collection of Miniature Ships' sixteen detailed miniatures; the Great Hall of Steam's history of steamships (plus an exhibit on the HMS Titanic); the Chesapeake Bay Gallery, which details this body of water's history and has an exhibit on shipbuilding (plus interactive computer games). A permanent exhibit on U.S. Navy history uses lively audiovisual displays to explore the history of sea power in Defending the Seas, from sailing ships to nuclear-powered submarines.

Allow time to enjoy the museum's parklike setting on 550 acres. You can rent boats, picnic, and walk a 5-milelong trail that surrounds Lake Maury. Children can get a **free** backpack (you have to leave your ID at the desk), which contains paper for leaf rubbing, water-testing kits, a bird book, binoculars, and a magnifying glass. Near the picnic tables there are kid-sized reproductions of ships that welcome crawlers.

Discount **Admission**

The **Newport News Combination Ticket** offers admission to seven attractions—Endview Plantation, The LeeHall Mansion, Mariners' Museum, Peninsula Fine Arts Center, SPCA Exotic Sanctuary and Petting Zoo, Virginia Living Museum, and the Virginia War Museum—at one (discounted) price. The ticket can be purchased at the Newport News Visitor Center, 13560 Jefferson Ave.; (757) 886-7777 or (888) 493-7386.

Virginia Living Museum (ages 3 and up)

524 J. Clyde Morris Blvd.; (757) 595-1900; www.thevlm.org. Open daily except Thanksgiving, Christmas Eve, Christmas Day, and New Year's Day. $–$$.

The exhibits look back at you at this indoor-outdoor museum. Outdoor paths lead you by raccoons, beavers, river otters, foxes, bobcats, deer, a bald eagle, forty species of birds, and many other animals in their natural habitats. Indoor highlights include a living replica of the James River, a touch tank where kids handle sea stars and horseshoe crabs, and an authentic dinosaur footprint made by a kayentapus (measure your foot size against it), plus a planetarium theater and observatory. The 5,500-square-foot Coastal Plain Aviary has more than sixteen species of birds that can be viewed from an 800-foot boardwalk that takes visitors 11 feet above Deer Park Lake and into the treetops. In the facility experience the cool, moist Appalachian Cove, which has a waterfall, a mountain stream, and a lake filled with mountain fish. The Coastal Plain Gallery features an open beach, a barrier island, and a salt marsh panorama. Transport yourself to the steamy world of a cypress swamp, complete with alligators and snapping turtles.

Kids will be in awe standing underneath the 6-foot-diameter globe showing Earth as it appears in space. Four hands-on discovery centers feature natural specimens that visitors can pick up and touch, ranging from animal skulls and pelts to fossils and minerals. Kids can view endangered red wolves, get close to loggerhead turtles, see moon jellies, and touch live spider crabs.

Every third Sat year-round is Story Time at the museum. Daily programs include watching aquarists scrub a turtle's back or feed the nurse shark, and presentations in the Planetarium theater.

At the Living Green House and Garden, homeowners, architects, and contractors, as well as children can see all the latest techniques and products available to build and maintain an earth-friendly home. Also, the 3,000 square-foot garden is a environmentalist's dream. The garden uses native plants, mulching, and composting to reduce the use of synthetic fertilizers and pesticides as well as landscaping to reduce storm water runoff while providing food, water, and shelter for wildlife.

Peninsula Fine Arts Center's Children's Interactive Gallery (ages 3 to 7)

101 Museum Dr.; (757) 596-8175; www.pfac-va.org. Open year-round except Thanksgiving, Christmas Day, and New Year's Day. $.

Little ones especially like this small art center. Kids color, paint, and craft collages and other artistic works in the Hands On for Kids gallery. Every third Thurs of the month, there's a family happy hour from 5:30 to 7 p.m. at which kids enjoy supervised activities in the gallery while their parents enjoy music and beverages in the center's Art Cafe. Check the calendar for the facility's special classes.

U.S. Army Transportation Museum (ages 9 and up)

10 miles east of Williamsburg on I-64 (Washington Avenue). Building 300, Besson Hall, Fort Eustis; (757) 878-1115; www.transchool.eustis.army.mil. Open Tues through Sun. Closed on all major holidays. All visitors must stop at the Fort Eustis Visitor Center to obtain a visitor pass. Those over 18 need a valid ID (driver's license or a photo ID) and vehicle registration to be issued a pass. **Free.**

See an array of military transportation vehicles, including a ship that "flies" and a truck that "walks," the first helicopter to land at the South Pole, and the army's largest helicopter, the *Flying Crane.* This facility traces more than 200 years of Army transportation history through film, miniature models, life-size displays, and nearly one hundred actual vehicles, aircraft, amphibians, rail equipment, and experimental craft. There are exhibits on Transportation Corp activities in Korea, the Cold War, Vietnam, and Iraqi Freedom, which portrays the lives of soldiers. Also displayed is the gun truck "Eve of Destruction," the only gun truck to return intact from Vietnam.

Endview Plantation (ages 8 and up)

362 Yorktown Rd.; (757) 887-1862; www.endview.org. Open Wed through Mon, with seasonal hours; closed Thanksgiving Day, Christmas Day, and New Year's Day. $.

The house and grounds, restored by the City of Newport News, are now the site of some children's programs throughout the year. Even kids who may not be that interested in the house's period furniture will want to spend some time in the gallery, where Native American, colonial-era, and Civil War artifacts from on-site archaeological digs are displayed. (Ask for the handouts just for kids.) A restored smokehouse on the grounds displays ways in which food used to be preserved.

During the summer there are Civil War camps, where kids ages 8 to 13 can learn all about camp life, including medicine, food, and musket care. At Miss Sallie's Academy, kids are invited to tea, as well as to learn the language of the fan and the Virginia reel. (Both are daylong, Mon through Thurs, extra fee.)

Virginia War Museum (ages 10 and up)

9285 Warwick Blvd.; (757) 247-8523; www.warmuseum.org. Open daily; closed Thanksgiving Day, Christmas Day, and New Year's Day. $.

An 1883 Gatling gun and one of the first battle tanks made during World War II are among the more than 60,000 artifacts on display in this museum. Established in 1923 to showcase articles from American military history, from 1775 until the present, the museum has uniforms, weapons, vehicles, and one of the largest propaganda poster collections in the United States. During the summer there are World War II camps where kids ages 8 to 13 can try on uniforms and learn the different ways past wars were fought. (Both are day-long, Mon through Thurs, extra fee.)

Newport News Regional Park (all ages)
13564 Jefferson Ave.; (757) 888-3333 or (757) 886-7912; www.nngov.com/parks-and-recreation. Open year-round. Free.

If the weather's wonderful, pack a picnic lunch and head for Newport News Park. With more than 8,000 acres, it's one of the country's largest municipal parks. After lunch hike the trails, take a paddleboat for a spin, bike ride, golf, canoe, or fish. There are 188 campsites available; call (800) 203-8322.

Along the White Oak Trail's 2.6 miles, you find bayberry shrubs, white oak trees, and Sycamore Creek, a good place to look for frogs and tadpoles. There's also a 5.3-mile designated bikeway (bikes are available for rent) that takes you from the park's campsite areas to George Washington's headquarters at Yorktown Battlefield. (Helmets required for those ages 14 and younger.)

Stop by the Newport News Park Discovery Center, 13560 Jefferson Ave. (757-886-7916), a temporary shelter for animals being rehabilitated. More than 400 orphaned and injured animals are cared for each year at this facility. Exhibits feature wildlife found in the park and Civil War artifacts. Ask about the Fri evening nature programs in the summer, such as Bats, Bats, Bats and Oh, Deer. Or play a round on the eighteen-hole disc golf course located near the entrance to the park.

Deer Park (all ages)
11523 Jefferson Ave.; (757) 886-7912; www.nngov.com/parks-and-recreation. Open year-round. Free.

This fifty-acre park's newest addition is the only Boundless Playground in Virginia. (Boundless Playgrounds are designed so children with and without disabilities can play together.) The playground's ground surface of rubber and wood mulch enhance accessibility for children in wheelchairs. Enjoy picnic areas, hiking trails, and floral gardens.

Newport News **Travel Tips**

Newport News has fourteen stops on its **Virginia's Civil War Trails** driving tour, many specifically related to the 1862 Peninsula Campaign. Ask about guided tours at the Newport News Visitor Information Center or look for the signage.

Amazing
Newport News Facts

- The **battle** for control of Hampton Roads during the Civil War saw the first fight between two ironclad ships: the USS *Monitor* and the CSS *Virginia* (Merrimack). At **Monitor–Merrimack Overlook,** Sixteenth Street, you can view the site of this historic battle fought on March 9, 1862. After four hours of combat, both sides claimed victory.

SPCA Exotic Sanctuary and Petting Zoo (all ages)
523 J. Clyde Morris Blvd.; (757) 595-1399; www.peninsulaspca.com/zoo.html. Open Mon through Sat; closed Thanksgiving Day, Christmas, and New Year's Day. $.

Younger children will love making friends with the ducks, turkey, sheep, goats, ostrich, and llama. Others will enjoy the exotic area, where kangaroos, jaguars, a lion, a tiger, and other critters reside.

Fort Fun (all ages)
9285 Warwick Blvd.; (757) 886-7912. Open daily. Free.

Just want to play? Then head to Fort Fun in Huntington Park. This 13,500-square-foot play area complete with mazes, towers, slides, swings, and lots of ladders makes for a great break from the rigors of touring. Here your kids are likely to find some local children with whom to romp.

Ferguson Center for the Arts at Christopher Newport University (ages 8 and up)
One University Place; (757) 594-8752; www.fergusoncenter.org. $$$.

This Performing Arts complex has three theaters, including a 1,700-seat concert hall and presents Broadway plays and ballet, as well as classical, rock, and country music concerts.

Where to Eat

What's a shore vacation without some seafood? Be sure to sample some of Newport News's many restaurants.

Bill's Seafood House, 10900 Warwick Blvd.; (757) 595-4320. A good lunch menu at moderate prices; dinner is more expensive but also good. $–$$

Captain D's Seafood Restaurant, 10158 Jefferson Ave.; (757) 596-1027. Open daily for lunch and dinner. $–$$

Chatfield's Grill, 950 J. Clyde Morris Blvd., (757) 952-1611. Open Mon through Sat for breakfast, lunch, and dinner, and brunch on Sun. $

Cheddar's Casual Cafe, 12280 Jefferson Ave.; (757) 249-4000. Open daily for lunch and dinner. Offers a variety of Mexican–American dishes. $–$$

Danny's Deli, 10838 Warwick Blvd.; (757) 595-0252. This hometown favorite serves lunch daily and dinner on Thurs and Fri. $

Gus's Hot Dog King, 10725 Jefferson Ave.; (757) 595-1630. Open daily for lunch and dinner. $

Monty's Penguin, 9607 Warwick Blvd.; (757) 595-2151. Open for breakfast, lunch, and dinner. $–$$

Rey Azteca, 10530 Jefferson Ave.; (757) 595-5956. Open for lunch and dinner. Mexican fare. $

Where to Stay

Comfort Inn, 12330 Jefferson Ave.; (757) 249-0200 or (800) 368-2477. Adjacent to the Patrick Henry Mall, it has an outdoor pool and a fitness center. Complimentary continental breakfast, coffeemakers in rooms. $$$$

Days Inn Oyster Point, 11829 Fishing Point Dr.; (757) 873-6700 or (800) 873-2369. The hotel has an outdoor pool and a fitness center. Complimentary continental breakfast, coffeemakers, microwaves, and refrigerators in rooms. $$$

Holiday Inn Express, 16890 Warwick Blvd.; (757) 887-3300 or (800) 248-0408. Outdoor pool (shared with the Mulberry Inn) and a fitness center. Complimentary continental breakfast; coffeemakers and refrigerators in rooms. Efficiencies with microwaves and stoves are available. $$–$$$

The Mulberry Inn, 16890 Warwick Blvd.; (757) 887-3000 or (800) 223-0404. The Mulberry has an outdoor pool as well as some efficiency rooms. Complimentary continental breakfast; coffeemakers and refrigerators in rooms. $$$

Omni Newport News Hotel, 1000 Omni Blvd.; (757) 873-6664 or (800) 843-6664. This hotel has an indoor pool, plus a restaurant. $$$$

Annual Events

For information on these and other events, contact the **Newport News Visitor Information Center** at (757) 886-7777 or (888) 493-7386.

MAY
Annual Children's Festival of Friends, Newport News Park; (757) 926-8451. Children and their families are the focus of one fun-filled day centered around ten themed pavilions providing pony rides, make-and-take crafts, rides and clowns, music, and food.

OCTOBER
Annual Fall Festival of Folklife, Newport News Park; (757) 926-8451. Southeast Virginia's largest celebration of traditional crafts, trades, and entertainment, with food and **free** children's activities.

For More Information

Newport News Visitor Information Center, 13560 Jefferson Ave., Newport News Park, VA 23603; (757) 886-7777 or (888) 493-7386; www.newport-news.org. Call for a **free** visitors guide and information about guided Civil War sites tour. For additional information on the state's Civil War history, call (888) CIVIL-WAR.

Norfolk

Home to the world's largest naval installation, Norfolk's history is tied to the sea. The renovated downtown harbor has many attractions, shops and a friendly-family feel. Norfolk is also a major cruise stop. The city's charms are not confined to port. Good bets to visit include the first-class botanical garden and the Chrysler Museum of Art. Just twenty minutes west of Virginia Beach, Norfolk is a good stop for families en route to the beach or those taking in Tidewater's attractions.

Nauticus, the National Maritime Center; USS *Wisconsin*; and Hampton Roads Naval Museum (ages 5 and up)

1 Waterside Dr.; (757) 664-1000 or (800) 664-1080; www.nauticus.org. Open daily, reduced hours Labor Day to Memorial Day; closed Thanksgiving, Christmas, and New Year's Day. $–$$.

Nauticus showcases the nation's maritime history through hands-on exhibits plus a real, battleship. The Nauticus campus includes the **Hampton Roads Naval Museum,** a facility contained within Nauticus's main building, as well as the USS *Wisconsin,* one of the largest and last of the country's battleships. Berthed adjacent to the museum in Norfolk harbor, the Wisconsin looms large at 887 feet and three inches long. Standing on her deck looking up at the huge guns gives us a first-hand sense of the ship's power. Each of the dozen 16-inch/50-caliber guns can fire a 1,900-pound projectile, equivalent to the weight of a VW Beetle, 23 nautical miles.

Nauticus makes that point dramatically clear. One of the indoor displays suspends in equilibrium a real VW and a real projectile. Battlescope, another exhibit, overlooks the USS Wisconsin. Point the scope at the ship and see the virtual result when laser cannons hit the vessel.

Kids can use other hands-on exhibits to land navy warplanes on an aircraft carrier, pilot a ship through the river and into the Chesapeake Bay, spell their name out in Morse code, and tie ropes like a sailor. At the National Oceanic and Atmospheric Administration's exhibits at Nauticus, you can "pet" cat sharks from the Pacific; handle horseshoe crabs, sea stars, and whelks at the touch tank; and enter a submersible to maneuver a nine-footlong robotic arm to pick up samples from the sea floor. At the Aegis Theater, test your mettle, making rapid fire decisions in a high-tech naval battle, and in Design Chamber: Battleship X race against others to design a WWII battleship.

In the Hampton Roads Naval Museum, one of only ten such museums operated by the U.S. Navy, find out about important battles in the Chesapeake Bay area, starting with Lord Dunmore's order to bomb Norfolk in the Revolutionary War on January 1, 1776. View ship models, see a video of underwater archeologists exploring a wreck and find out about the battle of the *Monitor* and the *Merrimac,* the first meeting of ironclad naval vessels and a significant battle of the U.S. Civil War that took place in the Hampton Roads area.

The Norfolk Naval Station (ages 9 and up)
9079 Hampton Blvd.; (757) 444-7955. The 45-minute bus tours run year-round from the Naval Base Tour Office, 9809 Hampton Blvd., Victory Rover, Nauticus, (757) 627-7406; www .navalbasecruises.com. Daily Apr through Oct. Nov, Dec, and Mar, Tues through Sun. Call ahead to check. Free.

Possible security restrictions may result in the base not being open to tours. It's best to call ahead. Also, those over 18 are required to show photo ID and vehicle registration.

Norfolk, the largest naval base in the world, occupies 4,300 acres and is home port to 75 ships and 134 aircraft. The tours take you past piers where you may see (depending on the ships in port) aircraft carriers, destroyers, and assault ships, as well as homes constructed for the 1907 Jamestown Exhibition.

Another way to see the modern Navy's battleships is on a cruise aboard the Victory Rover. The non-Navy vessel departs from Nauticus and motors up the Elizabeth River and into the Hampton Roads Harbor.

Fort Norfolk
On the banks of the Elizabeth River near Ghent, 810 Front St.; (757) 625-1720; www.norfolk historical.org/fort. Those over 18 are required to show photo ID and vehicle registration. Open Sat and Sun June through Aug. Call ahead for hours. Free.

The oldest fort on the Virginia waterfront, Fort Norfolk is one of the best-preserved War of 1812 sites in America. Visitors can walk the ramparts, visit the dungeon, tour the Officers' Quarters, and visit other restored areas. Military reenactments of the War of 1812 and the Civil War are staged throughout the year.

The Chrysler Museum of Art (ages 12 and up)
245 West Olney Rd. at Mowbray Arch; (757) 664-6200 or (757) 622-ARTS; www.chrysler.org. Open Wed through Sun; closed major holidays. Free.

The museum's vast collection includes textiles, ceramics, bronzes, and paintings from pre-Columbian, African, and Asian artists, plus an array of European paintings and American art from the 17th to the 20th centuries. The museum possesses a notable glass collection whose highlight includes many Tiffany items. Young visitors can go on a treasure hunt to see what they can find among the exhibits. Musical happenings in the summer include "The Art of Jazz" Wed nights and the "Cool It" concert series on Thurs year-round. And check out Family Days and Holiday Fest activities.

The Chrysler Museum manages two historic houses in downtown Norfolk. The Moses Myers House (757) 441-1526 takes visitors into the world of a prosperous 18th-century merchant and his family. Seventy percent of the items in the house are original. The Willoughby–Baylor House (757) 441-1526, renovated as the Norfolk History Museum, features changing exhibits highlighting Norfolk's maritime and military heritage as well as the city's decorative arts.

Norfolk Botanical Garden (all ages)

6700 Azalea Garden Rd. (located near the airport); (757) 441-5830; www.norfolkbotanical garden.org. Open daily. Visitor center closed Thanksgiving Day, Christmas, and New Year's Day. Tram tours daily from mid-Mar through Oct. $.

This don't-miss spot outside downtown Norfolk has, in season, 155 acres of blooms, including one of the East Coast's largest collections of azaleas (200,000) and roses (30,000). Stroll along 12 miles of garden pathways through more than 30 themed gardens. Kids, especially preschool ones, enjoy the canal boat, the tram tours, and the Kritter Crawlers painted to resemble ladybugs. The Family Fun Backpack, available upon request, provides kids with information and materials to use in the butterfly garden. Special events include History Alive! weekends, garden illuminations (Garden of Light), and Family Sleepovers. Bike and Kayak Nights in the spring and summer let families pedal and paddle on the canals through the petals. (Bikes not provided.)

At World of Wonders: A Children's Adventure Garden kids explore the connection between plants and different world cultures. Kids can explore such diverse re-created environments as an Australian red rock desert, a Serengeti savanna, and an Asian bamboo rainforest. Children can also romp through the dancing fountains on the map of the world.

Virginia Zoological Park (all ages)

3500 Granby St.; (757) 441-2706; www.virginiazoo.org. Open daily except Thanksgiving, Christmas, and New Year's Day. $.

Not large compared with some big-city zoos, the Virginia Zoo is a good size for younger kids, and the zoo train makes touring easy on little feet. Among its nearly 400 animals are Siberian tigers, a diamondback terrapin, a clouded leopard, a two-toed sloth, a Masai giraffe, gelada baboons, and a white rhinoceros. In the African exhibit, roaming animals such as elephants, rhinos, and zebras move about with other compatible animals they might encounter in their natural habitat.

The park's Cub Club and Kritter Kids include basic introductions to animals and reptiles for ages 2 and older. Its Keeper for a Day program (ages 16 and older) lets kids help prepare diets for the animals, clean exhibits, and work with keepers. Kids can also go

Mermaids on Parade

Reflecting the city's nautical heritage, civic pride, and diversity, Mermaids on Parade—more than two dozen mermaid sculptures measuring between 4 and 10 feet long—provides a touch of whimsy throughout downtown Norfolk. What started as a project to raise money for the arts has become a city trademark. Download a map at www.mermaidsonparade.com and see how many sea maidens your family can find.

Amazing
Norfolk Facts

- **General Douglas MacArthur,** best known for his leadership in the Pacific during World War II, is buried in Norfolk. A memorial to the general is located in Norfolk's renovated City Hall, (757) 441-2965.

- **St. Paul's Church.** The southeastern wall of St. Paul's Church still sports the British cannonball shot here on January 1, 1776, during a British attack during the American Revolution. Call (757) 627-4353 for visiting hours.

- Norfolk is the place credited with the **invention of the ice-cream cone.** Try Doumar's, 1919 Monticello Ave., (757) 627-4163.

behind the scenes on special tours to feed giraffes or meet the elephants. One-day Zoo Camps are offered during spring break and one-week camps during the summer. There's a Family Snooze (sleepover) at Halloween and other special events throughout the year.

Town Point Park, riverside in downtown Norfolk, is the site of numerous festivals, outdoor concerts and events. The recently renovated space also has walking paths. Check for scheduled events at www.festevents.org.

Fun Cruises

To really enjoy this port town, get out on the water. Some of the watery outings include:

American Rover Tall Ship Cruises (all ages)

333 Waterside Dr. The ship departs from Waterside Festival Marketplace; (757) 627-SAIL; www.americanrover.com. Tours run mid-Apr through late Oct. $$.

This three-masted topsail schooner offers two- or three-hourlong cruises. Along with seeing the sights, kids can help hoist the sails, learn how to navigate, and learn how to tie sailor's knots.

The *Spirit of Norfolk* (all ages)

Departs from Town Point Park next to Waterside Festival Marketplace; (757) 625-1463 or (866) 211-3803; www.spiritcitycruises.com. $$.

This ship offers two- and three-hour lunch and dinner cruises. Their Kid's Discovery Cruise includes a buffet, a DJ, and some history and geography shared in a fun way.

The *Victory Rover* (all ages)

Departs daily from Nauticus (757-627-7406); www.navalbasecruises.com. $$.

Offers narrated two-hour cruises of the naval base.

Sail Time
(757) 480-7254; www.sailtime.com.

Learn to sail in a weekend.

Go Green Bikes (all ages)
(757) 635-3202; http://gogreenbikerentals.com. $$.

The company drops off and picks up bikes to and from your hotel so that visitors can pedal through town. Bikes come with bike helmet and bike lock, and bike baskets are available by request.

Harbor Park Stadium (ages 5 and up)
150 Park Ave.; (757) 622-2222; www.norfolktides.com. $.

Located along the Elizabeth River, this park is home to the Norfolk Tides, a Triple A team for the New York Mets. In addition to baseball games, the 12,000-seat stadium hosts concerts and other events.

The Tide Light Rail system is scheduled to open in 2011.

Where to Eat

No Frill Bar & Grill, 806 Spotswood Ave., (757) 627-4262; www.nofrillgrill.com. Mon-Sat lunch and dinner and Sun brunch. This restaurant, offering moderately priced sandwiches, salads, and burgers, gains fame for its chili made with Jack cheese and served with cornbread. Children's menu available. $–$$

Doumar's Drive-in, 1919 Monticello Ave.; (757) 627-4163. www.doumars.com. This local landmark is also a legend. Smithsonian credits this town and this restaurant's owners' ancestors as having invented the ice-cream waffle cone. Kids love the eatery's 1950s, hamburger-joint style complete with curbside tray service, and parents love the inexpensive prices. Everyone likes the ice cream. $–$$

D'Egg Diner, 206 E. Main St., (757) 626-3447. Breakfast and lunch. This diner serves big portions of such traditional all-day breakfast fare as three egg omelets and steak and eggs as well as sandwiches for lunch. $

Byrd & Baldwin Brothers Steakhouse, 116 Brooke Ave., (757)222-9191; www .byrdbaldwin.com. This traditional steakhouse serves good-sized portions of steaks as well as some seafood. Reservations suggested. $$$

The Freemason Abbey, 209 West Freemason St.; (757) 622-3966. Lunch and dinner, Sun brunch. Located downtown, this restaurant is a good bet for seafood and steaks. $–$$

Rowena's Jam and Jelly Factory, 758 West Twenty-second St.; (757) 627-8699 or (800) 627-8699. Factory tours can be followed by a scrumptious afternoon tea. $–$$$

Where to Stay

Hampton Inn Norfolk Naval Base, 8501 Hampton Blvd., (757) 489-1000 or (800) 426-7866. Close to the naval base, this hotel has an indoor heated pool. Rooms have coffeemakers and refrigerators. Rates include a continental breakfast. $$$$

Norfolk Waterside Marriott Hotel, 235 East Main St.; (757) 627-4200 or (800)

228-9290. Located downtown, this family-friendly hotel has an indoor pool so that kids (and parents) can swim year-round. $$$$

Sheraton Norfolk Waterside Hotel, 777 Waterside Dr.; (757) 622-6664 or (800) 325-3535. Some rooms here have water views. The hotel is within an easy walk of Town Point Park, site of many outdoor events and festivals. $$$$

Where to Shop

D'Art Center at Selden Arcade, 208 E. Main St., (757) 625-4211; www.d-artcenter.org. Sat 10 a.m. to 5 p.m., Sun 1 to 5 p.m. More than 30 artists work and exhibit in their studios strung on either side of a glassed-in arcade in downtown Norfolk. The center has painters, print makers, sculptors, potters, jewelry makers, and fiber artists. Their pieces are often interesting and it's nice for kids to watch and chat with working artists.

The MacArthur Center, 300 Monticello Ave., Monticello Avenue and East Freemason Street; (757) 627-6000; www.shopmacarthur.com. Located in the heart of downtown Norfolk, the MacArthur Center has 145 stores, including Nordstrom and Dillard's, plus a food court, restaurants, eighteen movie theaters, and an indoor amusement center.

Annual Events

For information about events, contact the **Norfolk Convention and Visitor's Bureau,** (757) 664-6620 or (800) 368-3097; www.norfolkcvb.com.

APRIL–MAY

Virginia Waterfront International Arts Festival, along the city's waterfront; (877) 741-ARTS; www.vafest.com. Twenty-five days in Apr and May, featuring world-renowned artists, music, dance, opera, and family entertainment.

MAY

ARF'AM Fest is one of the largest family ethnic-cultural celebrations in the region, featuring music, food, and lots of children's activities.

JUNE

Harborfest, (757) 441-2345; www.festeventsva.org. Five days of celebration, with a parade of sails (tall ships), a pirate battle, water ski show, and fireworks, plus music and food. Town Point Park.

OCTOBER

Virginia Children's Festival, (757) 441-2345. For children age 10 or younger, fifty interactive activities, hands-on workshops, and arts and crafts.

For More Information

Norfolk Convention and Visitor's Bureau, 232 East Main St., Norfolk, VA 23510; (757) 664-6620 or (800) 368-3097; www.visitnorfolktoday.com.

For a visitor guide, call (800) 368-3097. Another tourist information office is located in Nauticus, the National Maritime Center, at 1 Waterside Dr., and another off I-64 at exit 273. It is also possible to chat online with a visitor guide.

Virginia Beach

With 35 miles of coastline and sandy—though sometimes crowded—ocean beaches, the shore and surf bring out the kid in even the most work-weary city dweller. Prime time is summer. With the high temperatures come crowds. A visit in spring and fall tends to offer more beach and fewer hordes.

Virginia Beach's boardwalk, a no-cars-allowed, long, flat stretch of sidewalk, is great for walking as well as cycling, as the path has a designated bike lane. You can rent bicycles as well as inline skates (Rollerblades) and surreys from the several bike stands set up along the boardwalk. Glide down the boardwalk with the sea breeze blowing in your hair.

Near Virginia Beach's see-and-be-seen strip of sand, you can still view the land as it was seen by America's first settlers. Located at the southernmost end of Virginia Beach, Back Bay National Wildlife Refuge and False Cape State Park share similar topography, but have different functions. Back Bay is mostly a wildlife refuge, whereas False Cape is primarily 10 miles of rustic beach area. At both Back Bay and False Cape, you can surf, cast for flounder, or sight white-tailed deer that dart through the thickets. Both serve as havens for nature lovers, because access is primarily by foot, bicycle, private boat, or by an open-air electric tram operated by False Cape State Park.

The Beach

Where you stay and where you park your beach blanket depends on what you like. The highest concentration of boombox, bikini, and college crowds are usually found in the resort area from Twentieth through Thirty-fifth Streets. The bodies can be blanket to blanket and the people-watching is prime, especially along the boardwalk, the 30-foot-wide paved path edging the sand.

If you prefer quieter stretches, then head to the North End, from Forty-third Street north toward **Fort Story,** or to the Sandbridge area in the southern end of town. Whatever stretch of sand you pick, time-honored traditions include swimming, sunning, and bodysurfing. Here you can look up from your sand castle and maybe see dolphins breaching the sea. On summer evenings Atlantic Avenue transforms into a family-style street party called "Beach Street USA," with a variety of entertainers, including crooners, strummers, magicians, and jugglers.

Back Bay National Wildlife Refuge (all ages)
4005 Sandpiper Rd.; (757) 721-2412; www.fws.gov/backbay. **Visitor Contact Station open daily; closed Sat Dec through Mar and on all public holidays except Memorial Day, Fourth of July, and Labor Day. Nov through Mar** Free**; Apr through Oct $.**

Back Bay's more than 9,000 acres are a managed area created as a waterfowl refuge (nearly 300 species of birds have been observed here). Egrets and herons dance on the water and turtles dive into pools along the 9 miles of dikes built to separate the man-made freshwater impoundments from the salt water of Chesapeake Bay. The sounds of geese and ducks echo through these gentle stretches of water. Approximately 10,000 snow geese and a large variety of ducks visit here during the peak of their migration, usually in Dec. For a quick tour, try the 1-mile boardwalk beach loop past dune barriers to the Atlantic or the 4-mile dike loop through marshlands. Be aware that venomous cotton-mouth snakes inhabit the marshes, so stay on the boardwalk. Pick up a free brochure at the Visitor Contact Station for information. There are many programs throughout the year

Virginia Beach **Travel Tips**

If your family is really into nature, the Back Bay National Wildlife Refuge and False Cape State Park offer a one-of-a-kind back-to-nature experience during the winter months on its beach mobile, called the *Terra Gator*. Designed to navigate the shoreline with thirty-six passengers, the *Terra Gator* takes families on a five-hour round-trip excursion, including a stopover at the park, with commentary throughout the journey. The trip is available on weekends Nov 1 to Mar 31. Reservations are required; call (800) 933–7275. $

at the refuge, such as wildlife walking tours, Creature Crafts, bike hikes, and the annual Family Fishing Festival, where kids (and parents) can learn the basics of fresh- and saltwater fishing. Preregistration is required.

False Cape State Park (all ages)

4001 Sandpiper Rd., 5 miles south of Back Bay. For camping and other information, call (757) 426-7128 or (800) 933-PARK; www.dcr.virginia.gov/state_parks/fal.shtml. Admission to the park is **free** but entry is through Back Bay National Wildlife Refuge, a site that charges admission Apr through Oct.

False Cape State Park is not for the novice camper. Sites are primitive: It takes work to reach the park, but if your family—older kids and teens—can handle this, do go. Leave behind the tourists and boomboxes for 5.9 miles of unspoiled beaches, thousands of acres of marshlands, and woods filled with songbirds. False Cape offers the changing interplay of beach, dune, and forest in one of the last undisturbed coastal environments anywhere. When here, think about the unspoiled beaches of False Cape and how this spot of what came to be Virginia Beach lured the New World dreamers.

To enjoy False Cape, you can hike 5 miles through Back Bay; rent a mountain bike from Conte's Bicycle and Fitness, 1805 Laskin Rd., (757) 491-1900; or take the tram (spring and summer) available from Little Island City Park, Sandbridge, (757) 498-2412. Be sure to bring your own water and lots of it. False Cape is a gift for the eye: 6 miles of beautiful shoreline graced by dunes, gulls, and sandpipers but inhabited by only a handful of people. At the height of the beach season, birds outnumber bathers, and the unspoiled arc of surf and sand stretches for miles. Other delights include walks through loblolly pine forests rising above tiers of blueberry patches, marshes speckled with white hibiscus, and sprays of gold asters. Along the Barbour Hill Trail, 2.4 miles, stop to go crabbing at the boat docks (bring your own gear), or dangle your feet in the cool water as you look across at Cedar Island, a 400-acre heron rookery. Camping is permitted year-round and reservations are required; call (800) 933-7275 for information. The park offers programs in astronomy, birding and night hikes, and bus tours, as well as special events in conjunction with the Virginia Aquarium and Marine Science Center and others.

First Landing State Park (all ages)

Highway 60 at Cape Henry, 2500 Shore Dr.; (757) 412-2300; www.dcr.virginia.gov/state_
parks/fir.shtml. $.

This park, with its 19 miles of hiking trails, is Virginia's most popular state park, attracting
more than one million visitors annually, yet it still offers a quiet respite. Paths lead you by
freshwater ponds and through thickets of large cypress trees draped with Spanish moss.
There is a special bicycle trail and bikes are permitted on park roads. (Bikes can be rented
at the Chesapeake Bay Center.) A boat ramp offers access to Broad Bay. The first section
of the Bald Cypress Trail is 1 mile long, crosses dunes and ponds, and is wheelchair accessible. Located in the park is the Chesapeake Bay Center, an environmental education center
that features wet labs and displays. The center also showcases Bay Lab, developed by the
Aquarium and Marine Science Center. This marine lab features aquariums, environmental
exhibits, classroom space, a wet lab, and touch tank. The visitor center includes a staging
area for adventure programs, enabling visitors to participate in such programs as sea kayaking and explore the Chesapeake Bay firsthand. For families who want something a little
closer to land, there are interpretive programs offered throughout the summer, such as
Night Over the Chesapeake (telescoping the moon and stars), Kritter Kids (kids learn about
resident critters), Cool Campfires (s'mores!), and Ospreys and Eagles. Families interested in
camping should call the State Parks Reservation Center at (800) 933-PARK, Mon through Fri,
to reserve a cabin or campsite. Some campsites here now have electricity and water.

Virginia Aquarium and Marine Science Center (ages 5 and up)

717 General Booth Blvd.; (757) 385-3474 ; www.virginiaaquarium.com. Open daily except
Thanksgiving and Christmas. $–$$.

At the Atlantic Ocean Pavilion and Main Building, visitors can see sand-tiger, nurse, and
brown sharks; stingrays; and other open-ocean dwellers in the 300,000-gallon Norfolk
Canyon Aquarium. There is also a 70,000-gallon sea turtle aquarium, a sea turtle hatching
laboratory, a jellyfish and octopus aquarium, a life-size model of a humpback whale, a 3-D
IMAX theater, and lots of hands-on exhibits. The Owls Creek Marsh Pavilion tells the story
of Owls Creek salt marsh, the waterway on which the museum is located. The exhibits are
clever and have kid-friendly touch-screen computers. In the whimsical Macro Marsh gallery where the "grass" is ten times larger than real life, visitors feel as tiny as hermit crabs.
In the Micro Marsh gallery little things such as mosquito heads come into view via microscopes. Apr through Sept there are half-hour pontoon boat tours through the marsh. Call
(757) 385-0278 for a schedule and fares.

VB Wave

The VB Wave is a nifty way to get around the oceanfront area from May
through Oct. Information on routes, schedules, and fares is available at (757)
222-6100 or www.hrtransit.org.

The dozens of aquariums and terrariums feature creatures such as river otters and seahorses, and at the one-of-a-kind interactive theater, children can test their knowledge about the local environment. Attached is a 0.5-acre outdoor aviary featuring more than fifty-five species, including cattle egrets, brown pelicans, turkey vultures, and great blue herons, all viewed from an elevated wooden walkway. Preschool Discovery Days and Fishy Fun Days offer kids 5 and under a fun way to learn about marine life through stories and crafts. Preregistration is required; (757) 385-0278.

Between the two pavilions is the Nature Trail, a 0.3-mile trail that meanders through ten acres of salt marsh preserve along Owls Creek. On this walk sweet gum and maple trees offer shade and circular loops jut out into the water to provide clear views of the gulls and great blue herons swooping down for fish. (You can almost ignore the steady hum of the traffic on busy General Booth Boulevard just 30 feet away. The contrast makes a powerful case for preserving wetlands such as this one.) A 30-foot observation tower and information boxes help visitors identify what they're seeing.

Informative fifteen-minute programs are held throughout the day in both pavilions and along the nature trail on a variety of topics. In addition, special family programs are held throughout the year at the Bay Lab in the Chesapeake Bay Center at First Landing State Park (see above). These range from simple ones, such as learning how sea stars protect themselves, to Exotic Aquatics: An Evening of Mystery, where participants (ages 6 to adult) are given clues to solve the mystery of what kind of animal has been pulled from the Chesapeake Bay. Overnights at the aquarium give families a chance to go behind the scenes while enjoying games, crafts, and animal interactions.

In winter sign on for the whale-watching trips sponsored by the museum. From Jan until mid-Mar, look for humpback whales as museum staff tell you about these leviathans. June to Oct the museum sponsors dolphin-watching trips. June through Aug Ocean Collection boat trips give visitors the opportunity to examine sea life up close, with sea creatures pulled from the ocean and brought on deck. Call (757) 385-3474 for information.

The Old Coast Guard Station Museum (ages 5 and up)
Twenty-fourth Street and Boardwalk; (757) 422-1587; www.oldcoastguardstation.com. Open daily in the summer, Tues through Sun the rest of the year; closed Thanksgiving, Christmas, and New Year's Eve and Day. $.

Housed in a 1903 Coast Guard Station, this museum looks at another aspect of sea life. Learn about lifesaving techniques from the early days of shipwrecks to the submarine-mined waters of both world wars. Check out its TowerCAM to get an up-close view of the ocean, beach, and nearby objects. By using the video monitor and video camera, kids can learn the identity of the vessels visiting the port of Hampton Roads. Special exhibits throughout the year highlight the history and activities of the station.

Old Cape Henry Lighthouse (ages 5 and up)

Northeastern tip of Virginia Beach, on the grounds of the U.S. Army's Fort Story. A photo ID card is needed to enter Fort Story; (757) 422-9421; www.apva.org/capehenry. Open year-round. Closed Thanksgiving Day, Christmas, and New Year's Eve and Day. $.

This lighthouse, built in 1791, marked the entrance to the Chesapeake Bay until 1881. The lighthouse is open for tours and climbs to the top.

Psychic Travels: Association for Research and Enlightenment
(ages 9 and up)

215 Sixty-seventh St. and Atlantic Avenue; (757) 428-3588 or (800) 333-4499; www.edgar cayce.org. Open year-round except Thanksgiving, Christmas, and New Year's Day. Free.

Turn-of-the-20th-century seer Edgar Cayce obeyed instructions he received in a trance to move to Virginia Beach in 1925 to establish a hospital. Cayce, frequently called the "sleeping prophet," garnered his information from higher states of consciousness when he was in a trancelike state. Cayce gave readings in which he diagnosed people's illnesses and prescribed cures, skills he never possessed in his waking state. Visitors here can browse through one of the most extensive metaphysical libraries in the world, containing Cayce's transcribed readings. At the bookstore expand your beach reading with tomes on holistic health, numerology, dream interpretation, meditation, and channeling. Daily tours include films, lectures, meditation classes, and ESP demonstrations. Spa treatments are also available.

Hit the Water (all ages)

Getting out on the water is a favorite family activity. You can rent a boat, kayak, or canoe at Surf and Adventure Co., 577 Sandbridger Rd.; (757) 721-6210 or (800) 695-4212; www.surfandadventure.com, or try out their ocean kayaking and dolphin tours. Book a day of deep-sea fishing or parasailing with the Virginia Beach Fishing Center at 200 Winston Salem Ave. at the Rudee Inlet Bridge; (757) 491-8000 or (800) 725-0509; www .virginiafishing.com.

Ocean Breeze Waterpark (all ages)

849 General Booth Blvd,; (757) 422-4444 or (800) 678-WILD; www.oceanbreezewaterpark .com. Open daily Memorial Day through Labor Day. $$.

Families who want something a little more active than lying on the beach should head here, where the Virginia Beach icon Hugh Mongous (looking something like King Kong as a Hawaiian tourist) welcomes visitors. The park's sixteen water slides range from the fast-and-furious Bahama Mamma and the Hurricane to the Little Amazon and South Seas Silly Slides for small kids. There is also a candy store, a gift shop, lockers, and three food outlets.

The Chesapeake Bay Bridge–Tunnel (all ages)

32386 Lankford Hwy., Cape Charles; (757) 331-2960; www.cbbt.com. $$.

Even if it costs $12 each way ($5 to cross back if within 24 hours) to cross the 17.6-milelong Chesapeake Bay Bridge–Tunnel, the fee is worth it, at least once. As the structure loops over and under the bay, it's easy to savor the sense of space and joy common to open roads, panoramic water views, and sea breezes. In Sept and early May, hundreds of bird-watchers come to observe this mid-Atlantic flyway for migratory sea birds. (Permission to make brief stops on the four man-made islands must be obtained in writing.) Families also will enjoy the view and menu offered at Seagull Pier and Restaurant, midway across the structure.

Where to Eat

Virginia Beach offers the hungry the usual array of cheap eats plus some good restaurants.

Aldo's Ristorante, Le Promenade Shopping Center, 1860 Laskin Rd.; (757) 491-1111. Open daily for lunch and dinner. Italian fare and homemade desserts. $$

The Jewish Mother, 3108 Pacific Ave.; (757) 422-5430. This informal restaurant offers deli sandwiches with enough variety for even the most finicky kid. Breakfast is served all day, lunch and dinner. Some evenings there is live music. $–$$

Lynnhaven Fish House, 2350 Starfish Rd.; (757) 481-0003. If you're in the mood for something special, this fine restaurant is family-oriented and has a children's menu and a wonderful view of Chesapeake Bay. $$$

Where to Stay

There are many hotels in the Virginia Beach area. Decide whether you want to be beachfront in the heart of the action, on the sand in the quieter northern area, or a few blocks from the water. Here are some family-friendly suggestions. Visitors planning on a longer stay should consider real estate rentals. Several rental agencies are available.

Affordable Properties, (757) 428-0432 or (800) 639-0432; www.affordablepropertiesvb .com, and **Siebert Realty–Sandbridge Beach,** (757) 426-6200 or (877) 422-2200; www.siebert-realty.com.

Barclay Towers Resort Hotel, 809 Atlantic Ave.; (757) 491-2700 or (800) 344-4473. This is an all-suite hotel whose rooms have kitchenettes. Five- and seven-night package plans are available. Complimentary continental breakfast, indoor pool, sauna, and video game room. $$–$$$

The Belvedere Motel, Oceanfront at Thirty-sixth St.; (757) 425-0612 or (800) 425-0612. This lodging in the quiet end of town offers families motel rooms and efficiencies with refrigerators. $$$$

The Cavalier Hotel, Forty-second and Atlantic Avenue; (757) 425-8555 or (800) 446-8199. This property has two locations, one on the beach and one nearby. Both sites have balconies and children under 18 stay **free.** Indoor and outdoor pools, bikes, and tennis courts. There's a Camp Cavalier and Kids' Cafe for the little ones. $$$$

The Holiday Inn SunSpree Resort, Thirty-ninth and Atlantic Avenue; (757) 428-1711 or (877) 863-4780. This property has outdoor and indoor pools, an exercise room, and a Kids Activity Center. Also offers refrigerators and coffeemakers in rooms. $$$$

The Holiday Inn, 2607 Atlantic Ave.; (757) 491-6900 or (877) 863-4780. In the heart of the "action," this property offers rooms and suites plus an indoor pool. Refrigerators in rooms. $$$$

Wyndham Hotel & Resort, 5700 Atlantic Ave.; (757) 428-7025 or (800) 365-3032. This beachfront property is a good choice for those who want to stay in the quieter north end of town. The facility has indoor and outdoor pools, plus an exercise room, and microwaves, refrigerators, and coffeemakers in rooms. $$$$

Annual Events

Virginia Beach has many festivals and special events throughout the year. Here are a few of them. For more information, call (800) 822-3224.

MARCH

Annual Virginia Beach Shamrock Sportfest for kids who are into running ½ Marathons. There's a world-class marathon, 8K, and children's races. (757) 412-1056.

MAY

Memorial Day Weekend. Visitors enjoy live music in the parks on the oceanfront. For strawberry lovers, there's the **Pungo Strawberry Festival,** with homemade delicacies, live music, a children's activity area, and arts and crafts; (757) 721-6001.

What better month than May for the Annual **Panorama Caribbean Music Festival.** Kick off your shoes and dance on the sand; (757) 491-7866.

JUNE

Boardwalk Art Show and Festival. More than 450 artists and craftspeople sell their handmade creations along the boardwalk; (757) 425-0000.

AUGUST

East Coast Surfing Championships. Catch a wave—at least vicariously; (757) 465-1535.

SEPTEMBER

Annual Blues at the Beach Festival, 17th Street Park.

Neptune Festival Boardwalk Weekend, held the last weekend of Sept. This grand finale to summer has an internationally renowned **North America Sandsculpting Competition,** daily concerts, more than 250 artisans at the craft show, food, and fun scattered along 30 blocks of the boardwalk.

OCTOBER

Brewfest brings an **Octoberfest** atmosphere to the beach, with samplings of beers, microbrews, and cider surrounded by authentic German music and food.

For More Information

The **Virginia Beach Convention and Visitor's Bureau,** 2100 Parks Ave., Virginia Beach, VA 23451; information (800) 822-3224; (800) VA-BEACH; www.vbfun.com.

Virginia's Northern Neck

Boat on the water, breeze in our faces, ospreys nesting on pilings: these are some of the pleasures of Virginia's Northern Neck, a boater's dream and a naturalist's delight.

With the sun glinting off the Rappahannock River, the birds appear as a splash of white fluff and brown feathers as we cruise on the wide Rappahannock River, the Northern Neck's southern border. The Chesapeake Bay is the region's eastern border and the Potomac River, the northern border. The Northern Neck offers more than 1,200 miles of tidal coastline as well as 6,500 acres of natural areas, including marshes, state parks and preserves.

The Tides Inn　(all ages)

480 King Carter Dr., Irvington; (804) 438-5000, (800) 843-3726; www.tidesinn.com. Closed New Year's Day until Mar. $$–$$$.

The Tides Inn, a 106-room, waterfront, Four Diamond property, serves as a good base for families exploring the region. The resort, situated about three hours from D.C. and one hour from Richmond, features comfortable rooms, an outdoor pool, good food, and an imaginative children's program. The front lawn blooms with bougainvillea, roses, crape myrtles, and wildflowers that edge an executive, par 3-golf course, a great place for teaching the fundamentals of the game to budding duffers. Nearby, is the resort's Golden Eagle Golf Club, an 18-hole course. At Crab Net Kids, available Memorial Day to Labor Day, the supervised children's program, ages 4–12 swim in the pool, kayak on Carters Creek, play croquet, and do crafts. In summer there is an on-site sailing school.

George Washington Birthplace National Monument

Oak Grove, (804) 224-1732; 1732 Popes Creek Rd., Colonial Beach. www.nps.gov/gewa. Open daily 9 a.m. to 5 p.m. $.

George Washington was born on this plantation, February 22, 1732. Although Washington lived at the plantation (now 550-acres) until he was three-and-a half-years, he returned as an adolescent to practice surveying at the property. An informative film using excerpts of Washington's own diaries sets the tone about life on a tobacco farm. Now only the foot-print of the original home remains, but you can tour a reconstructed 18th century upper-class plantation house (not like the one George inhabited).

Stratford Hall

Stratford, 483 Great House Rd., on Rt. 214 off Rt. 3, Stratford, (804) 493-8038; www.strat fordhall.org. Open daily 9:30 a.m. to 4 p.m. $.

Stratford Hall, Stratford, the plantation home built in the 1730's by the Lee family, is one of Virginia's grand manor houses. Richard Henry Lee and Francis Lightfoot Lee, both sign-ers of the Declaration of Independence, grew up at this plantation whose green lawns roll toward the Potomac River, and Robert Edward Lee was born in the residence on January 19, 1807. Surrounded by 1,670-acres, the brick mansion, seen by guided tour, is impres-sive. Lee resided here until he was three-years and 11 months old, spending much of his time in the nursery. Visit the gardens, kitchen, caretaker's office, the "Negro" cabins, and the barns.

Northern Virginia

Northern Virginia features history both distant and still in the making: Alexandria and Mount Vernon, George Washington's plantation, are steeped in colonial history, while the Pentagon Memorial commemorates September 11, 2001. Arlington National Cemetery and related military museums and memorials pay tribute to wars past and present. The region also features natural attractions like the C&O Canal and Great Falls Park.

Arlington

Arlington, just across the Memorial Bridge from the District of Columbia, is well known for Arlington National Cemetery. The area has many other historical attractions and war memorials, too. Visit the ones most likely to interest your kids. Remember, seeing all of them might cause your children to rebel, while a little bit of well-chosen history goes a long way.

Let the kids' individual interests guide you—are they interested in learning about brave women? See the Women in Military Service Memorial, dedicated to women who

TopPicks in Northern Virginia

1. **Arlington National Cemetery,** Arlington
2. **Mount Vernon Estate,** Mount Vernon
3. **Wolf Trap National Park for the Performing Arts,** Vienna
4. **Mount Vernon Bicycle Trail,** Alexandria
5. **Women in Military Service for America Memorial,** Arlington
6. **Great Falls Park,** Great Falls

NORTHERN VIRGINIA

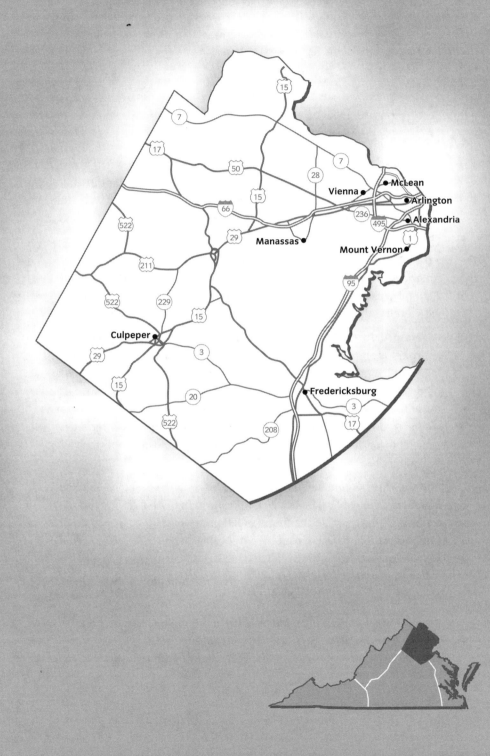

have served in the Armed Forces. Would they recognize the iconic Iwo Jima tableau? See it at the Marine Corps War Memorial. And if they're old enough to remember September 11, the Pentagon Memorial would be especially meaningful. Break up the history lessons with shopping at some of the region's favorite malls.

Amazing
Wartime Facts

- **Elizabeth Van Lew** of Richmond, Virginia, received Confederate military plans and encoded them before carrying them to the Union Army. She also smuggled food and clothing to Union prisoners jailed in Richmond's Libby Prison.

- **Sarah Osborne** accompanied her husband Aaron to war during the American Revolution, cooking for him and his fellow soldiers. When General Washington asked her if she was afraid of bullets, she said, "It would not do for the men to fight and starve, too."

- **Women Airforce Service Pilots (WASP)** was a civilian organization of approximately 1,000 women who worked closely with the Army during World War II. These women performed essential services such as flying aircraft from factories to air bases and towing, in the air, targets for antiaircraft artillery students to practice shooting at. This task was so dangerous—thirty-eight WASPs died while doing this—that men refused to perform this duty, stating that they'd rather risk their lives in combat.

- **Phoebe Jeter** commanded a platoon of fifteen men assigned to identify incoming enemy SCUD missiles and destroy them during Operation Desert Storm. She became the first woman in her battalion to earn an Army Commendation medal while in Saudi Arabia.

- **Sybil Ludington** rode 40 miles on horseback—farther than Paul Revere—in 1777 to warn the people around Ludington, Connecticut, that the British were attacking.

- **Grace Banker** served in World War I as a telephone switch operator, receiving and sending messages from troops on the front line to soldiers at headquarters. For her work she received the Distinguished Service Cross.

Arlington National Cemetery (ages 7 and up)

Take the Metro's Blue Line to the Arlington National Cemetery station; (703) 607-8000; www.arlingtoncemetery.org. Open daily. $.

See where America's military heroes, presidents, and other public figures have been honored, memorialized, and buried. This cemetery isn't just historical; there are an average 27 to 30 military funeral services a day, so don't be surprised if you come upon a service. Start at the visitor center near the Metro stop and obtain historical information, gravesite locations for notables, and information on **Arlington House** (also known as the Robert E. Lee Memorial, 703-235-1530, www.nps.gov/arho/index.htm). Tour buses (for a fee) shuttle between four stops inside the cemetery gates: the visitor center, John F. Kennedy grave site, Tomb of the Unknowns, the Challenger Space Shuttle Memorial (www.arlingtoncemetery.net/challengr.htm) and Arlington House.

Visit the **Tomb of the Unknowns,** which overlooks the Washington, D.C., skyline. The tomb contains the remains of unidentified soldiers from World War I, World War II, Korea, and Vietnam. The tomb itself is guarded 24 hours a day by the 3rd U.S. Infantry Regiment, also known as the Old Guard. Changing of the guard, a solemn and impressive ceremony, occurs every half hour from Apr 1 through Sept 30 and every hour on the hour from Oct 1 through Mar 31. The guards change at two-hour intervals during night hours year-round.

There is more method to the guards' marching than one might think. The guard paces from his post and across the crossway in twenty-one steps, turning to pause while facing the memorial for twenty-one seconds. Turning once more, the guard pauses for another twenty-one seconds before repeating the process. "Twenty-one" represents the highest honor of salutation, matching the twenty-one-gun salute.

Additional graves of notables include those of General Philip Henry Sheridan, U.S. Army, a Civil War soldier; Lt. Commander Roger Bruce Chaffee, U.S. Navy, Apollo astronaut, who died while performing test operations for the Apollo One space mission; Lt. Colonel Virgil I. ("Gus") Grissom, U.S. Air Force, Apollo astronaut, the second American in space on the Mercury mission (1961), first person to make two space trips on the two-man Gemini flight (1965); the commingled remains of the seven astronauts who died aboard the space shuttle *Challenger* in 1986; William Jennings Bryan, presidential candidate, secretary of state; Oliver Wendell Holmes Jr., Civil War veteran, Supreme Court Justice; Joe Louis (Barrow), heavyweight boxing champion; Rear Admiral Robert E. Peary, U.S. Navy, explorer; and William Howard Taft, president, chief justice of the United States Supreme Court. Jacqueline Kennedy's and John F. Kennedy's gravesites are home to the Eternal Flame. Your child may well ask how the flame stays lit: There is a constantly flashing electric spark near the tip of the gas nozzle that relights the flame if it should go out in the rain or wind.

The visitor center and parking facility are open during cemetery hours. There are special events at Arlington House offered throughout the year including a St. Patrick's Day bagpipe procession to the Custis family grave and madrigal singers during winter holidays.

Women in Military Service for America Memorial (ages 7 and up)

At the entrance to Arlington National Cemetery; (703) 533-1155 or (800) 222-2294; www .womensmemorial.org and www.nps.gov. Open daily year-round except Christmas.

This memorial, dedicated in October 1997, was built to honor all women who have served in, and with, the military. The education center and 196-seat theater portray the history of women in the armed forces beginning more than 220 years ago. Children may be surprised to learn that women played important roles in war as far back as the Revolution. The Hall of Honor recognizes women who have made a significant sacrifice, such as those who were prisoners of war or died in service, and those who were recipients of the highest awards for service and bravery. The Computer Registry makes it possible to locate and view the records of friends and relatives who were, or are, servicewomen. Activity books for children are available by calling in advance.

The Marine Corps War Memorial (ages 7 and up)

Marshall Drive between US 50 and Arlington National Cemetery; (703) 289-2500; www.nps .gov. Open 24 hours, year-round.

This Marine Corps memorial, commonly referred to as the Iwo Jima Memorial, can be reached from the cemetery. (Ask at the cemetery's visitor center for directions.) The capture of Iwo Jima, a noted incident in World War II, was immortalized on film when news photographer Joe Rosenthal photographed five marines and one Navy corpsman raising a large American flag. Felix W. de Weldon's sculpture of that scene honors not only those marines who fought in World War II but every marine who has died defending America since 1775.

The Netherlands Carillon, a gift from the Dutch people in gratitude for American aid during World War II, is adjacent to the memorial. Carillon concerts are held on national holidays and on Sat. In May and Sept the concerts are from 2 to 4 p.m., and in June, July, and Aug, from 6 to 8 p.m.

In the summer, from June through mid-Aug, the U.S. Marine Drum and Bugle Corps and the Marine Corps Silent Drill Platoon present an hourlong Sunset Parade every Tues evening beginning at 7 p.m. This is open to the public, no charge and no reservations. The precision drill, solemn and fascinating, enchants children.

Air Force Memorial (ages 7 and up)

One Air Force Dr. (located off of Columbia Pike near Highway 244; the Pentagon Metro station is within walking distance); (703) 979-0674; www.airforcememorial.org. Open daily.

Three stainless-steel spires, the tallest at 270-feet, soar on a site that overlooks the Potomac River, the Pentagon and the Washington, D.C., skyline. Evoking a sense of flight and precision teamwork, the memorial honors the more than 54,000 airmen who died in combat while in the Air Force.

Pentagon (ages 7 and up)

Take the Metro's Yellow and Blue lines to the Pentagon station; (703) 697-1776; http://pentagon.afis.osd.mil.

Due to security concerns, the Pentagon is not available for tours by the public. As of press time, tours of the Pentagon are available only to schools, educational organizations, and other select groups and only by reservation. Check out the Web site for a virtual tour that includes the Military Women's Corridor, the Flag Corridor, and the Hall of Heroes.

Pentagon Memorial (ages 7 and up)

1 Rotary Rd., on the Pentagon Reservation, Arlington. Limited parking; take the Metro's yellow or blue lines to the Pentagon station; www.pentagonmemorial.net/home.aspx. Open daily, 24 hours.

A powerful memorial to the 184 people who died when terrorists crashed Flight 77 into the Pentagon on September 11, 2001, this spare park is a place of reflection on lives lost and on the impact of that day on the nation and the world. The gravel field is scattered with elegant benches hovering over individual light pools, one for each of the victims; they are arranged in a timeline from the youngest victim, age 3, to the oldest, age 71. Each is distinguished further by the direction it faces: toward the open sky, for the 59 victims on Flight 77, and toward the Pentagon for those working inside that day. Guided tours are not available, as the memorial is designed to experienced on a personal level.

Drug Enforcement Administration (DEA) Museum and Visitor Center (ages 10 and up)

This museum is across the street from the Pentagon City Shopping Mall and one Metro stop from Arlington National Cemetery; 700 Army Navy Dr.; (202) 307-3463 (note that the area code is 202, even though the museum is located in Virginia); www.deamuseum.org. Open Tues through Fri; closed major holidays. Free.

This chronological exhibit on drugs in America spans more than 150 years and is heavy on photographs, but kids will be interested in the items on display about such cultural icons as Coca-Cola, which contained cocaine until 1903 and was advertised as a medicine that would "ease the tired brain," or Bayer Aspirin, whose precursor was Bayer Heroin, advertised as "highly effective against coughs." There's a literature rack just for kids, with brochures about the museum and information on the dangers of drug use. A scavenger hunt for children from kindergarten through sixth grade is available if you call ahead.

Amazing
Pentagon Facts

- The **Pentagon,** which covers twenty-nine acres, is one of the world's largest office buildings and has 17.5 miles of corridors.

Theodore Roosevelt Island (all ages)

Located off the George Washington Memorial Parkway heading north; (703) 289-2500; www.nps.gov/this. Open daily 6 a.m. to 10 p.m. year-round.

This island, in the middle of the Potomac River, serves as an 88-acre respite from the big city just across the river and provides sanctuary for beavers, box turtles, opossums, gray squirrels, raccoons, rabbits, birds, and non-venomous snakes. Its 2.5 miles of walking trails make it something of an oasis—if you ignore the jet noise from nearby Ronald Reagan Washington National Airport. You can bird-watch and walk through swamp, marsh, and forest. The upper trail leads through woods filled with elms, tulip poplars, oaks, and red maples. In the center of the island is a 47-foot monument of Teddy Roosevelt. Call ahead or check out the Web site for the schedule for the ranger-led tours given throughout the year.

Where to Eat

Cafe Parisian Express, 4520 Lee Hwy.; (703) 525-3332. Open Mon through Sat for breakfast, lunch, and dinner, Sun for brunch. This French bistro features soups, sandwiches, crepes, and quiches. $

Faccia Luna Pizzeria, 2909 Wilson Blvd.; (703) 276-3099. Open daily for lunch and dinner. Good Italian food in a family atmosphere. Children's menu available. $–$$

Hunan Number One, 3033 Wilson Blvd.; (703) 528-1177. Open daily for lunch and dinner. Specialties of this Cantonese restaurant are sesame chicken with lemon sauce, sizzling black-pepper steak, and the Hunan No. 1, a combination of shrimp, chicken, beef, broccoli, straw mushrooms, and snow peas in a brown sauce. $–$

Red, Hot, and Blue, 1600 Wilson Blvd.; (703) 276-7427. Open daily for lunch and dinner. Memphis-style ribs, pulled pork, beans, barbecued chicken, and catfish are staples at this lively restaurant. Children's menu available. $–$$

Silver Diner, 3200 Wilson Blvd.; (703) 812-8600. Open daily for breakfast, lunch, and dinner, breakfast served all day. Basic hamburgers, salads, and fish plates, plus great desserts. Children's menu available. $–$$

Where to Stay

Embassy Suites Crystal City, 1300 Jefferson Davis Hwy.; (703) 979-9799 or (800) EMBASSY. The suites offer families more space and privacy than a single room. There is a refrigerator in each guest room and rates include full American breakfast. $$–$$$$

Hyatt Arlington at Washington's Key Bridge, 1325 Wilson Blvd.; (703) 525-1234 or (800) 233-1234; http://arlington.hyatt.com. The Hyatt is well located across Key Bridge from Georgetown. The family-friendly property has children's menus. $–$$$$

For more lodging, check out www.stay arlington.com.

Where to Shop

For a break from history and government, Arlington offers four shopping centers with lively cafes and myriad opportunities to spend.

Ballston Common, 4238 Wilson Blvd.; (703) 243-8088; www.ballston-common .com. Located 2 blocks from the Ballston Metro station on the Orange line; connected via the skywalk from Mall Level 2. This nifty neighborhood mall offers more than one hundred stores, including Macy's, Curious Kids, East Bay Watches, and Champs Sports, plus twelve movie screens, a large food court, and seven restaurants. Comedy Sport, a comedy club featuring family-friendly "clean" humor, is a nice place to spend an evening.

Crystal City Shops, Crystal City Underground and Crystal City Drive; (703) 922-4636. Located above and below ground, this center features more than 150 shops and eateries. Legal Seafood, McCormick & Schmicks, and Jaleo are among the restaurants.

Fashion Centre at Pentagon City, 1100 South Hayes St.; (703) 415-2400; www.fashioncentrepentagon.com. Take the Metro's Blue or Yellow line to Pentagon City station. The more than 170 shops include Macy's and Nordstrom;

the usual chains of women's, men's, and kids' clothing stores; plus restaurants, and computer, electronics, and toy stores.

Pentagon Row, 1101 South Joyce St.; (703) 413-6690; www.pentagonrow.com. Adjacent to the Fashion Centre, this row of shops features popular chain stores such as Ann Taylor Loft, DSW Shoe Warehouse, and others, as well as outdoor cafes, an ice rink (Nov through Mar) and a summer outdoor concert series.

For More Information

Arlington Convention and Visitors Service, (800) 677-6267; www.stayarlington.com.

Alexandria

Alexandria was a flourishing seaport long before rebelling from the Crown was even a whisper. It was the river and the promise of riches that lured the first settlers to Alexandria's shores in the early 17th century. The area grew with the aspirations of its residents. By 1749 the town became a city as 120 lots were auctioned off. George Washington, a young surveyor's assistant, helped pace off these parcels. The heart of this original sixty-acre tract still beats as Old Town, an enclave that wears its historic past with a gracious air.

To see beyond the bustle of northern Virginia back to colonial times, take a walking tour of Old Town Alexandria and use your imagination to see these streets as the early colonists did. When you stroll along King, Cameron, Queen, and Duke Streets, names that hark back to the town's colonial past, you'll discover amid the modern businesses and traffic the outlines of this thriving river town, which captured the imaginations of its first citizens.

Merchants and money made Alexandria grow. By the 18th century this city bustled as the third-largest seaport in the colonies. The prosperity created a thriving merchant class who talked business over port in front of fires in tastefully appointed drawing rooms. Remember that with young kids, one historic house goes a long way; it's the rare child who wants to see them all. Allow time to browse Alexandria's shops, stroll the waterfront, or take a scenic cruise.

Carlyle House (ages 8 and up)

121 North Fairfax St.; (703) 549-2997; www.nvrpa.org/parks/carlylehouse/index.php. **Open Tues through Sun. $.**

Reminiscent of country houses of Scottish gentry, this sandstone manor embodied the dreams of John Carlyle, a prosperous merchant. Completed in 1753, the two-story mansion, built on two choice lots, stands in contrast to the smaller brick town houses that are flush with the sidewalk. Furnished with donated period furniture, an unrenovated bedroom also shed some interesting light on 18th-century building techniques, as the old beams reveal the careful carpentry of the era. Be sure to pause amid the aster and fox-glove in the gardens. Although not faithful to Carlyle's plan, these flower and herb beds conform to 18th-century ideals of symmetry and usefulness.

There are family programs throughout the year (fee, registration), including Hands-On History, the Read-See-Do program, which involves a museum-related craft (monthly or by appointment) and period reenactments, including an 18th-century funeral. Call or check the Web site for schedules.

Market Square (ages 4 and up)

On the 300 block of King Street on Historic Market Square in front of City Hall; (703) 838-4343.

The front of Carlyle's house faces what is still among the oldest continuous markets in the country. If you're up early on a Sat, between 5 and 10 a.m., browse the stalls set up for fresh bread, pastries, and fruit. Kids like the happy commotion and cheap eats.

Torpedo Factory Art Center (ages 5 and up)

105 North Union St.; (703) 838-4565; www.torpedofactory.org. Open daily. Free.

The art center overlooks the waterfront. This space, once a factory for torpedo shells for our fighting men in World War II, now booms as the Torpedo Factory Art Center, where professional artists not only work at their craft but display their wares. You can wander through the studios, chat with the artists, and watch them at work. More than 160 artists work or present at the Torpedo Factory. Kids and adults enjoy browsing the brightly colored pottery, glass vessels, jewelry, and wearable art. Look for the World War II torpedoes on display. Throughout the year there are programs for families and for kids, including live music, art activities, and a summer art camp through an on-site school.

Amazing Virginia Facts

- **Robert E. Lee** spent part of his childhood in Alexandria.
- **Revolutionary War general** "Light Horse" Harry Lee lived in Alexandria.
- **George Washington** became the Masonic Lodge's Charter Master in 1788.
- **George and Martha Washington** danced at Gadsby's Tavern.

Market Square Pass and Tricorn Pass

For discounts to a number of the most popular museums in Alexandria, get a Market Square and Tricorn pass, available at the Alexandria Visitor Center at Ramsay House. The passes, at $12 each, include admission to Gadsby's Tavern, Carlyle House, and the Stabler–Apothecary Museum. The Tricorn pass covers Gadsby's Tavern, Carlyle House and the Lee–Fendall House.

Alexandria Archaeology Museum (ages 7 and up)

Number 327, 105 North Union St.; (703) 838-4399; http://oha.alexandriava.gov/archaeology. Open Tues through Sun; closed major holidays. **Free.**

Watch archaeologists research Alexandria's history in the museum's laboratory. There might be a volunteer piecing together an 18th-century pot or examining bones from a 17th-century family's meal; Fridays are the most likely days to see activity here. There are hands-on Discovery Kits for kids, and Family Dig Days (requires fee, registration), spring through fall.

Lee–Fendall House (ages 9 and up)

614 Oronoco St.; (703) 5481789; http://leefendallhouse.org. Open Wed through Sun. Occasionally closed on weekends for special events, so call ahead. $.

Find out about the Lee family as you peruse the memorabilia of thirty-seven Lees who resided here over a period of more than 118 years. The house, constructed in 1785 and renovated to an 1850 Greek-revival style, also features special events like tea tastings, Easter Egg hunts, and candlelight ghost tours.

The Lyceum, Alexandria's History Museum (ages 8 and up)

201 South Washington St.; (703) 838-4994; http://oha.alexandriava.gov/lyceum. Open daily; closed Thanksgiving, Christmas Eve, Christmas Day, and New Year's Day. $.

A Greek-revival structure built in 1839 and used as a hospital in the Civil War, the Lyceum houses 300 years of historical items, such as Civil War artifacts, photos, ceramics, furniture, and 19th-century stoneware. In the South Gallery, materials are provided for children to color pictures of colonial life and draw maps of Alexandria. The gift shop has a nice selection of children's books explaining colonial life and heroes.

The Alexandria Confederate Memorial is just outside the Lyceum at the intersection of Prince and South Washington Streets. A plaque on the corner in front of the Lyceum tells you the statue commemorates the one hundred Alexandrians who died during the Civil War.

Alexandria's African-American History (ages 6 and up)

Trace Alexandria's African-American history with *A Remarkable and Courageous Journey*, a twenty-page **free** booklet available at the Alexandria Visitor Center, 221 King St.; (800) 388-9119; www.VisitAlexandriaVa.com.

Learn about Benjamin Banneker, the mathematician who assisted with the survey for the new city of Washington; Moses Hepburn, the wealthiest African American in northern Virginia; and Dr. Albert Johnson, the only African-American physician practicing in Alexandria in the early 1900s.

Find out about the Bottoms, an 18th-century neighborhood where the town's first free slaves lived, and about Hayti, an area established in the early 1800s around the 400 block of South Royal Street, home to the only successful slave uprising in the western hemisphere. A map pinpoints these sites and others, including the Franklin & Armfield Slave Office & Pen, headquarters for Isaac Franklin and John Armfield, the owners of one of the largest slave-trading companies in the United States, as well as the 1834 Roberts Memorial United Methodist Church, one of the oldest African-American church buildings in Alexandria.

Another important resource is the **Alexandria Black History Museum,** 638 North Alfred St.; (703) 838-4356; http://oha.alexandriava.gov/bhrc. Open daily, Tues through Sat.

Gadsby's Tavern Museum (ages 10 and up)

134 North Royal St.; (703) 838-4242; http://oha.alexandriava.gov/gadsby. Open Wed through Sun Nov to May, daily Apr to Oct. Occasionally closed for special events, so call ahead. $.

In the 18th and 19th centuries, as now, nightlife sparkled. George and Martha Washington danced here in the second-floor ballroom. Frequent guests to this gentlemen's pub, which dates to 1785, included the Marquis de Lafayette, James Madison, and Thomas Jefferson. On the tavern museum tour, you can envision these notables sipping ale and swapping political stories. There's an open house on Tavern Day, held every summer, with storytelling and fencing matches.

Gadsby's Tavern is also a restaurant serving lunch and dinner. (See Where to Eat, below.)

Christ Church (all ages)

118 North Washington St.; (703) 549-1450. Open daily. Free.

For the warmth of salvation, the locals flocked to this still-active church designed by James Wren in 1767 and consecrated in 1773. It was originally called the Church in the Woods because of its setting on the outskirts of town. The notable parishioners who rode

Amazing
George Washington Facts

- **The tale of** George Washington chopping down the cherry tree is merely a legend created, perhaps, to portray his honesty.
- **The myth of** George Washington's wooden false teeth is not true; however, he did have false teeth made out of ivory, animal, and human teeth.

Bike **the Sites**

The **Mount Vernon Bicycle Trail** totals a hearty 19 miles, but it's only an 8-mile bike trip from Alexandria to Mount Vernon. Rent bikes at Bike and Roll (One Wales Alley, Alexandria, VA 22314; http://bikeandroll.com/washington dc) or opt for hiking and running on this paved path along the Potomac. Trail maps are available at Alexandria Visitor Center at Ramsay House (221 King St., Alexandria, VA 22314, (703) 746-3301.

to services here included George Washington, whose family pew is marked and maintained, and Robert E. Lee. Now docents lead tours three days a week and services are held every Sunday. Call for times.

Potomac Riverboat Company (all ages)

Alexandria City Marina; (703) 548-9000; www.potomacriverboatco.com. $$–$$$.

Another way of seeing Alexandria that is easier on your feet than walking is to take a forty-minute narrated cruise that reveals history, legends, and a view of Admiral's Row, where sea captains once lived. The company also offers a Pirate Cruise in the summer, with tales and songs of piracy on the Potomac, and a narrated boat tour of Washington landmarks, passing the Lincoln and Jefferson Memorials and the Washington Monument and turning around in Georgetown Harbor.

Alexandria Colonial Tours (ages 4 and up)

(703) 519-1749; www.alexcolonialtours.com. $–$$.

A costumed pirate leads young buccaneers ages 4 to 7 on a hunt through Alexandria's hideouts on Trail of the Pirate's Treasure, offered Sat mornings at 10 a.m., by reservation only, spring through fall. Purchase the Old Town Scavenger Hunt and follow the clues for a self-guided history trip. Packets lead you to information on either George Washington; Dr. James Craik, Washington's friend and physician; or William Ramsay, a wealthy tobacco merchant. Ghouls and spirits star in the Ghost & Graveyard Tour, open to ages 11 and older.

Where to Eat

Austin Grill, 801 King St.; (703) 684-8969; www.austingrill.com. Open daily for lunch and dinner. The Tex-Mex cuisine features enchiladas, tacos, and fajitas. $–$$

Bilbo Baggins, 208 Queen St., Old Town; (703) 683-0300; www.bilbobaggins.net. Open daily for lunch and dinner. A casual family restaurant set in a more-than-120-year-old town

house, it is known for its fresh-baked bread and desserts. Kid-size portions are available, and parents will like the thirty-two kinds of wine by the glass and ten microbrews on tap. $$–$$$

The Fish Market, 105 King St.; (703) 836-5676; www.fishmarketva.com. Open daily for lunch and dinner. Crab-cake sandwiches

Information **Central**

For a plethora of information on all things Alexandria, spend some time exploring the Web site, www.visitalexandriava.com. You'll find descriptions and Web links to attractions, lists of shops, and recommended restaurants plus practical tools like an interactive map and schedules for public transportation and the **free** trolley. A calendar of events helps plan your trip, and links allow you to make reservations at hotels and restaurants right online.

and seafood stew are two of the noteworthy dishes at this popular seafood restaurant. $$

Gadsby's Tavern, 138 North Royal St.; (703) 548-1288; www.gadsbystavernrestaurant.com. Open daily for lunch and dinner. Reservations suggested. This historic tavern operated in the colonial period, when it served George Washington and his friends as well as other founding fathers. Now it's been featured on the Food Channel for its evocation of the colonial era, with period furnishings, pewter dishes, and costumed servers. Period fare includes signature Sally Lunn bread and peanut soup, and a changing menu features George Washington's favorite duck, chicken roasted on an open fire, and high-quality beef, as well a children's menu. $$$

The Hard Times Cafe, 1404 King St.; (703) 837-0050; www.hardtimes.com. Open daily for lunch and dinner. This cafe offers both Texas- and Cincinnati-style chili and thirty-one brands of beer plus burgers, dogs, and chicken. $

King Street Blues, 112 North Saint Asaph St.; (703) 836-8800; www.kingstreetblues.com. Enjoy Southern comfort food from po'-boy sandwiches to low-country shrimp and award-winning barbecued ribs. Look for whimsical art and colorful papier-mâché characters. $-$$

Scoop Grill & Homemade Ice Cream, 110 King St.; (703) 549-4527. Open for

breakfast, lunch, and dinner. Frozen custard, homemade soups, and ice cream. $-$$

Torpedo Factory Food Pavilion, 5 Cameron St. The pavilion offers splendid views of the Potomac and some cheap eats. $

Union Street Public House, 121 South Union St.; (703) 548-1785; www.unionstreetpublichouse.com. Open daily for lunch and dinner. $-$$

Where to Stay

Embassy Suites—Old Town, 1900 Diagonal Rd.; (703) 684-5900 or (800) EMBASSY. This all-suite hotel includes the cost of breakfast in the room rate and is located across the street from the King Street Metro station. On weekends the complimentary Kids Corner at the reception desk offers refreshments. Refrigerators and microwaves in the rooms. $$-$$$$

Hampton Inn—King Street Metro, 1616 King St.; (703) 299-9900. New hotel conveniently located 2 blocks from the Metro station and a **free** trolley comes every 20 minutes for a ride through Old Town. Complimentary continental breakfast and Internet service. $$$-$$$$

Hawthorn Suites, 420 North Van Dorn St.; (703) 370-1000 or (800) 368-3339. Rooms have fully equipped kitchens, and a complimentary hot buffet breakfast is served. $-$$$$

Residence Inn by Marriott, 1456 Duke St.; (703) 548-5474 or (800) 331-3131. This hotel has an indoor pool, rooms with fully equipped kitchens, and a complimentary buffet breakfast and complimentary light dinner Mon through Thurs. $–$$$$

Annual Events

FEBRUARY

George Washington's Birthday Celebration. Alexandria claims to have the largest in the country. The celebration features a parade complete with George Washington himself, plus games, food, and music.

Revolutionary War Encampment and Skirmish, George Washington's Birthday weekend, 3401 West Braddock Rd. at Fort Ward Park; (703) 838-9350. Costumed interpreters reenact camp life and maneuvers.

JUNE

Alexandria Red Cross Waterfront Festival, second weekend in June, Oronoco Bay Park; (703) 549-8300. Admission. This festival focuses on the city's historic seaport. Check out the visiting ships, arts and crafts, music, and special children's events.

SEPTEMBER

Alexandria Festival of the Arts, on King Street in Old Town; (703) 746-3301. A weekend of paintings, sculptures, jewelry, glassware, and photography, plus music and food.

OCTOBER

Art on the Avenue shows off Alexandria's Del Ray neighborhood, known for its lively arts scene. Enjoy live music, kids activities, and street food along Mount Vernon Avenue, the first Sat of the month.

DECEMBER

Holiday Boat Parade of Lights. On the first Sat in Dec, leisure boats lit up for the holidays cruise along Alexandria's waterfront.

First Night Alexandria, Dec 31. Ring in the new year with singing, dancing, clowns, and other family-friendly activities. Event hotline (703) 883-4686.

For More Information

Alexandria Visitor Center at Ramsay House, 221 King St., Alexandria, VA 22314; (703) 746-3301 or (800) 388-9119; www .VisitAlexandriaVA.com. Open daily. Located in historic Ramsay House, the visitor center has brochures for museums, attractions, and walking tours as well as information about restaurants and shops. Out-of-town visitors can get a free parking proclamation (a worthwhile item) at the visitor center or online. Constructed in 1724 and rebuilt after a fire in 1942, the building was named for William Ramsay, a Scottish merchant and city founder.

Mount Vernon Region

Mount Vernon is best known for the attraction after which it's named: George Washington's estate.

George Washington's Mount Vernon Estate
and Gardens (ages 5 and up)
Located at the south end of George Washington Memorial Parkway, 8 miles south of Alexandria; (703) 780-2000; www.visit.mountvernon.org. Open daily year-round. The George Washington: Pioneer Farmer exhibit is open Apr through Oct. $$.

For anyone who hasn't taken the drive to Mount Vernon, the trip is well worth it. Mount Vernon, a lovingly restored riverfront property, was George and Martha Washington's estate, where the first president lived (although he spent a good deal of his time away from it).

Additional reasons to visit include the surrounding facilities: the Ford Orientation Center, the Donald W. Reynolds Museum and Education Center, and a remodeled slave cabin. Start your tour by watching the 18-minute film narrated by Pat Sajak—yes, the pick-a-vowel emcee—at the Ford Orientation Center. The film showcases Washington against the background of life at Mount Vernon and his exploits in the French and Indian War and the Revolutionary War.

The 23 galleries in the Donald W. Reynolds Museum and Education Center present George Washington the boy and man as opposed to the legend. Highlights include the three life-size wax figures of Washington—as a 19-year-old surveyor, a 45-year-old general, and a 57-year-old president. To create these figures, especially the faces, the museum employed a sculptor, a forensic anthropologist, a computer specialist, and a good deal of high-tech equipment. The result: some of the most accurate likenesses of Washington anywhere.

Along with the physical re-creations of our first president, the galleries present Washington the boy, military leader, farmer, and husband through eleven films and hundreds of artifacts. The museum also talks about Martha, his loving wife. In 1799 she wrote, "The day you died. I could not speak or cry. I did not go to the funeral. I locked our chamber door never to sleep again in the bed we shared."

At the Hands-On History room, in Reynolds Museum and Education Center, kids can try on colonial-era clothes, piece together pottery shards similar to those found on the estate by archaeologists, and assemble woodblocks and trussing rings to craft buckets as coopers did.

The tour of the historic house may not be the most exciting for kids, but the guides are good at mentioning details that bring Washington's character to life. Much of the furniture in the 7,000-square-foot mansion is authentic. The dining room, the most ornate room, lacks a main table and the chairs are placed against the wall. Constant hosts, the Washingtons never knew exactly how many guests to expect. Rather than set a formal table, trestle tables were set up to accommodate whomever arrived. After dinner these were dismantled so the room could be used for dancing, something Washington loved to do.

Allow time to explore Mount Vernon's grounds, especially the Pioneer Farmer site. From Apr to Oct the facility offers hands-on opportunities such as cracking corn, visiting the animals in the sixteen-sided "round" barn, making a fishnet, or hoeing the fields with "farmers" in period dress. The gardens on the grounds contain trees, flowers, and herbs selected and planted by Washington himself. Washington chose a nearby setting as the grounds for the family tomb.

In September 2007 Mount Vernon debuted a newly reconstructed slave cabin, a tiny 14-by-16-foot dwelling with a clay floor. It was the hard work of the slaves who served at Mount Vernon that created the splendid estate that Washington loved.

George and Martha Washington are buried at Mount Vernon and a nearby plaque marks the burial grounds of the plantation's slaves.

Picnicking is not allowed on the grounds, but tables and chairs are outside the gates. The property offers a food court and the expanded Mount Vernon Inn Restaurant (see Where to Eat, below).

George Washington's Gristmill and Whiskey Distillery

(ages 7 and up)

Located 3 miles west of Mount Vernon Estate, 5514 Mount Vernon Memorial Hwy.; (703) 780-2000; www.mountvernon.org. Open daily Apr through Oct. Combination tickets to Mount Vernon and George Washington's Gristmill may be purchased at Mount Vernon's main gate. $.

This reconstruction of a mill once owned (and designed) by George Washington is operated by interpreters dressed as 18th-century millers who use the water-powered wheel to grind grain into flour just as it was done more than 200 years ago. George Washington's whiskey distillery is open for visiting, too.

Woodlawn Plantation   (ages 8 and up)

Intersection of US 1 and Highway 235, 9000 Richmond Hwy.; (703) 780-4000; www.woodlawn1805.org. Open Thurs through Mon, Apr through Dec; closed Thanksgiving and Christmas. $.

Designed by the first architect of the U.S. Capitol, Dr. William Thornton, this Georgian-style brick home and its grounds were a gift from George Washington to his nephew Major Lawrence Lewis and adopted daughter, Eleanor Parke Custis ("Nelly"). Visitors can view the Washington and Lewis heirlooms and paintings from the federal period, and enjoy the colonial-revival garden, which features a large array of 19th-century rose species. There are programs throughout the year for families, such as Grandparents Day in the summer (when grandparents are admitted **free**) and a very popular Haunted History tour on Halloween weekend (fee, reservations required).

Combination tickets for Woodlawn and the Pope–Leighey House are available.

Frank Lloyd Wright's Pope–Leighey House (ages 8 and up)

At the Woodlawn Plantation; (703) 780-4000; www.popeleighey1940.org. Open Thurs through Mon, Apr through Dec, closed Thanksgiving, Christmas and New Year's Day. $.

Frank Lloyd Wright designed this home as a model of Usonian architecture—the principle that people of moderate means deserved beautiful, well-designed homes. Made of cypress, brick, and glass, the house is intended to blend in with its natural surroundings, reflecting many of Wright's important contributions to architecture. The furnishings were selected or designed by Wright. Your kids might be surprised how "modern" this house looks, despite the fact that it was built in 1940. After being saved from demolition, the house was moved to this site in 1964.

There are picnic grounds on-site, and admission is **free** every June 8—Frank Lloyd Wright's birthday.

Gunston Hall (all ages)

6 miles south of Mount Vernon. 10709 Gunston Rd. (Highway 242), Mason Neck; (703) 550-9220; http://gunstonhall.org. Open daily, closed Thanksgiving, Christmas, and New Year's Day. $.

George Mason, who drafted the Virginia Declaration of Rights and was a framer of the Constitution, lived at this 19th-century manor home originally set on 5,000 acres. Mason, in the end, refused to sign the Constitution because it did not abolish slavery. The film at the visitor center presents some background on Mason's life. The house is known for its intricately carved woodwork, particularly apparent in the Palladian Room. Children on the tour are given a Sleuth Score Card and asked to solve a mystery that takes them through all the rooms. The gardens, recreated with only plants found in colonial times, is noted for its tall boxwood and view of the river. Kids like the nature trail that leads past George Mason's original deer park and along the river. They'll also love special programs like the annual kite festival, plantation Christmas, and archaeology day. Check the Web site for dates.

Where to Eat

Food Court Pavilion, located on the Mount Vernon estate; (703) 799-5225. Open daily for breakfast, lunch, and snacks. If you don't have time—or the kids don't have the patience—for a sit-down lunch, stop by for hamburgers, hot dogs, salads, and sandwiches as well as fresh-baked muffins, cakes, and jumbo hot pretzels. $

Mount Vernon Inn Restaurant, 3500 Mount Vernon Memorial Hwy., located on the grounds of the estate; (703) 780-0011. Open for lunch daily, dinner Mon through Sat. Call ahead, sometimes closed for private parties.

This restaurant offers meals in a colonial setting, complete with fireplaces, hand-painted murals, and a costumed staff. Some of the entrees are salmon fillet, stuffed pork loin, and roast duck. The old standby, chicken fingers, is available for children as well as a children's menu and smaller portions of the entrees. $$–$$$

RT's Restaurant, 3804 Mount Vernon Ave., Alexandria; (703) 684-6010; www.rtsrestaurant.net. Open Mon through Sat for lunch and dinner; Sun for dinner only. Reservations recommended. The Cajun and Creole dishes draw raves from diners; particularly note-worthy are the crawfish, gumbo, and pecan-crusted chicken. $$$

Where to Stay

See accommodations listed for Alexandria page 94.

For More Information

Visit **Fairfax (Fairfax County Convention and Visitors Corporation),** 7927 Jones Branch Dr., Suite 100 West, McLean, VA 22101; (703) 790-0643. There are two Visitor Information Centers—one in Lorton, off I-95 and one inside Tysons Corner Center. For visitor information call (703) 550-2450 or (800) 7-FAIRFAX; www.fxva.com.

McLean

Although McLean is best known as a bedroom community for people who work in Washington, D.C., it has several attractions of its own. Most notable is Great Falls National Park. Shopaholics like the upscale shops of the Tysons Galleria and the variety of stores at Tysons Corner Center.

Patowmack Canal and Great Falls Park (all ages)

9200 Old Dominion Dr., McLean; (703) 285-2966; and 11710 MacArthur Blvd. (at the end of MacArthur Boulevard), Potomac; (301) 299-3613; www.nps.gov. Open daily year-round. The entrance fee admits a carful of people or an individual to either side for three consecutive days. C&O Canal tours begin during the first two weeks in Apr and end in early Nov. Tours run Wed through Sun. Certain conditions may necessitate canceling tours, so it's best to call or check the Web site first. $.

Commonly referred to as Great Falls Park, this is a definite must-do. This 800-acre park has 15 miles of hiking trails, ranging from easy to strenuous, 20-foot waterfalls, and 5 miles of trails for horseback riding and biking. For out-of-town visitors, it may seem confusing as to which side of the park to choose. Separated by the Potomac River, each side offers hiking trails, visitor centers, and snack pavilions, but only the Maryland side of Great Falls Park has the C&O Canal. Both the Virginia and the Maryland sides can be reached easily from the Beltway (I-495) and are just minutes from each other.

I must confess that my family prefers the Maryland side because of the canal towpath. Along this flat, slightly elevated trail removed from any vehicles, we taught our children to ride bicycles. (Bring your own bicycles.) We've spent many pleasant weekends bicycling on the Maryland side and also, sometimes, exploring the Virginia side.

Great Falls, Maryland, also offers canal boat rides from Apr through Oct. Mules pull these barges upstream and you can watch a barge going through one of the canal's locks. Claimed as a national monument in 1961, then named a National Historical Park in 1971, the C&O Canal remains a technological treasure. Its system of lift locks raises the canal's waters from near sea level in Georgetown, Washington, D.C., to 605 feet above sea level at Cumberland, Maryland, 184.5 miles upstream.

At Great Falls, Virginia, take the opportunity to hike the park's trails. The brand new visitor center, completed in 2009, includes interactive exhibits about the park's resources, touchable displays and videos as well as maps and brochures, and an informative eight-minute slide show. There is a snack pavilion, and grills are provided for cookouts. (Just remember to bring your own charcoal.) Ranger-guided walks and special programs (such as Swamp Tromp, Snakes and Bunnies, and Kids Crafts) are available weekends year-round. Call for the schedule or check out the Web site.

Claude Moore Colonial Farm at Turkey Run
(ages 2 to 7)

6310 Georgetown Pike; (703) 442-7557; www.1771.org. Open Apr through mid-Dec, Wed through Sun, except Thanksgiving and Independence Day. $.

This living-history museum re-creates tenant farm life in the 1770s. The one hundred acres of land are tilled, planted, and cultivated by hand by folks who dress and talk the way tenant farmers did over 200 years ago. Visitors are welcome to help with farm chores, such as carding wool, weeding gardens, or hoeing the fields, as well as helping the farmer's wife mix hoecake batter or prepare vegetables. Children will see the usual assortment of farm animals, including cows, pigs, chickens, geese and turkeys. There are festivals in the spring, summer, and fall.

Colvin Run Mill Historic Site (all ages)

5 miles west of Tysons Corner, 10017 Colvin Run Rd. (Highway 7) in Great Falls; (703) 759-2771; www.fairfaxcounty.gov/parks/crm. Open Wed through Mon year-round. Call ahead for a weekly operating schedule. $.

This site once served as a crossroads for farmers from the Shenandoah Valley and tradesmen from the busy port of Alexandria. A 19th-century gristmill and miller's house are on the site. The property also has an early-20th-century general store where you can still buy items ground at the mill, which operates from Apr through Oct (call for schedule). Special events include children's shopping and country Christmas in Dec, maple syrup boildown in late winter/early spring, and ice cream making in summer. Check the Web site for other activities.

Smithsonian Air & Space Museum
Steven F. Udvar–Hazy Center (ages 7 and up)

Located at Washington Dulles International Airport, south of the main terminal, near the intersection of Highway 28 and US 50; www.nasm.si.edu/museum/udvarhazy.

The Smithsonian Institution's National Air and Space Museum built this facility to restore and display its collection of aviation and space artifacts. The center includes exhibit hangars (with 163 aircraft and 154 large space artifacts), an observation tower to watch planes taking off and landing at Dulles, an IMAX theater, dining facility, and gift shops.

Where to Eat

Kazan Restaurant, 6813 Redmond Dr.; (703) 734-1960. Open Mon through Fri for lunch and dinner, Sat for dinner only; closed Sun. The Turkish cuisine includes lamb and chicken shish kebabs as well as shrimp and rice dishes. $$

Maggiano's Little Italy, Tysons Galleria, 1790-M International Dr. (Highway 123), Tysons Corner; (703) 356-9000. Open daily for lunch and dinner. Huge portions perfect for sharing and reasonable prices make this chain eatery popular with families. Children's menu. $$

Taste of Saigon, 8201 Greensboro Dr., Tysons Corner; (703) 790-0700. Open daily for lunch and dinner. Even the fussiest of kids will like the rice, and the rest of the family will enjoy a wide variety of tasty Vietnamese dishes at this popular restaurant. $$

Where to Stay

Hilton McLean Tysons Corner, 7920 Jones Branch Dr.; (703) 847-5000 or (800) HILTONS; www.mclean.hilton.com. Enjoy the indoor pool, fitness center, and a restaurant. $–$$$$

Crowne Plaza Tysons Corner, 1960 Chain Bridge Rd.; (703) 893-2100. This property has an indoor pool, and a **free** scheduled shuttle to the Metro. $–$$$$

The Ritz-Carlton, 1700 Tysons Blvd.; (703) 506-4300; www.ritzcarlton.com. This upscale hotel offers large rooms, concierge service on selected floors, an indoor lap pool, and a spa. Attached to Tysons Galleria Mall. $$$$

Where to Shop

McLean has two well-known malls.

Tysons Galleria, 2001 International Dr.; (703) 827-7700; www.tysonsgalleria.com. This mall has one hundred shops and restaurants, including Macy's, Neiman Marcus, and Saks Fifth Avenue.

Tysons Corner Center, 1961 Chain Bridge Rd.; (703) 893-9400 or (888) 2TYSONS; www.shoptysons.com. Nearby, Tysons Corner Center is a true "shop till you drop" place with more than 250 stores, including Nordstrom, Bloomingdale's, Lord & Taylor, Eddie Bauer, Williams–Sonoma, and The Disney Store. Pottery Barn has Kids Concerts weekends in the summer.

For More Information

Visit **Fairfax (Fairfax County Convention and Visitors Corporation),** 7927 Jones Branch Dr., Suite 100 West, McLean, VA 22101; (703) 790-0643. There are two Visitor Information Centers—one in Lorton, off I-95 and one inside Tysons Corner Center. For visitor information call (703) 550-2450 or (800) 7-FAIRFAX; www.fxva.com.

Vienna

From May through Sept Vienna's Wolf Trap Park National Park for the Performing Arts offers a wide variety of performances on a covered outdoor stage.

Wolf Trap National Park for the Performing Arts (all ages)

1624 Trap Rd.; (703) 255-1900 or (703) 255-1860 for ticket information; www.wolftrap.org. Open from late May through mid-Sept for performances; the park is open year-round. $–$$$.

An easy drive from both Alexandria and Washington, D.C., Wolf Trap is the only national park for the performing arts. Performances are held at the Filene Center, an outdoor covered pavilion. The National Park Service also offers backstage tours of the Filene Center from Oct through Apr. Kids love the concerts, which range from classical to jazz, rock, and pop. Lawn seats allow kids running room (but arrive early with your picnic supper). The informal park atmosphere adds to the fun. From July to Aug Wolf Trap features the Children's Theatre-in-the-Woods program, with performances and workshops that teach kids how to mime, act like a clown, and become a puppeteer. Each Sept Wolf Trap hosts the International Children's Festival with outstanding performing artists, including puppeteers, magicians, storytellers, and children's theater productions.

The Barns at Wolf Trap offer performances throughout the fall, winter, and spring months as well.

Meadowlark Botanical Gardens

9750 Meadowlark Gardens Ct.; (703) 255-3631; www.nvrpa.org/parks/meadowlark/. Open year-round; closed Thanksgiving, Christmas, New Year's Day, and when snow or ice covers the trails. $.

Ninety-five acres of woodlands, park, flowers, and three sparkling lakes make this place a nice respite from sightseeing. There are picnic areas, a snack bar, and a gift shop, plus educational programs (some for children) throughout the year. Check the Web site for the schedule.

Where to Eat

Amphora Restaurant, 377 East Maple Ave.; (703) 938-7877; www.amphoragroup.com. Open 24 hours a day. A local landmark, Amphora is the place to go for a snack or a meal, and breakfast is served at any hour. $

Anita's, 521 East Maple Ave.; (703) 255-1001. Open daily for breakfast, lunch, and dinner. This predictable but reliable Mexican food includes enchiladas, tacos, fajitas, and burritos. Traditional American breakfasts are served but so is Mexican-style chorizo con huevos (sausage with eggs). Children's menu available. $

The Olive Garden, 8133 Leesburg Pike; (703) 893-3175. Open daily for lunch and dinner. There's plenty of pasta, chicken, and lasagna at this Italian restaurant. Children's menu available. $–$$

Where to Stay

See accommodations for McLean, page 101.

For More Information

Visit **Fairfax (Fairfax County Convention and Visitors Corporation),** 7927 Jones Branch Dr., Suite 100 West, McLean, VA 22101; (703) 790-0643. There are two Visitor Information Centers—one in Lorton, off I-95 and one inside Tysons Corner Center. For visitor information call (703) 550-2450 or (800) 7-FAIRFAX; www.fxva.com.

Prince William County/Manassas

Manassas is rich in Civil War history and historical sites. In 2003 it was honored with the Great American Main Street Award by the National Trust for Historic Preservation. Its Old Town section has dozens of interesting museums, shops, and restaurants.

Manassas National Battlefield Park (ages 9 and up)

12521 Lee Hwy., Manassas; (703) 361-1339; www.nps.gov/mana. Open daily year-round sunrise to sunset; visitor center open 8:30 a.m. to 5 p.m. Closed Thanksgiving, Christmas, and New Year's Day. $.

The battlefield is Manassas's most famous attraction. This is the site of the first major land battle of the Civil War, as well as the second Battle of Manassas, better known as the Battle of Bull Run. Begin your battlefield tour at the visitor center, where a 45-minute video and battle map illustrate the strategy and tactics behind the campaigns. The First Battle of Manassas is a self-guided, 1-milelong walking tour along the site up to Henry Hill, the climactic point. Exhibits and audio recordings along the trail provide information. The Second Battle of Manassas route is 12 miles long, so it's best to tour this by car. At the twelve stops along the way, exhibits help you visualize the fighting. Obtain folders, maps, and audio cassettes from the visitor center.

Civil War Heritage Trail

Manassas Visitor Center, 1914 Train Depot, 9431 West St., Manassas.

Twenty-five Civil War Heritage Sites and Museums in Prince William County and Manassas. Brochures available at the Battlefield (see above) and the Manassas Visitor Center.

Manassas Museum (ages 4 to 7)

9101 Prince William St. in Old Town; (703) 368-1873; www.manassasmuseum.org. Open Tues through Sun and Mon that fall on federal holidays; closed Thanksgiving, Christmas, and New Year's Day. $.

This small museum details northern Virginia's history, emphasizing the Civil War. There are exhibits, photographs, artifacts, and videos. Artifacts include Civil War weapons and uniforms, Victorian clothing and quilts, furniture, and store signs from the 1800s. Children can ask for the scavenger-hunt sheet at the front desk. Geared to specific age groups, the sheets help kids focus on exhibits. A completed sheet earns them a bookmark. The museum's gift shop has a nice selection of children's books and period dolls.

Old Town **Manassas**

Old Town Manassas serenades visitors with **free** concerts on Sat evenings from June through Aug at 6:30 p.m. on the Manassas Museum Lawn.

In summer there are **free** concerts and movies on the lawn. Call (703) 368-1873 for concert schedule.

National Museum of the Marine Corps (ages 9 and up)

18900 Jefferson Davis Hwy., Triangle, VA (not far from Manassas and 36 miles south of Washington, D.C.); (877) 635-1775; www.usmcmuseum.org. Open daily year-round except Christmas.

Find out what boot camp is really like and why no recruit ever forgets his or her drill instructor at the National Museum of the Marine Corps. Also discover the Marines' sacrifices and contributions in the Vietnam and Korean Wars as well as World War II and other conflicts. When available, **free** guided tours for families and individuals depart from the Leatherneck Gallery at 10 a.m., noon, and 2 p.m. Reservations are not necessary.

SplashDown Water Park (all ages)

Take exit 47A off I-66 West to Highway 234 South and follow the signs to the park in Manassas; (703) 361-4451; www.splashdownwaterpark.com. Open Memorial Day through Labor Day. $$.

Cool off during Virginia's hot summers at this thirteen-acre facility where you can float down the lazy river on tubes, twist down slippery slides, and swim in a giant pool. Little ones have their own area, Sandcastle Kid's Club, with child-size slides, climbing equipment, and a kiddie pool.

Prince William Ice Center (all ages)

5180 Dale Blvd., Dale City; (703) 730-8423; www.pwice.com. Open daily year-round. Hours vary.

Year-round indoor National Hockey League arena and an Olympic-size arena, plus skate rentals, an arcade, and cafe.

Prince William Forest Park (all ages)

Take Highway 234 South to Route 619 East for about 7 miles and follow signs to the park; (703) 221-7181; www.nps.gov/prwi. Open daily; closed Thanksgiving, Christmas, and New Year's Day. Center located at 18100 Park Headquarters Rd., Triangle. Park entrance fee is good for admission for seven consecutive days. $.

Hike, bike, picnic, fish, and camp at this forest park with 37 miles of hiking trails and 21 miles of bike roads and trails. Obtain information at the visitor center. If you have a Virginia fishing license, you can try your luck catching bass, bluegills, pickerel, or crappies. The park also offers tent, RV, and backcountry camping year-round. During winter when weather permits, cross-country skiing and snowshoeing are allowed. (Bring your own equipment.)

Loy E. Harris Pavilion (all ages)

Corner of West and Center Streets in Old Town; (703) 361-9800; www.harrispavilion.com.

Located in the heart of Old Town, the pavilion offers ice-skating from mid-Nov through Mar (call for limited hours), as well as concerts, children's programs, and other events during the spring, summer, and fall.

Freedom Museum

10400 Terminal Rd.; http://freedommuseum.org. Open daily except Thanksgiving, Christmas, and New Year's Day.

At this museum, affiliated with the Smithsonian Institution, kids may very well have an opportunity to interact with one of the World War II veterans who staff the collection of memorabilia, photography, artifacts, and interactive displays on U.S. wars in the 20th century. Being located at Manassas Regional Airport affords it the space to have an impressive outdoor display of military vehicles, plus air shows.

Potomac Mills

Exit 156 off I-95, 2700 Potomac Mills Circle in Prince William; (703) 643-1885 or (800) VA-MILLS; www.potomac-mills.com. Open daily year-round.

Potomac Mills is a large off-price mall that advertises shopping discounts of 20 to 70 percent. Some locals swear by the bargains on furnishings and back-to-school clothes. With more than 200 stores, anchors include Neiman Marcus Last Call, Saks Fifth Avenue Outlet OFF 5TH, Nordstrom Rack, COSTCO, and Modell's Sporting Goods; specialty stores include Polo Ralph Lauren Factory Store, Brooks Brothers Factory Store, and Banana Republic Factory Store. There are also some twenty-five places to eat and eighteen movie screens if you're ready for a break from shop-til-you-drop.

Where to Eat

City Square Cafe, 9428 Battle St.; (703) 369-6022. Open Mon through Sat for "international bistro" lunch and dinner, breakfast on Sat, brunch on Sun. $$

Deli Depot, 8961 Center St.; (703) 368-0714, www.thedelidepot.com/deli. New York-style deli open Mon through Sat for lunch. $

Thai Secret Restaurant, 9114 Center St.; (703) 361-2500. Open Tues through Sat for lunch and dinner, Sun dinner only. If your kids don't like the traditional spicy Thai cuisine, ask for a rice and vegetable dish. $–$$

Where to Stay

Family accommodations in Manassas include these three moderately priced hotel/motels:

Best Western Manassas, 8640 Mathis Ave.; (703) 368-7070. Refrigerators and microwaves in all the rooms. $–$$

Days Inn, 10653 Balls Ford Rd.; (703) 368-2800 or (800) 329-7466. Outdoor pool, continental breakfast, and microwaves and refrigerators in all the rooms. $$–$$$

Four Points by Sheraton, 10800 Vandor Lane; (703) 335-0000 or (800) 465-4329. Indoor and outdoor pools. Microwaves and refrigerators in all rooms. $$–$$$$

Annual Events

MAY–NOVEMBER

Four Farmers' Markets in the area offer fresh produce and the bustle of farmers hawking their harvest in the open air. Manassas Farmers' Market, at West and Center

Streets in Old Town, (703) 361-6599, www
.harrispavilion.com; Downtown Haymarket,
(804) 493-1070 www.townofhaymarket.org;

Occoquan, (571) 334-7357, www.occoquan
merchantsassociation.com; and Nokesville,
(703) 794-7057.

JUNE

Annual Manassas Heritage Railway Festival, at the Historic Train Depot; (703)
361-6599. A day filled with memorabilia,
full-size and model exhibits, living-history
programs, storytelling, food, and live
entertainment.

AUGUST

Civil War Weekend at the Henry Hill Visitor Center in late Aug, outside the Manassas
Museum. Costumed interpreters talk of war-
fare and period weapons.

OCTOBER

Fall Jubilee, early Oct. This annual festival in
historic Old Town Manassas features music,
children's entertainment, food, rides, and
juried crafts. For additional information about
these and other events, call Historic Manassas, Inc., at (703) 361-6599.

For More Information

Prince William County Visitor Center,
200 Mill St., Occoquan, VA 22125; (703)
491-4045; www.visitpwc.com or Prince William County/Manassas Convention & Visitors
Bureau at (703) 396-7130 or (800) 432-1792.

Manassas Visitor Center, a historic 1914
train depot, 9431 West St., Manassas; (703)
361-6599; www.visitmanassas.org. Brochures
are available for self-guided tours of Old
Town Manassas.

Culpeper

If you're traveling from Manassas to Fredericksburg, Culpeper makes for a nice stop. It's
about 38 miles south of Manassas on US 29 and features Civil War history sites, an eques-
trian center, and an outdoors outfitter.

Civil War Battlefields

(540) 825-8628; www.visitculpeperva.com.

At Culpeper Chamber of Commerce & Visitor Center, 109 South Commerce St., pick up a
driving brochure to Culpeper County's three major Civil War battlefield sites: Brandy Station, Cedar Mountain, and Kelly's Ford.

Civil War Walking Tours

Call (540) 825-9147 or e-mail morton@edgehillbooks.com. $.

Virginia Morton, author of the book *Marching through Culpeper,* offers two-hour Civil War
Walking Tours of Historic Downtown Culpeper. You learn about "Extra Billy" Smith, two-
time governor of Virginia, the oldest general in either army, General J. E. B. Stuart, and
other characters. Tours are by appointment only. Profits are donated to the Friends of
Cedar Mt. Battlefield.

The Graffiti House

19484 Brandy Rd., Brandy Station; (540) 727-7718; open 11 a.m. to 4 p.m. Wed and Sat, Nov through Mar; Wed, Fri, Sat, and Sun, Apr through Oct; www.brandystationfoundation .com. $.

Located adjacent to the Brandy Station Battlefield, the Graffiti House gets its name because on the walls of the second floor are more than 200 inscriptions, drawings, messages, and signatures of Civil War soldiers. The building, believed to have been built in 1858, was likely used as a hospital by both Union and Confederate forces.

HITS, Inc. Commonwealth Park (all ages)

13246 Commonwealth Parkway; (540) 825-7469; www.hitsshows.com. Open Wed through Sun, Mar through Nov. Admission charge on Sun only.

HITS stands for "Horse Shows in the Sun." If you're in the area when shows are held, this is definitely worth a visit, especially if you have children who ride or are "in love" with horses. The riding, hunting, and jumping events in three different rings enthrall kids. Call ahead and check the schedule.

Mountain Run Lake Park (all ages)

Route 29 South to right on Mountain Run Lake Rd. (Route 718), go exactly 2.3 miles, on left will be J. B. Carpenter Jr. Dr. and the entrance to the lake and park; (540) 829-8260; www .culpeper.to/departments/planning/parks_recreation.htm.

Adjacent to Mountain Run Lake, this park, set in the rolling countryside of western Culpeper County, offers stunning views of the Blue Ridge Mountains but is just fifteen minutes from downtown Culpeper. This is a good place for a picnic and romp with the kids. Mountain Run Lake is a popular fishing lake. For fishing information, check out www.visit culpeperva.com/fishing.cfm.

Rappahannock River Campground (ages 6 and up)

33017 River Mill Rd., Richardsville; (800) 784-PADL or (540) 399-1839; www.canoecamp .com. Open Apr through Oct. Reservations required. $ ($9 to$11 per person, $30 to $35 per family).

Rappahannock River Campground can set you up for a self-guided canoe, kayak, or tubing trip down class two rapids of the Rappahannock River. All participants must know how to swim. Children must be at least 6 years old. You can picnic in the shade of the pine trees, fish the river or stocked pond, or camp overnight (forty-five rustic campsites), with a camp store and hot showers available.

Where to Eat

Baby Jim's Snack Bar, 701 North Main St.; (540) 825-9212. An old-fashioned outside snack bar, specializing in hamburgers, hot dogs, and milkshakes. $

CJ's Soft Serve Ice Cream, 237 Southgate Shopping Center, adjacent to Luigi's; (540) 825-1166. Ice-cream treats. $

Dee Dee's Family Restaurant, 502 North Main St.; (540) 825-4700. Open daily for breakfast, lunch, and dinner. Known for its down-home cookin', this eatery features hickory-smoked pork ribs, barbecued beef sandwiches, burgers, and seafood platters. Locals like the crab-stuffed mushrooms. Children's menu available. $–$$

Frost Cafe, 101 East Davis St.; (540) 825-9212. 1950s-style decor complete with booth jukeboxes. $

It's About Thyme, 128 East Davis St.; (540) 825-4264, www.thymeinfo.com. Open Tues through Sat for lunch and dinner. The continental cuisine features staples such as fettuccini Alfredo and Italian pot roast. $$

Luigi's Italian Restaurant, 235 Southgate Shopping Center; (540) 829-4688. Good pasta, seafood, and meat dishes plus pizza and subs. A children's menu is available. $–$$

Pancho Villa Mexican Restaurant, 910 South Main St.; (540) 825-5268; http://panchovillava.com. Open daily for lunch and dinner. If you're hungry for something spicy, try the Enchilada Supreme. Children's menu available. $–$$

Tea, Lace & Roses, 123 West Davis St.; (540) 829-9700; www.teaandroses.com. A Victorian teahouse and gift shop. Open Tues and Sat 11 a.m. to 4:30 p.m. Groups of eight or more can make special reservations. $–$$

Where to Stay

Comfort Inn of Culpeper, 890 Willis Lane, US 29; (540) 825-4900 or (800) 4-CHOICE. This property has an outdoor pool and provides a complimentary continental breakfast. Refrigerators and microwaves in rooms. $–$$

Best Western Culpeper, 791 Madison Rd.; (540) 825-1253 or (800) 572-3167. This is a moderately priced lodging with an outdoor pool. Refrigerators and microwaves in all rooms. $–$$$

For More Information

Culpeper County Chamber of Commerce & Visitor Center, 109 South Commerce St., Culpeper, VA 22701; (540) 825-8628 or (888) 285-7373; www.culpeper vachamber.com. Located in a historic train depot, the visitor center provides brochures and maps.

Fredericksburg

If George Washington could visit his birthplace in Fredericksburg, he would probably recognize some of it because the building facades are restored to their 18th- and 19th-century appearance. Fredericksburg, situated halfway between the two Civil War capitals of Richmond and Washington, D.C., also served as a critical Civil War locale. The city features historic homes and four Civil War battlefields. The battles took place from 1862 to 1864 within a 17-mile radius of Fredericksburg and are now encompassed in the Fredericksburg and Spotsylvania County Battlefields Memorial National Military Park (more commonly known as Fredericksburg/Spotsylvania National Military Park). Your best bet is to pick and choose carefully to hold your kids' interest. Don't attempt to see all the battlefields and historic homes. Remember, overkill will bore your kids, but a well-chosen tour or two will be welcome.

Fredericksburg/Spotsylvania National Military Park
(ages 7 and up)

Open daily; visitor centers open year-round except Thanksgiving, Christmas, and New Years Day. Call one of the visitor centers in Fredericksburg for specific directions or more information on one or all of the four battlefields: Chancellorsville Battlefield Visitors Center, Highway 3 West, (540) 786-2880; and Fredericksburg Battlefield Visitors Center, 1013 Lafayette Blvd., (540) 373-6122; www.nps.gov/frsp.

The national military park stretches more than 8,300 acres, includes four different battlefields, and is run by the National Park Service. The entire drive is about 75 miles, including driving between and within the parks. In the parks you can see the Old Salem Church, the Spotsylvania Court House, and the Marye's Heights National Cemetery along with trenches, historic buildings, interpretative trails, exhibit shelters, maps, monuments, and, of course, the landscape where these important battles were fought. The tours take about three hours for each battlefield, so plan a couple of days if you want the full tour. Be selective. For an audiotape driving tour or other information, stop in one of the two visitor centers that cover all four battlefields in the park.

The battlefields include Fredericksburg, Chancellorsville, Wilderness, and Spotsylvania Court House.

Fredericksburg Battlefield, December 11–15, 1862. The Battle of Fredericksburg took place on Sunken Road and the Stone Wall at Marye's Heights. Look for the Marye's Heights National Cemetery and the Lee Hill Exhibit Shelter, which are located in this battlefield. Chatham Manor has a 12-minute film and exhibits, as well as knowledgeable volunteers. Also stop by the Old Salem Church on your way to the Chancellorsville Battlefield.

Chancellorsville Battlefield, April 27–May 6, 1863. This was the site of a strategic military maneuver by Robert E. Lee and General Stonewall Jackson. But that same day ended sadly when Jackson was fatally wounded by his own troops. Visit the artillery positions at Hazel Grove and Fairview, the remains of the Chancellor House, and the Unfinished Railroad in this battlefield.

Wilderness Battlefield, May 5–6, 1864. This battlefield saw the military confrontation of generals Ulysses S. Grant and Robert E. Lee. You might want to pause at the Wilderness Exhibit Shelter and Ellwood, a historical home open on summer weekends. Stonewall Jackson's arm, amputated after a battle wound, is buried at this battlefield.

Spotsylvania Court House Battlefield, May 8–21, 1864. Troops fought for two weeks here in some of the most intense hand-to-hand fighting of the war, in a place called the

Trolley **Tours**

It's always a good idea to get the lay of the land before setting out on a day of touring, and trolleys are a fun way to do it. Daily seventy-five-minute tours leave from Charlotte Street, next to the Fredericksburg Visitor Center. Call (540) 373-1776 or (800) 678-4748 for the schedule.

The Timeless **Ticket**

The Timeless Ticket provides a 40 percent discount on admission to many of Fredericksburg's main attractions, including the battlefields. The ticket is valid until all participating sites have been visited and allows **free** admission for one student (ages 6 to 18) visiting with an adult. Available at the Fredericksburg Visitor Center, 706 Caroline St.; (540) 373-1776 or (800) 678-4748.

"Bloody Angle." On view are the Spotsylvania Court House, the Spotsylvania Confederate Cemetery, and one of three house sites.

The park is currently undergoing a face-lift, with more than one hundred new wayside exhibits being installed. A new film on the life of civilians shows at the Chancellorsville Visitor Center.

Fredericksburg has several historic sites associated with famous people. For many children, especially younger ones, the often static displays and roped-off rooms may be of little interest. Choose carefully.

Belvedere Plantation

1601 Belvedere Dr.; (540) 373-4478 (market) and (540) 371-8494 or (800) 641-1212 (plantation); www.belvedereplantation.com. Open daily in Oct and Nov. $.

This 1,000-acre, 245-year-old farm is the setting for family adventures that include the Great Adventure Maize Maze and pumpkin picking. The Fun Barn includes pedal tractors for the little ones, talking pipes, and a straw jump pile. There's a barnyard with pygmy goats, chickens, ducks, and calves, plus a market with farm produce, crafts, and fresh-baked pies on weekends.

Fredericksburg Area Museum

Old Town Hall and Market House, 907 Princess Anne St.; (540) 371-3037; www.famcc.org. Open Thurs through Sun afternoons, store open daily, except Thanksgiving, Christmas Eve and Day, and New Year's Eve and Day. $.

Three floors of exhibits range from dinosaur prints to Native American history, plus Civil War pistols and swords and late-19th-century wooden toys. **Free** children's programs include puppet shows and living-history demonstrations.

Kenmore (ages 10 and up)

1201 Washington Ave.; (540) 373-3381; www.kenmore.org/kp_home.html. Open daily Mar through Dec, except Thanksgiving, Christmas Eve and Day, and New Years Eve. Open Sat and Sun in Jan and Feb. $.

The plantation home of Betty Washington, George's sister, is worth a visit for its 18th-century furnishings and its tours designed for children. On the History Hunt (kindergarten to grade 2), kids hear stories about George Washington's boyhood. Steps into the Past (grades 3 to 5) takes kids into the daily lives of the people who lived on the Kenmore plantation. With Learning to Read (grades 6 to 12), kids explore ways to use documents to study the past. Call or check the Web site for schedules. Kenmore is undergoing a major renovation, and its tours have been designed to work around the construction. Tours include information on how buildings were constructed 200-plus years ago. Kids will be intrigued by mysteries like whose fingerprints are fired in the bricks and what the butler saw in the servants' passage.

James Monroe Museum and Memorial Library (ages 10 and up)

908 Charles St.; (540) 654-1043; www.umw.edu/jamesmonroemuseum. Open daily; closed Thanksgiving, Christmas Eve and Day, and New Year's Eve and Day. $.

This museum, operated by the University of Mary Washington, contains hundreds of artifacts from Monroe's law practice, including the desk where he signed the Monroe Doctrine, his collection of Louis XVI furniture, and his wife's gems and gowns. There's an activity center with reproductions of period items for children to touch, including hats and glasses to try on.

Rising Sun Tavern (ages 10 and up)

1304 Caroline St.; (540) 371-1494. Open daily; closed Thanksgiving, Christmas Eve and Day, and New Year's Eve and Day. Reduced hours in winter. $.

Eighteenth-century life is re-created in the restored taproom with its costumes and artifacts. This house, once owned by George Washington's youngest brother, was later turned into a tavern. Guided tour helps visitors imagine staying at a tavern in the 1700s.

Mary Washington House (ages 10 and up)

1200 Charles St.; (540) 373-1569. Open daily; closed Thanksgiving, Christmas Eve and Day, and New Year's Eve and Day. $.

This was the home of Mary Washington, the mother of George Washington. It offers visitors a chance to see period decorations and a garden with a sundial.

A Children's Walking Tour of
Historic Fredericksburg

This self-guided tour, which was created by a class of fourth-graders, begins at the Fredericksburg Visitor Center and takes families past twenty-six points of interest, including Kenmore, the Hugh Mercer Apothecary Shop, and Rising Sun Tavern. Ask at the visitor center (706 Caroline St.) or call (540) 373-1776 or (800) 678-4748 for more information.

Hugh Mercer Apothecary Shop (ages 7 and up)

1020 Caroline St.; (540) 373-3362. Open daily Mar through Dec; closed Thanksgiving, Christmas Eve and Day, and New Year's Eve and Day.

This may interest the kids: Here they can learn about leeches, lancets, snakeroot, crab claws, and other 18th- and 19th-century treatments and surgeries. You can also see silver-plated pills, a rosewater "still," and hand-blown glass apothecary jars.

Lake Anna State Park (all ages)

Off Highway 208 in Spotsylvania; (540) 854-5503; www.dcr.virginia.gov/state_parks/lak .shtml. Open daily year-round. Parking fee.

For a break from history, head to where 13 miles of trails, a boat ramp (boat rentals available), and a lifeguard-patrolled beach offer diversions. This area was the site of the Goodwin Gold Mine in the early 1800s, and visitors can still pan for gold in the river. A tour of the gold mine is offered on summer weekends between Memorial Day and Labor Day. There are also pontoon boat tours, astronomy programs, and interpretive programs at the visitor center in summer, plus a fishing pond for children and those with physical challenges.

George Washington's Ferry Farm (ages 10 and up)

268 Kings Hwy., Highway 3 at Ferry Road; (540) 373-3381; www.kenmore.org. Open daily year-round except Thanksgiving, Christmas, and New Year's Day. $.

George Washington resided here from ages 6 to 20, the period of his formal education and the years in which he taught himself the art of surveying. Only the icehouse and surveyor's shack still stand from Washington's childhood. Visitors may see white-tailed deer, red fox, opossum, raccoons, rabbits, beaver, box turtles, salamanders, hog-nose snakes (nonvenomous), herons near the river, and wild turkeys. Kids are given handouts of pages to color and a scavenger hunt. Every Sat during the winter months, there's a special family program on varying themes related to Washington's life and times. From May to Oct, the program "I Dig George" introduces children to the techniques of archaeology.

Where to Eat

Basil's Italian Market and Pizzeria, 909 Caroline St.; (540) 899-5414. Open daily for lunch and dinner. Salads, subs, and pizza. $$

Brock's Riverside Grill, 503 Sophia St.; (540) 370-1820. Open daily for lunch and dinner. Chicken, seafood, beef, and pasta dishes,

with a great view of the Rappahannock River. $$–$$$

Virginia Deli, 101 William St., (540) 371-2233. Open daily for lunch, with a menu of sandwiches. $

Where to Stay

Quality Inn, 543 Warrenton Rd.; (540) 373-0000 or (800) 4CHOICE. A traditional motel/hotel property. Microwaves and refrigerators in most rooms. $

Comfort Inn Southpoint, 5422 Jefferson Davis Hwy.; (540) 898-5550. Indoor pool, sauna, and exercise room, plus a deluxe continental breakfast. $

Days Inn North, 14 Simpson Rd.; (540) 373-5340 or (800) DAYSINN. This lodging has an outdoor pool and includes a continental breakfast in the room rates. $

The Kenmore Inn, 1200 Princess Anne St.; (540) 371-7622 or (800) 437-7622; www.kenmoreinn.com. Four of the nine guest rooms at this colonial-style inn feature working fireplaces. Dinner is served in either a casual or formal dining room. Children are welcome. Look on the Web site for live music and other events. $$-$$$

For More Information

Fredericksburg Visitor Center, 706 Caroline St., Fredericksburg; (540) 373-1776 or (800) 678-4748; www.visitfred.com. The visitor center offers several walking tours. One leads through historic neighborhoods, one tours African-American sites, and another "relives" the events of December 1862.

Spotsylvania County Visitor Center, 4704 Southpoint Parkway, Fredericksburg; (540) 891-8687 or (877) 515-6197. Offers maps, brochures, discount touring tickets, and a ten-minute orientation film on the area's history and attractions.

The Eastern Shore

D riving through the small towns of Virginia's Eastern Shore takes you back centuries. Accomac, for example, has buildings that date to 1632. On Tangier Island, accessible only by boat, the residents can trace their ancestry back to Elizabethan times. Virginia's 70-mile portion of the Delmarva Peninsula (named for Delaware, Maryland, and Virginia) is dotted with small towns that received their names from Native American words such as Chincoteague, Wachapreague, and Onancock.

As much as possible, my family tries to get off US 13, a modern byway dotted with gas stations and strip malls. We prefer Seaside Road, sometimes called Route 600. This curvy country lane and its branches take us past roadside stands bursting with sweet corn and tomatoes and pickup trucks whose beds are piled high with wobbly green pyramids of watermelons. In the morning seagulls flutter like angels above fields of soybeans, sorghum, and sweet potatoes. At dusk the setting sun falls gently on the frame farmhouses, turning the surrounding fields of cut corn stalks to spun gold.

In season at the dock in Oyster, a town just a few blocks long, you're likely to see fishermen unloading their crab pots. In Wachapreague fancy boats are moored at the Island House Marina, where the shore's gentry lunch on succulent crabcakes. On Assateague Island the breezes may bring you the sounds of snow geese honking and the neighs of wild ponies. A walk here takes you along sunlit beaches and past wetlands where thousands of ducks roost and deer and otters dot the marsh.

TopPicks in the Eastern Shore

1. **Chincoteague and Assateague Islands**

2. **Ferry to Tangier Island**

3. **Kiptopeke State Park**

4. **Chesapeake Bay Bridge–Tunnel**

THE EASTERN SHORE

Assateague
Island

Chincoteague

Onancock

Wachapreague

Cape Charles

Go slowly to explore Virginia's Eastern Shore. Drive the backroads or bicycle from place to place so that you may sample the charms of these shore towns.

Chincoteague and Assateague Island

Chincoteague is 83 miles north of Virginia Beach.

Although Misty, the pint-size pony from Marguerite Henry's book *Misty of Chincoteague*, may have made this area famous, there's a lot more than horses here. Chincoteague is for people. This town has shops, restaurants, camping areas, and hotels and also provides the only Virginia access to Assateague Island, home to Assateague Island National Seashore and Chincoteague National Wildlife Refuge. This barrier island has 37 miles of wild beach, and the only inhabitants include 320 different species of birds, the endangered Delmarva fox squirrel, white-tailed deer, sika elk, and wild ponies. Grazing or galloping across a field, the ponies impart a sense of power and freedom to this landscape. Cars are allowed only in limited areas, so your best bet for enjoying the wildlife and undeveloped beaches is to hike or bike.

Both Chincoteague and Assateague also have museums where you can learn about the island's wildlife and the environment. Each year thousands of people visit the island to watch the famous pony penning held the last Wed and Thurs in July. The wild ponies are herded into the channel to swim to Chincoteague, where they are auctioned off to benefit the volunteer fire department.

Chincoteague National Wildlife Refuge and Assateague Island National Seashore (all ages)

Except for small parcels of land, the entire Virginia portion of Assateague Island comprises Chincoteague National Wildlife Refuge. When the entire island was designated Assateague Island National Seashore, the Virginia portion of the island remained Chincoteague National Wildlife Refuge. The National Park Service, Assateague Island National Seashore, helps to administer public uses on an assigned area of the beach that includes land from parking lot #1 south. $.

The refuge ends at the Virginia–Maryland border. The Virginia side and the Maryland side each contain about 9,000 acres. The Maryland side offers more beach and primitive camping facilities, while the Virginia side has more winter waterfowl, denser pine forests, and a Victorian lighthouse.

Summer is certainly the prime time for families to visit here. The water's right for swimming and the shore can be crowded. The farther you walk away from the main beach access areas, though, the thinner the crowds. Take time in summer to drive or bicycle through the cool loblolly pine forests populated by white-tailed deer and sika elk. With luck you'll encounter some of the island's famous wild ponies. Do not get too close and do not pet these animals; they are wild and may bite or kick. In summer, spring, and fall, rangers lead guided walks (check at the visitor centers for details).

Besides swimming, try such shore staples as surf fishing, clamming, and crabbing. The best place for surf fishing is at the southernmost tip of the island, just beyond the public beach. Crabbing is permitted along the banks of Swans Cove, and clams can be found in the saltwater marshes of Tom's Cove. Generally you don't need a permit for these activities, but you should obtain information at one of the visitor centers.

Fall and winter are special times to visit, too. There are 18,000 acres of natural landscape—no motels, condominiums, or fast-food restaurants to mar your communing with nature—and few crowds except during the peak of the fall migration. The island is located on the eastern flyway, so the sky is filled with thousands of migrating waterfowl in fall. Here the crisp, clear air vibrates with strange sounds, such as the high-pitched honk of snow geese and the throaty duck calls that carry from marsh to marsh. At this time of year there's enough space to walk hand-in-hand with your children along the shore, admiring how an arc of sunlight is caught in a wave.

In winter you can walk the miles of wild beaches bordered by dunes, bike through the acres of marshlands, and observe scores of black ducks, snowy egrets, and great blue herons. This is a special winter refuge, not just for the migratory waterfowl, but for beach lovers, bird-watchers, animal enthusiasts, and especially burned-out city dwellers. Both sides of the island offer unusually striking scenery: windblown dunes, gnarled pines, and storybook ponies. It's a world of subtle earth hues, from the wheat-colored reed grass caught in frozen freshwater ponds to the soft browns of tree bark and shrub thickets.

To learn more about the refuge, visit the Herbert H. Bateman Educational and Administrative Center, a state-of-the-art, green building with an array of interactive, educational exhibits in a sustainable-design facility. Here, children ages 8 to 13 can pick up the *Junior Refuge Manager* or *Junior Birder* booklets for educational activities and earn a handsome patch for completing them. The Toms Cove Visitor Center, nearer the beach, is also well worth a stop. "You can pet slimy things!" exclaimed one recent visitor, handing over a snail from the touch tank.

Amazing Chincoteague Facts

- **Chincoteague Ponies.** No one knows how the ponies arrived. Legends abound, including speculation that the first ponies swam ashore from wrecked Spanish galleons or were driven to the barrier island in the 1680s by colonists avoiding livestock taxes and the cost of fencing.

- Six inches shorter than saddle horses, the brown, white, or dappled Chincoteague ponies are stockier than other breeds.

Some Interesting **Pony Facts**

- Just like us, if one pony in a group yawns, the others follow suit.
- The ponies may look fat to us; that's because the seaweed they eat is salty and they need to drink twice as much freshwater as domestic horses.
- There's a pony hierarchy. The higher-ranking ponies get first access to water and seaweed.
- Some mares are continually pregnant, since gestation lasts for almost one full year.
- Ponies may look tame, but they are wild. Do not pet or feed the ponies.

Hikes

The Virginia end of Assateague features more than 15 miles of winding trails through marshes and forests. Hikers can also explore the 10 miles of wild undeveloped beaches along the Atlantic. These are some suggested hikes:

Woodland Trail: A good path, especially for biking, is the beautiful 1.6-mile trip through a shaded loblolly pine forest. If your kids keep quiet, they might spot white-tailed deer, sika elk, and Delmarva fox squirrels. If you're here in the spring or fall, listen for songbirds along the way. This trail also leads to an overlook where, with luck, you'll catch sight of the wild ponies, and in fall and winter see waterfowl. Another good pony-spotting point is in Black Duck Marsh along Beach Road.

Wildlife Loop: Open to bikers and hikers daily during refuge hours, open to vehicles 3 p.m. to dusk. After 3 p.m. you can drive the loop, but to get the best view of the shorebirds and the waterfowl, walk or ride the 3.2-mile trail.

Toms Cove Beach: Be sure to pause here. If you want to bicycle here, take the Swans Cove Trail from the Wildlife Loop. The 1.25-mile Swans Cove Trail ends at beach parking lot #1.

Swimming Beaches: From Memorial Day to Labor Day, lifeguards patrol a section of the beach, which is designated by flags. Swim here especially if you have young children. Certain areas of Tom's Cove on the bayside are open for swimming, too. Please obey posted signs that indicate beach closings because of nesting birds.

Assateague Lighthouse: An easy walk is the quarter-mile loop to this historic lighthouse and back. Originally built in 1833, the current lighthouse was constructed in 1866–67. It is one of many lights operated by the U.S. Coast Guard to warn ships as they approach the barrier islands of the East Coast. Open Fri through Sun, 9 a.m. to 3 p.m., Easter weekend through Thanksgiving weekend. $

Kayaking

Gliding along the surface of saltwater marshes between Chincoteague and Assateague islands, weaving among acres of marsh and mussel beds, is a great way to get close to the wildlife teeming along Virginia's Eastern Shore. One kayak outfitter and a rental service in Chincoteague and two outfitters based nearby offer you the opportunity to sneak up on great blue herons, nesting bald eagles, the snakey-necked cormorant, and maybe even a pod of dolphins. No experience is necessary; each outfit reviews technique and tailors trips to its guests, who can choose single or tandem boats.

Assateague Explorer (757-336-5956 or 800-PONY SWIM, www .assateagueisland.com/kayaktours.htm) offers three- to six-hour tours daily, plus sunset tours when requested. Owner "Captain" Mark Colbourne comes from a long line of islanders—his family was here in the early 1800s, once lived on Assateague before the village there was shut down, and his grandfather was in the movie *Misty*. Though he rarely leads kayak tours himself, Colbourne's years of experience as a waterman come through as he advises his guides about the best places to spot wild ponies and other wildlife. Colbourne also skippers the *Misty*, a pontoon boat he's used for nature tours since 2001. In the winter, Colbourne lives in Hawaii guiding scuba tours and surfing, so Assateague Explorer is a seasonal business, May through Oct.

Farther afield is **Southeast Expeditions** (32218 Lankford Hwy., Cape Charles; 877-22KAYAK or 757-331-2680; www.southeastexpeditions.net), based in Cape Charles but offering paddling adventures all over the Eastern Shore, including the Historic Onancock Creek Tour and a half day Schooner Bay Beach Adventure to a remote Chesapeake Bay beach. In addition to two-, four-, or eight-hour tours, adventurers can try multiday tours, kayak camping, fishing, or instruction. Southeast also rents kayaks or kiteboards.

Up a Creek With a Paddle (27369 Phillips Dr., Melfa; 757-693-1200; www .upacreektours.com) offers guided kayak tours with Virginia Ecotour guides and instructors. You can try the sunrise or sunset tours, a half day, or a full day. Every tour includes kayak, gear, and a brief paddling lesson. Locations include Chincoteague National Wildlife Refuge as well as sites along the Chesapeake Bay.

East Side Rentals and Marina (7462 East Side Rd., Chincoteague; 757-336-5555) may look like a bait shop, but it also rents skiffs, fishing boats, and pontoon boats, plus canoes and kayaks during summer. Rent by the hour, half day, or full day.

For More Information

Chincoteague National Wildlife Refuge, 8231 Beach Rd., P.O. Box 62, Chincoteague, VA 23336; (757) 336-6122; www.chinco.fws .gov.

Toms Cove Visitor Center, Beach Road, P.O. Box 38, Chincoteague, VA 23336; (757)

336-6577; www.nps.gov (National Park Service) and www.fws.gov (Fish and Wildlife Service).

Assateague Island National Seashore, 7206 National Seashore Lane, Berlin, MD 21811; (410) 641-1441.

Camping

No camping is allowed on the Virginia side of Assateague, not even backcountry camping. It's an 11-mile hike from Virginia over to Maryland, where backcountry camping is allowed with a permit, but this is too long a trek for most families. The Maryland side of the island offers some established camping areas. There are several campgrounds on Assateague Island; the Maryland State Park Service manages one campground, which is open late Apr through late Oct; two others are run by the National Park Service and are open year-round. For more information about Maryland camping, contact one of the Assateague offices: Campground/Ranger Office for Assateague Island National Seashore, (410) 641-3030; and Assateague State Park Campground Office, (410) 641-2918 in season or (410) 641-2120 year-round.

Oyster and Maritime Museum (ages 5 and up)

7125 Maddox Blvd.; (757) 336-6117; www.chincoteaguechamber.com/oyster/omm.html. Open daily in summer, weekends in spring and fall; closed winter. Free.

Learn about local history, from the details of harvesting oysters to the operation of the old lifesaving station and the impressive Fresnel lens at the Assateague lighthouse. The ever-changing exhibit includes an Ice Age walrus tusk, Native American artifacts, shipwreck relics, photographs from the village on Assateague—taken before residents floated their homes across the bay on barges—and a display showing the variety of places that oysters will colonize, such as bottles, pipes, and even inner tubes. $

Memorial Park and Skate Park (all ages)

At the west end of East Side Drive, Chincoteague.

This lovely waterside park overlooks the Assateague Channel and has a great view of the lighthouse. Parents can gaze across the water or get in some fishing off the pier while kids enjoy the free skateboarding park. It's likely they'll meet the locals there, shredding across two half-pipes and grinding rails and ramps. Helmets, knee pads, and elbow pads are required, and it's skate at your own risk; an occasional visit from the town police helps enforce the rules.

NASA/Wallops Visitor Center (ages 5 and up)

Located on Highway 175, 5 miles from Chincoteague; (757) 824-1344; www.wff.nasa .gov/vc. Open daily during July and Aug, Thurs through Mon, Mar through June and Sept through Nov, and Mon through Fri Dec through Feb.

In 1945 NASA established a launch site on **Wallops Island** that was then known as the Langley Research Center. Research is still done at this facility. The visitor center is designed so the public can learn about the NASA Wallops Flight Facility, which is located on nearby Wallops Island. Exhibits include life-size models of planes, probes, and rockets. Special events are the model-rocket demonstrations on the first Sat Mar through Nov and first and third Sat of July and Aug, and living-in-space demonstrations every Sun at 1 p.m., from Mar through Nov. The facility also offers puppet shows depicting life aboard the space shuttle every Sat and Sun at 11 a.m., and there is a rocket launch or children's program at 1 p.m. every Sat Mar through Nov. See Web site for other events.

Chincoteague **Treats**

What's a trip to the beach without ice cream to cool sunburned brows? Chincoteague's three popular parlors each offer a different twist on frozen treats. At **Muller's** (4034 Main St.) take in town history surrounded by Victorian decor. Built by a 19th-century undertaker, the house, according to legend, hosts a resident ghost. Owners John and Mary Lou Lynn, teachers during the academic year, serve ice-cream cones, fresh fruit sundaes, ice-cream sodas, draft root beer from a shining brass keg, and New York egg creams from an antique soda fountain. Their towering Belgian waffle with fresh peaches and homemade whipped cream is plenty for two. Check out their hot-sauce shop out back.

The **Island Creamery** (6243 Maddox Blvd.) offers deliciously rich ice cream made right behind the counter. Some of the flavors scooped into oversized waffle cones were invented by local schoolchildren, who take an annual field trip to the shop. (How about Pony Tracks? Or Mr. Chocolate's Candy Explosion?) Conquer the Round Up—five scoops of ice cream, three toppings, and more—and your photograph goes on the electronic bulletin board.

Mr. Whippy (6201 Maddox Blvd.), the island icon—a cartoon-character ice-cream cone—beckons you to try soft-serve ice cream done up in dozens of combinations—with dips, sprinkles, and waffle cones and in sandwiches and sundaes. There are also snowballs and slushes, smoothies and "cyclones," with candy folded in. Look for the Mr. Whippy ice-cream truck in the campground, or use the drive-through window at the shop.

Fishing

Bluefin, yellowfin, king mackerel, wahoo, dolphin, shark, sea bass, flounder. The fishing around Chincoteague is phenomenal, and visitors can get in on the action by signing on for a fishing trip or renting gear and heading off to the local pier. No license is required at Memorial Park, near where the ponies swim on the Assateague Channel side of the island. Bait shops and charter boats abound. See the Chincoteague Island Charter Boat Association, www.chincoteague.com/charterboats, or pick up a brochure at the chamber of commerce, on the circle at Maddox Boulevard.

Where to Eat

Main Street Shop and Coffeehouse, 4288 Main St.; (757) 336-6782; www.mainstreet-shop.com. Open daily during summer, weekends in fall and spring; closed in winter. Part coffee shop, part art gallery, and part gift shop, the coffeehouse is a popular spot to park the bikes and come in for a cuppa. Pastries and other sweets complement coffee and tea, and while you're waiting to pick up your order, you can check out wearable art, housewares, and one-of-a-kind art both upstairs and down. Tables look over Main Street, and a little porch is pleasantly surrounded with flowers and greenery. $

Sea Star Gourmet Carryout, 4121 Main St.; (757) 336-5442. Open daily July 4 through Labor Day, Thurs through Mon the rest of the year; closed Dec through Feb. This small kitchen packs great flavor, with innovative wraps and sandwiches made from the freshest veggies and meats. Lots of vegetarian options, multigrain breads and sprouts, hummus and pita, black-bean soup, plus full-bore pastrami, smoked turkey, tons of cheeses, and other deli standards. $

Steamer's, 6251 Maddox Blvd.; (757) 336-5300; www.steamersallyoucaneat.com. This is the place for crab feasts—and shrimp, oysters, clams, and flounder, pasta, steak—the works. A get your elbows dirty-style crabhouse, it can get crowded so plan accordingly. $$$

The Village, 6576 Maddox Blvd.; (757) 336-5120. Open year-round except five or six weeks in winter (call first); closed Christmas & New Year's. This family-owned restaurant has a leg up on the freshest seafood on the island, as the owner is a well-connected former waterman himself. He and his family offer a full seafood menu plus steaks and sides. Lots of folks come for the seafood-stuffed tomato, full of crab imperial, shrimp, and scallops and topped with cheese. $$$

Woody's Fried Chicken and Woody's Beach Barbecue, 6700 Maddox Blvd. at the traffic circle; www.woodysbeachbbq.com. Equal parts eatery and hangout, Woody's offers tetherball, volleyball, and other distractions at a retro surf camp adorned with quirky details like benches made from surfboards, vintage drink coolers and funky driftwood art. Get fried chicken from one wagon, BBQ from the other—and since there are no tables, it's takeout, beach chairs, or stand-around-and-eat. Everything we've tried here has been terrific—crispy chicken, delicious pulled pork (try a sandwich with onion rings in it), and plenty of sides like gingered applesauce, succotash, and cheesy mashed potatoes.

Where to Stay

Chincoteague offers motels, vacation homes, and cottages for weekly and extended stays as well as several inns and bed-and-breakfasts. Keep in mind that most lodgings close for the winter and not all inns and bed-and-breakfasts welcome children. For rental homes, we've had good luck with Island Properties (757-336-3456, http://island prop.com) and Harbour Rentals (757-336-5490, 800-221-5059, www.harbourrentals .net). Contact the chamber of commerce at (757) 336-6161 for more information.

Best Western Chincoteague Island, 7105 Maddox Blvd.; (757) 336-6557 or (800) 553-6117. Open year-round, this lodge overlooks the wildlife refuge. **Free** deluxe breakfast, Internet, and pool. Some rooms have a view of the Assateague Lighthouse. $–$$$

Maddox Family Campground, 6742 Maddox Blvd.; (757) 336-3111. Close to Assateague and also near the shops and restaurants of Chincoteague, this campground has beautiful water views, a pool, playground, grocery store, laundry room, and modern bathhouse. Activities include shuffleboard, horseshoes, an arcade, crabbing, and bird-watching. Open Mar 1 through Nov 30. $

Refuge Inn, 7058 Maddox Blvd.; (757) 336-5511 or (888) 257-0034; www.refugeinn.com. Open year-round except Feb, this inn offers accommodations near the wildlife refuge and the beach, a refrigerator in every room, and a pool. $–$$$$

Tom's Cove Family Campground, 8128 Beebe Rd.; (757) 336-6498; www.tomscove park.com. The campground offers waterfront camping plus a boat ramp and marina, pool, playground, and fishing and crabbing piers. Sites have hookups for water, electricity, and sewer. Open Mar 1 through Nov 30. $

Annual Events

APRIL–DECEMBER

Art Stroll, every second Sat between Apr and Dec. For a taste of the thriving art community in Chincoteague, a fun variety of participating galleries and shops open from 6 to 10 p.m. and offer, besides their displays, live music, wine tastings, book signings, and sometimes a group painting project. Our favorite shop is Egret Moon, at 4044 Main St., where resident Meghan McCook sells her own pottery, paintings, and woodwork along with the work of other island artists: jewelry, hanging art, fabric creations, and more. Expect quirky, creative, and fun.

APRIL

Easter Decoy and Art Festival, Easter weekend. Local and noted carvers and wildlife artists from around the country display their work.

MAY

International Migratory Bird Celebration, (757) 336-6122. Enjoy birdhouse building, guided walks, and other activities from 9 a.m. to 4 p.m.

JULY

Annual Pony Swim and Auction, last consecutive Wed and Thurs of July. Wild ponies from Assateague Island are rounded up for their swim to Chincoteague for a foal auction with "saltwater cowboys" and spectators in boats and kayaks lined up to watch. This is reputed to be the oldest roundup in the United States.

Chincoteague Volunteer Fireman's Carnival, every weekend in July and the last full week of July, not including Sun. This is an old-fashioned carnival with rides, food, entertainment, prizes, and auctions.

Old Fashioned Fireworks Display, July 4. Chincoteague Volunteer Fire Company Carnival Grounds.

SEPTEMBER

Chincoteague National Wildlife Refuge beach cleanup, mid-Sept, call for dates; (757) 336-6122. Many regulars at Chincoteague schedule their vacation around this event. Participants don **free** T-shirts and join the locals to do their part in preserving the wild beach.

OCTOBER

Chincoteague National Wildlife Refuge Archery Hunt; (757) 336-6122. Hunters are chosen by lottery to hunt the sika elk living in designated areas of the refuge. Other sportsmen's events include gun hunting for whitetail deer during Dec, and for sika elk through some winter months, and the Wallops Island hunt for white-tail deer in Nov and Dec. Fees. For an application and for specific dates, call the Fish and Wildlife Service, (757) 336-6122.

National Wildlife Refuge Week, Columbus Day weekend; (757) 336-6122. More than 500 wildlife refuges celebrate the diversity of wild places. Sign up for birding walks, workshops on wildlife, and other activities.

Oyster Festival, Sat of Columbus Day weekend. The festival offers all-you-can-eat oysters, crabs, clam fritters, and hot dogs.

NOVEMBER

Waterfowl Weekend, Thanksgiving weekend; (757) 336-6122. Celebrate the marvel of migration; the refuge opens its 7-mile service road, just off the Wildlife Loop, to vehicles, noon to 3 p.m., and the Wildlife Loop 9 a.m. to dusk for the Thanksgiving weekend. Guided walks are held as well.

Chincoteague hosts many festivals. Check with the chamber of commerce for details: (757) 336-6161.

For More Information

Chincoteague Chamber of Commerce, 6733 Maddox Blvd., Chincoteague, VA 23336; (757) 336-6161; www.chincoteaguechamber .com.

Eastern Shore of Virginia Tourism Commission, 24391 Lankford Hwy., P.O. Box 72, Tasley, VA 23441; (757) 787-8268; www .esvatourism.org.

Onancock

One of the oldest towns in America, Onancock has buildings that date to the 17th century. Established on Chesapeake Bay in 1680 as Port Scarburgh, Onancock continues to be a fishing community. Onancock is popular, too, because it's one of the departure points for the ferry to Tangier Island, a classic Eastern Shore day trip. Staying overnight in Onancock makes it convenient to catch the morning ferry.

Ker Place (ages 7 and up)

69 Market St.; (757) 787-8012; www.kerplace.org. Open Tues through Sat Mar through mid-Dec. $.

This is the headquarters of the Eastern Shore of Virginia Historical Society. This museum was once the home of John Shepard Ker, a wealthy merchant, who built his house in 1799. On the first floor you'll find the house as he lived in it, with furnishings and artifacts representative of the early 1800s. On the second floor learn about local history through pieces such as the Custis trunk, brought by settlers in the 1620s, and artifacts from John Cropper, leader of the Accomack County Minutemen.

Walking Tour of Onancock (ages 12 and up)

Map available at the town office, 15 North St., or Ker Place (see above); (757) 787-3363.

While walking along the shady lanes, you pass 19th-century homes with decorative trim and wraparound porches, as well as older homes.

Art Galleries

Onancock has an eclectic mix of art from locals and from artists who have moved from more metropolitan areas, making a tour of galleries especially rewarding. Among them: **Crockett Gallery** (39 Market St., 757-787-2288, www.williecrockett.com) features paintings evocative of the gentle tidal rhythms of the area from artist Willie Crockett, born and raised on Tangier Island; **Gallery Onancock** (8 North St., www.galleryonancock.com), run by three area women, offers an assortment of local artists; and **gardenART,** admittedly not a gallery but an artistically creative garden, housewares, and art shop where you can rent a bike, plan a kayak trip, buy garden accoutrement or art, or visit with the resident Portuguese Water Dog, Lulu.

Fishing

Get a true flavor of the Eastern Shore by getting out on the water and fishing. Contact Fish N'Finn Charters at the town dock, (757) 787-3399; or James Gang Sportfishing, 4 Frances St., (757) 787-1226.

Tangier Island (all ages)

P.O. Box 27, Tangier Island, VA 23440; (757) 891-2240. Cruises run daily Memorial Day through Labor Day. Closed during winter and early spring. $25 round-trip adults, half price children ages 6 to 12, under 6 free.

On Onancock's town dock you can purchase tickets for the one-and-a-half-hour tour-boat ride to Tangier Island. Situated in the middle of Chesapeake Bay, 6 miles south of the Virginia/Maryland border, the 500-or-so-resident island is accessible only by boat or plane. Visitors stay on the island for two hours, enough time for lunch and a walk, before catching the ferry back.

Oystering and crabbing have been legacies on Tangier for generations, probably since its settlement in 1686. Still true to its watery traditions, Tangier sports work sheds along the wharf and narrow lanes of whitewashed houses, many with centuries-old gravestones in their front yards, a sight my teenage daughter finds unnerving.

Day-trippers come for the boat ride, the food, and a glimpse of a more traditional and quiet way of life. When we visit we eschew the locals' offers of island tours in golf carts and instead rent bicycles or meander along the lanes and the wharf. On one outing we watched a young mother bicycling home from the grocery store with her young child propped in the basket, a black Labrador retriever excitedly trotting into an inlet to accompany a fisherman, and children playing catch.

Like most of the ferry passengers, we lunch at the Chesapeake House, a simple, family-style restaurant reputed to serve the best crab cakes in Virginia (some say in Maryland,

Custis **Farms**

Custis Farms, 6118 Seaside Rd. in Nassawadox; (757) 442-9071 or (800) 428-6361. Open Mon through Sat year-round. This retail and wholesale nursery, operated by Phil and Barbara Custis, includes a nationally known woodland birding trail as well as a Victorian garden to explore. Fall and spring are popular among birders. All ages.

too). Fisherman's Corner Restaurant, run by three wives of watermen, has terrific soft-shells, the island's signature dish (757-891-2900). Unlike most, we stroll around the island first to avoid the midday dining crowd. My daughter Alissa, who doesn't even like seafood, relishes tasty crab cakes served at Hilda Crockett's with big portions of clam fritters, potato salad, corn pudding, and home-baked bread. Sated, tanned, and happily tired, we board the ferry back. As the waves break over the bow, splashing us into giggles, we can taste the salt spray and the Chesapeake Bay history, too.

Three places to stay on the island are Hilda Crockett's Chesapeake House (757-891-2331, www.chesapeakehousetangier.com), Sunset Inn (757-891-2535, http://tangierisland sunset.com), and Bay View Inn (757-891-2396 http://tangierisland.net).

The Tangier History Museum (16215 Main Ridge, 302-234-1660, www.tangierhistory museum.org, open daily in summer) is a great place to get a feel for the island's past and present, with hands-on displays and seashell checkerboard games on the porch, plus kayaks out back that are available **free** to anyone who wants to paddle the marshy channels around the island. For a first-hand look at crabbing, sign up for an hour-and-a-half boat ride with a local captain to visit a crab shanty, where soft shell crabs molt, and learn about the ecology of the area (757-891-2331 www.chesapeakehousetangier.com/tours or for a shorter crab shanty-only tour, 757-891-2269, www.fishermanscornerrestaurant.com/baycrabs).

Another way to reach the island is via Tangier & Chesapeake Cruises, aboard the *Chesapeake Breeze*. The one-and-a-half-hour narrated cruise leaves from Buzzard's Point Marina in Reedville, Virginia, every day at 10 a.m. and returns at 3:30 p.m.; (804) 453-2628; www.tangiercruise.com.

Annual Events

MAY–DECEMBER

Second Fridays in Onancock, each second Fri of the month Onancock shops and galleries open their doors to showcase local talent, from 5 to 8 p.m. Look for craft demonstrations, gallery openings, wine tastings, restaurant discounts, and a lot of friendly company in a town that combines down-home attitude with sophisticated art and cuisine.

JULY

Art in the Park, early July, Barrier Island Park, Machipongo; (757) 787-2460. Juried festival of local and visiting artists.

SEPTEMBER

Harbor Fest, early Sept; (757) 787-3363. Paper boat competitions, carnival rides, games of chance, face painting, food vendors.

DECEMBER

Christmas Parade, mid-Dec; (757) 787-3363. A homey display of firefighting trucks and equipment, community and school bands, scouts, and other small-town treasures.

Onancock Christmas Homes Tour, children 12 and over, early Dec; (757) 787-2460. Tour historic homes gaily decorated for the holidays, with shops open and offering a cup of cheer, along with live music at the historic Cokesbury Church.

Where to Eat

Bizzotto's Gallery and Cafe, 41 Market St.; (757) 787-3103. Open daily, closed Sun after Labor Day. Offers lunch and dinner specializing in international cuisine with an emphasis on local seafood. Dine amidst one-of-a-kind artisans' work including the owner's fine leather handbags and briefcases. $$$

Blarney Stone, 10 North St.; (757) 302-0300. A family-oriented classic Irish pub serving lunch and dinner, which includes American fare along with traditional Irish dishes and gourmet dinner specials. $$$

Mallard's at the Wharf, Two Market St.; (757) 787-8558; www.mallardsllc.com. Open daily for lunch and dinner. Right on the water, this restaurant serves local seafood (and other selections) with a view. The menu offers lots of sandwiches, including crab cakes; salads like the Onancock Cobb; and a handful of entrees at dinner. Chef Johnny Mo may haul out his guitar and sing with his band if he's on site—he has two other Malard's in the area. The historic Hopkins and Brothers building

has been here since 1847, and the front room has displays of local yarn crafts. $$

Flamenco European Restaurant, 4 North St.; (757) 787-7780. Features a long menu of Eastern European-influenced food from Czech owners; the locals rave about the goulash. $$$

Where to Stay

Charlotte Hotel and Restaurant, 7 North St.; (757) 787-7400; www.thecharlottehotel .com. This eight-room boutique hotel welcomes children over 10 to what was once the White Hotel, built in 1907. Rooms include continental breakfast; the award-winning, internationally influenced New American cuisine restaurant is open for dinner as well. $$$–$$$$

Colonial Manor Inn, 84 Market St. (5 blocks from the harbor); (757) 787-3521; www.colonialmanorinn.com. This large Victorian home, on the town's main street, has served as an inn for more than sixty years. There are six rooms, all with private baths. Guests are welcome to relax in the Victorian gazebo or curl up with a book on the quiet glassed-in sun porch. The inn welcomes families with well-behaved children. Pets allowed in some rooms. Kids love collecting breakfast eggs from the resident chickens. Rates include a full breakfast. $–$$

Spinning Wheel Bed and Breakfast, 31 North St.; (757) 787-7311; (888) 787-0337; www.1890spinningwheel.com. This 1890s home, furnished with period antiques including the eponymous spinning wheels, includes five guest rooms and is open year-round. Guests can use house bicycles, play croquet or badminton on the lawn, or rock away the afternoon on the porch. Children over age 8 are welcomed. One room accommodates pets. $–$$

For More Information

Eastern Shore of Virginia Tourism Commission, P.O. Box 72, Tasley, VA 23441; (757) 787-8268; www.esvatourism.org or www.onancock.org.

Wachapreague

Many people think this little fishing village has the most scenic waterfront on the Eastern Shore. Known as the Flounder Fishing Capital of the World, Wachapreague is rich with other sorts of wildlife, too. More than 250 species of birds pass through the area as they travel along the Atlantic Flyway.

Boat Rentals

Charter a boat with a captain for offshore fishing or rent one for a day and captain it yourself (if you know how). Wachapreague is located between two favorite places for sport fishermen—Ocean City, Maryland, and Virginia Beach. Charter boats are less expensive than in many beach areas.

For boat charters, May through Oct, contact Wachapreague Hotel Marina, (757) 787-2105; the Wachapreague Town Marina, 15 Atlantic Ave., (757) 787-1930; and Wachapreague Seaside Marina (757) 787-4110. Ask about 16-footlong fishing boats that handle up to four people as well as chartered boats for up to six people. Bait is also for sale.

Where to Eat

Island House Restaurant, 17 Atlantic Ave.; (757) 787-4242. Located near the Wachapreague Motel, the Island House is a popular eatery with locals. In summer you'll see fancy boats tied up at the dock so their skippers can lunch on the restaurant's crab cakes. Children's menu. $$

Where to Stay

Garrison Bed and Breakfast, 34000 Seaside Rd. (Route 600), Painter; (757) 442-9446; http://garrisonbandb.com. This colonial bed-and-breakfast has four bedrooms, expansive grounds, and a shady front porch. Hosts Barbara and Cleo Hargis are especially proud of their hearty Southern breakfast. Located 7 miles from Wachapreague, Garrison is close enough for "Captain Cleo" to take you on a fishing trip aboard his 24-foot skiff. Children age 6 and older are welcome. $–$$

Virginia Landing, camping and cabins located at the end of County Road 605 in Quinby; (757) 442-4853. Open Apr 15 through Oct 31. Call to make reservations. Quinby is the closest town to Wachapreague with a campground. Amenities include a fishing pier, fish-cleaning station, minigolf, volleyball courts, baseball fields, paddle boats, and canoes. $–$$$

Wachapreague Motel and Marina (also called Hotel Wachapreague), 15 Atlantic Ave.; (757) 787-2105. The motel has rental and charter boats as well as a bait-and-tackle shop. Apartments, an efficiency, and motel rooms available year-round. Pets are allowed. $–$$

Annual Events

APRIL

Wachapreague Spring Flounder Tournament, mid-Apr. Angling enthusiasts fish for trophy-size catches.

JULY

The Fireman's Carnival. This small-town fête, with carnival rides and games of chance, is always popular with families.

AUGUST

Annual Fish Fry, late Aug. Local fare is served.

Tuna Tournament. Fishing enthusiasts angle for big tuna.

For More Information

Eastern Shore of Virginia Tourism Commission, P.O. Box 72, Tasley, VA 23441; (757) 787-8268; www.esvatourism.org.

Cape Charles

Cape Charles and its environs offer families the outdoors Eastern Shore-style, and a recent growth spurt is directing this once bustling railroad town back to its former glory. In addition to the gentle bay beach and fishing pier, there are harbor parties throughout the summer, interesting shops, quaint B&Bs, and several eateries.

Kiptopeke State Park (all ages)

3540 Kiptopeke Dr.; (757) 331-2267; www.dcr.virginia.gov/state_parks/kip.shtml. **Open year-round. $.**

On 375 acres of beachfront, woods, and farm fields, Kiptopeke gives families a chance to unwind away from the crowds. My family fell in love with Kiptopeke for its simplicity. The 0.5-mile of Chesapeake Bay beach is not particularly picturesque, but it's rarely crowded, and it's always calm due to the sunken World War II ship that serves as a breakwater for the waves. Young kids tumble in and out of tire tubes (bring your own), happily using the gradually sloping shoreline as a playground.

At the south beach, a primitive swath of shore backed by wild grasses, locals angle for flounder or croakers from the fishing pier, a former ferry terminal. Scheduled activities include ranger-led fishing clinics, nighttime bonfires, lessons in becoming a "chicken-necker" (crabbing by using poultry necks as bait), as well as canoe treks through the salt marshes of nearby Raccoon Creek.

A mile and a half of hiking trails afford plenty of opportunities for sighting birds. Nature paths wind over sand dunes through groves of loblolly pines, sassafras, and wild cherry trees. The Baywoods Trail, a 1-mile loop, passes the gazebo that seems to flutter to life in Sept as a bird-banding

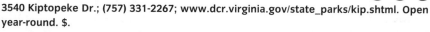

station for hundreds of migratory birds, songbirds, shorebirds, and hawks. In summer, though, the benches offer lazy hikers like us a pleasant place to picnic and pause to watch for rabbits and deer and to listen for quail rustling in the red oak and bayberry trees.

Kiptopeke also has basic and full-service campsites as well as RV, cabin, and bunk-house rentals. (Reservations are required, call 800-933-7275.)

The Eastern Shore of Virginia National Wildlife Refuge
(all ages)
5003 Hallet Circle; (757) 331-2760. Open daily year-round; call for visitor center hours.

It's easy to drive right by the Eastern Shore of Virginia National Wildlife Refuge, because it's just before the northern terminus of the Chesapeake Bay Bridge–Tunnel. The wildlife refuge is a surprise with 1,100 acres of forests, myrtle thickets, grasslands, and ponds. At this roadside oasis, the distant sounds of traffic are almost obliterated by the twittering of scores of birds and the swish of bushes and leaves in the breeze. The **Observation Trail** leads through an abandoned World War II bunker to an observation platform overlooking a salt marsh. If you visit in summer, remember that it's hot in these grasslands. Wear a hat, use sunscreen, and tote water. Stop at the visitor center for information. The refuge is a must-visit during fall's migratory season. Species such as the bald eagle and peregrine falcon, along with many other birds and monarch butterflies, use the refuge's ponds and woods. Between late Aug and early Nov, you can see hundreds of hawks, falcons, and songbirds in flight.

The Palace Theater
305 Mason Ave.; (757) 331-2787; www.artsentercapecharles.org.

The 1941 art deco theater was given a rebirth by a nonprofit organization, Arts Enter Cape Charles, which features locally produced plays, dance performances, and touring productions year-round, as well as art education and exhibit space.

Cape Charles Museum
814 Randolph Ave.; (757) 331-1008.

Exhibits of local historical interest are on display daily from Apr through Nov.

Ecotours

Touring the deserted seaside barrier islands by boat is a great Huck Finn-type adventure. Experienced captains and local guides will show you the tidewater environment and take you on custom tours that could include shelling, surf fishing, birding, cultural history, geography, and more, on land or water. Two to try are: **Broadwater Bay Ecotours** (757-442-4363; www.broadwaterbayecotour.com) and **Eastern Shore Adventures** (757-615-2598; http://easternshoreadventures.com).

Chesapeake Bay Bridge–Tunnel
to Virginia Beach

Highway 13; (757) 331-2960. Cars pay $12 one-way and another $5 to cross back, if it's within 24 hours.

This is the world's longest bridge-tunnel complex, stretching 17.6 miles from Virginia Beach/Norfolk to Virginia's Eastern Shore. As the structure loops over and under the bay, savor the sense of space and joy common to open roads, panoramic water views, and sea breezes. More than just a bridge, this structure has a 625-foot fishing pier, making it the only place where you can fish 3.5 miles offshore without a boat. The Seagull Pier Restaurant and a souvenir shop are other one-of-a-kind stops, and several telescopes give you a unique view of the bay and the Eastern Shore. All ages.

At the tunnel's terminus, a new visitor center in Cape Charles is a great place to pick up brochures and information about the area, with revolving exhibits showcasing area businesses like regional food vendors, restaurants, art galleries and wineries.

Where to Eat

The Cape Charles Coffee House, 241 Mason Ave.; (757) 331-1880. Breakfast and lunch in a restored 1910 downtown building. Bistrolike fare with daily specials, lots of seafood, salads, soups, sandwiches, accompanied by sides. $$

Rayfield's Pharmacy, 2 Fig St.; (757) 331-1212. Breakfast and lunch. The old-fashioned lunch counter and soda fountain lives on, complete with jukebox. $

Sting-Ray's Restaurant, Highway 13 in Capeville, a 5-mile drive from Cape Charles; (757) 331-2505. Open daily for breakfast, lunch, and dinner. From the outside, Sting-Ray's looks more like a convenience store attached to a gas station than a restaurant. A favorite among the locals, it's famous for crabs caught in nearby bays, seafood, plus a popular and spicy chili. $

Where to Stay

Cape Charles House Bed and Breakfast, 645 Tazewell Ave.; (757) 331-4920; www.capecharleshouse.com. This colonial-revival frame house, built in 1912, is furnished with antiques and features extensive landscaping with herb and perennial beds. Blocks from the bay beach. $$–$$$

Kiptopeke Inn, 29106 Lankford Hwy., Highway 13; (757) 331-1000 or (800) 331-4000, www.kiptopekeinn.net. This is a traditional 103-room motel right next to the park. **Free** boat parking, fish cleaning stations, and a pool. $–$$

Sea Gate, 9 Tazewell Ave.; (757) 331-2206; http://seagatebb.com. This bed-and-breakfast invites guests to enjoy the bay breeze from its porches. Four traditional rooms; full country breakfast at individual tables. Children over 7 welcome. $–$$

Sunset Beach Resort, Highway 13; (757) 331-1776 or (800) 899-4-SUN; www.sunset beachresortva.com. Pool, private beach, beachfront cafe, and kayak tours next to the property. Adjacent to wildlife refuge. $–$$$

Annual Events
SEPTEMBER
Seasonal Festival, Cape Charles; (757) 331-3259. Crafts and live music are part of this festival.

OCTOBER
Eastern Shore Birding Festival; (757) 787-8268; early Oct. Located at various sites including Kiptopeke State Park and Sunset Beach. The two-day-long festival coincides with the peak of the fall migration. Check out the workshops, exhibits, children's activities, crafts, and bird art.

Eastern Shore Harvest Fest; (757) 787-8268. Held the first Wed in Oct, Harvest Fest celebrates the foods—such as seafood, sweet potatoes, crab, and chicken—that make Virginia's Eastern Shore famous. Craft vendors sell their wares.

Between the Waters Bike Tour, fourth Sat of Oct; (757) 678-7157; www.cbes.org. This fund-raiser for Citizens for a Better Eastern Shore gives riders a choice of 20-, 40-, 60-, or 100-mile rides on back roads of the Eastern Shore. Riders are given snacks and lunch at rest stops along the way as well as sag wagon services, if they're needed. An oyster roast ends the day. **Free.**

For More Information
Eastern Shore of Virginia Tourism Commission, P.O. Box 72, Tasley, VA 23441; (757) 787-8268; www.esvatourism.org.

Central Virginia

Central Virginia offers families a wide variety of vacation possibilities including scenic rolling hills; lakes, rivers, and streams; a rich historical heritage; and cities that include the capital, Richmond, also the capital of the Confederacy during the Civil War.

Home to Appomattox, where Lee surrendered to Grant and ended the South's hopes for its own Confederate nation, central Virginia offers children meaningful and memorable lessons about American history and the consequences of war. Be sure to prepare your children beforehand with books and videos, or, with younger kids, simple explanations about the Civil War.

The central section of the state, flanked by the Blue Ridge Mountains to the west and tidal rivers to the east, is particularly distinguished for being the home of notable patriots and presidents. Thomas Jefferson and Patrick Henry were born and lived here; James Madison and James Monroe made their homes in central Virginia.

With so much history, there's much to see. It's important to keep in mind that not every historic house, monument, and battlefield is going to fascinate a child, particularly younger ones. Try to offer a balance. Pick and choose your historic sites and be sure to complement these with time out to enjoy the area's parks, forests, and theme parks.

TopPicks in Central Virginia

1. **Wintergreen Resort, Nelson County, and the Blue Ridge Mountains**

2. **Monticello,** Charlottesville

3. **Pamplin Historical Park and the National Museum of the Civil War Soldier,** Petersburg

CENTRAL VIRGINIA

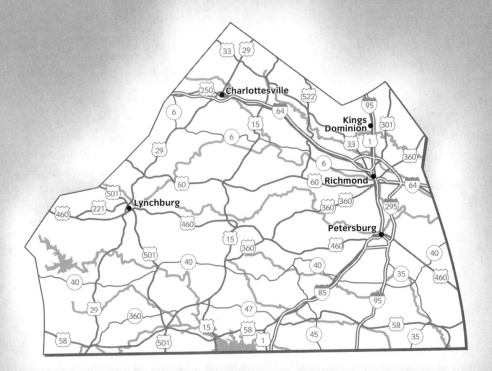

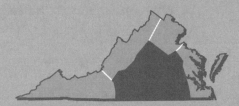

Charlottesville and Albemarle County

Charlottesville, located in the foothills of the Blue Ridge Mountains along I-64, is the home of the University of Virginia, which was founded and designed by Thomas Jefferson, third president of the United States. Jefferson's influence is very strong in this city of some 40,000 and in the surrounding Albemarle County. If you have school-age or older kids, they may enjoy a visit to the home of a former president. Not far from Charlottesville is Monticello, the home of Thomas Jefferson; Ash Lawn–Highland, the home of James Monroe; and Montpelier, home of James Madison.

For additional information, check out www.pursuecharlottesville.com (an information-packed Web site worth checking before you go).

Monticello (ages 5 and up)

931 Thomas Jefferson Parkway (Va. Route 53), about 2.5 miles from I-64 exit 12; (434) 984-9822; www.monticello.org. The house and visitor center are open daily year-round except Christmas, with reduced hours Nov through Feb. $$.

Designed by Jefferson and built over the span of forty years, this mountaintop-plantation is considered to be an architectural classic, not to mention a stunning, eye-catching beauty set in peaceful surroundings. Jefferson moved here in 1771, although construction continued until 1809.

To get the most out of your family's visit, start at the Thomas Jefferson Visitor Center. After purchasing or picking up your tickets and getting the children's guide *Exploring Monticello,* view the 15-minute introductory film, *Thomas Jefferson's World,* shown three times each hour in the theater on the center's courtyard level.

Families with children ages 6 to 11 should be sure to visit the Griffin Discovery Room, located on the lower level of the center, a please-touch activity space that includes replicas of items from the Monticello house and plantation. The two-level Smith Gallery contains four exhibitions, including the interactive multimedia display *Thomas Jefferson and "the Boisterous Sea of Liberty."*

Guided tours are offered of the imposing main house, where many belongings of Jefferson and his wife, Martha, remain. Most of the furnishings are original. Jefferson's innovative thinking resulted in some unusual architectural touches throughout Monticello. For example, because he didn't like staircases (neither their appearance nor the amount of space they require), most are very narrow or not visible. Jefferson got a jump on the green revolution with doubled glass doors and windows to keep out the cold.

Jefferson was a brilliant thinker and a number of gadgets he created or improved upon to make life easier can be viewed throughout the house, such as a two-pen device that enabled him to make a copy of whatever he was writing. (All the more remarkable when you consider that Jefferson lived in a time when there were few gadgets.) The

Monticello's **Tour for Families**

Families with children ages 6 through 11 can smell vanilla beans, examine 18th-century nails, decipher secret codes, and learn about Jefferson's grandchildren on children-friendly house tours focusing on hands-on learning. These tours are offered six times daily from mid-June through early Sept. Inquire at the ticket office or reserve online.

seven-day calendar clock, which he designed, is still in working order and is on display in the house's main entrance hall.

Visitors can also take tours through the restored orchard, vineyard, and vegetable gardens (offered daily Apr through Oct) and view Jefferson's grave in the family burial grounds. Allow time to explore the "dependencies"—the work spaces under the house. From the house you can take a shuttle bus back to the parking lot or take a walk through the woods along a guided path that passes the family cemetery. This huge property requires a fair amount of time to tour. Written guided tours of Monticello are available in Braille, Chinese, French, German, Italian, Japanese, Korean, Spanish, and Russian. Reserve tickets online to be sure you get in.

Ash Lawn–Highland (ages 5 and up)
1000 James Monroe Parkway, 4.5 miles southeast of Charlottesville on County Road 795 and 3 miles southwest of Monticello; (434) 293-9539; www.ashlawnhighland.org. Open daily year-round except Thanksgiving, Christmas, and New Year's Day, with reduced hours Nov through Mar. $.

This was the estate of James Monroe, fifth president of the United States. The 535-acre site is just a few miles from Monticello, and its proximity is no coincidence: Jefferson himself selected the site for Monroe and even sent over his gardeners to plant orchards for his neighbor.

This small and cozy place is actually larger than it was when Monroe lived here; a later owner built additions onto what was a very simple farmhouse. Remember that Monroe was the first president to come from the middle class, which may explain the lack of grandeur.

There are picnicking spots that offer marvelous views of the Blue Ridge Mountains in the distance. Kids especially enjoy the peacocks, sheep, and cows on the grounds. Daily guided tours of the main house offer a glimpse into the past. Special celebrations are held on Monroe's birthday, April 28. On selected summer weekends, the plantation offers hands-on crafts and colonial games. Check the schedule for Ash Lawn Opera Festival's summer season (434-979-0122 or 434-293-4500) and for Ash Lawn's Sounds of the Season Concerts after Christmas.

The Rotunda and the Academical Village, University of Virginia: Rotunda (ages 9 and up)

On University Avenue, near what is known as "The Corner" (Main Street and University Avenue); (434) 924-7969; www.virginia.edu.

The University of Virginia sprawls along Old Main Street. The highlight of the original "Academical Village" designed by Jefferson, the university's founder, is the Rotunda that Jefferson modeled after Rome's Pantheon. The Rotunda is still used for lectures and academic events, much as Jefferson intended.

Free walking tours of the Rotunda by University of Virginia students are offered year-round, except during a three-week Dec/Jan holiday, although families with young kids might prefer a self-guided stroll around the campus. For a preview tour of campus, see www.virginia.edu/uvatours/slideshow.

Follow the lawn extending from the south portico of the Rotunda. The Jeffersonian design of this older part of the University of Virginia stands the test of time; the classically designed buildings are still occupied as student dorms, and the lawns are typically dotted with young people studying or trotting off to class. Lawns make for great Frisbee tossing. Along the walkway, pavilions built (and still used) for faculty housing are each influenced by a famous classical building. Behind each is a decorative garden, originally used by faculty members to grow vegetables and tend livestock. The original student dorms are located behind the gardens; although they now have central heating, they still have working fireplaces. Edgar Allan Poe was a student here, and his living quarters (Room 13, West Range) are open for public viewing. For more on this area, see www.virginia.edu/academicalvillage.

Michie Tavern ca. 1784

Highway 53, 683 Jefferson Davis Parkway; (434) 977-1234; www.michietavern.com. The restaurant serves lunch year-round. The museum is open year-round, with guided tours of the tavern given daily Apr through Oct, self-guided tours Nov through Mar. $.

One of the oldest homesteads still standing in Virginia, this is now a restaurant with costumed hostesses who welcome you as "strangers," the 18th-century term for "traveler." The "ordinary" log cabin serves tasty fried chicken and other lunch fare at a bountiful buffet. Come from Apr to Oct for Living History, when you can step to a colonial dance, write with a quill pen, and taste a tavern punch. An annual yuletide dinner gives a peek at holiday history.

Michie Tavern opened in 1784 as an "ordinary," a place to dine, rest, and socialize along the stagecoach route. While gentlemen passed time in the tap room, ladies enjoyed a decorated room in which they could sew or read while waiting for the next stagecoach to arrive. In 1927 the tavern was dismantled piece by piece and moved to its present location from Old Buck Mountain Road, in Northwest Albemarle, about 17 miles northwest of where it is now. Behind the building are re-created dependencies, including a log kitchen, smokehouse, dairy, and a "necessary" (outhouse). Three unique shops complete the 18th-century experience. Kids ages 5 and under eat **free** with a paying adult.

Amazing
Thomas Jefferson Facts

- **Thomas Jefferson's daughter,** who had spent some time in France, is said to have introduced the Round Dance to society at a party at Michie Tavern. She also reputedly danced the first waltz in America with a young French officer, who shocked the crowd when he put his arm around her waist.

Virginia Discovery Museum (ages 2 to 10)

524 East Main St., at the east end of the Downtown Mall (a 10-blocklong pedestrian mall) near city hall; (434) 977-1025; www.vadm.org. Open Tues through Sun, closed Mon and some holidays. $.

The Virginia Discovery Museum offers toddlers through kids age 10 opportunities for interactive fun. Most of the activities, however, are geared for young kids.

Inside, in addition to exhibits that change every four months, young children can step inside a reconstructed 18th-century pioneer log cabin filled with such period furnishings as a rope bed, cradle, and cooking hearth. Kids enjoy the walk-in kaleidoscope, Virginia Faces, the dress-up area, and the Puppet Tree. Weekly self-directed art programs are offered in the Art Corner. Throughout the year there are **free** (with admission) drop-in programs with changing themes: Tuesday Travelers, who explore geography and cultures; the Poetry Club on Tues afternoon; Wednesdays' Toddler Time; and Art Adventures on Fri. During the school year (Oct to June), a Magic School Bus Science Club meets weekly, staging hands-on activities for the family to do together.

Montpelier (ages 3 to 12)

11407 Constitution Highway, 28 miles northeast of Charlottesville on Highway 20, 4 miles southwest of the town of Orange; (540) 672-2728; www.montpelier.org. Open daily year-round except Thanksgiving and Christmas, with reduced hours Nov through Mar. $$.

This home of James Madison, fourth president of the United States, was spruced up considerably in 2001 in celebration of the 250th anniversary of Madison's birth. Start with a fifteen-minute presentation at the new visitor center. The house is in the process of being restored to reflect Madison's period and visitors can witness artisans at work on the transformation. A hands-on restoration tent lets you make a brick or saw a log; an active archaeological dig shows research in action. A cabin built in 1870 by George Gilmore, born a slave of Madison, has been restored, and tours reveal what the daily life of a slave might have been like.

The acoustiguide relates the history of the family and buildings. The guided tour lasts one to two hours, so younger children may get impatient. Check for special events like pony races to spark their interest, including Wed morning programs, July through mid-Aug, geared separately toward children ages 3 through 6 and 7 through 12.

Paddling **Fun**

The James River is famous among river rats—those folks who tote kayaks on their cars and jump into white water every chance they get—as the only Class IV river that runs through a city (further south, in Richmond). That's impressive, but even better is the charm it holds for families.

The River Sojourns organized by the Alliance for the Chesapeake Bay are affordable, weeklong journeys, along various area waterways including the James River, that combine camping, paddling (canoes or kayaks), environmentalism, and a heavy dose of play. The James River Sojourn takes a different section of the river each year, but has previously included such treats as a tour of an organic farm (one 10-year-old girl got to harvest an egg from free-range chickens and carry it back on the hay wagon), a boat cruise catered by the local pizza joint, and a guitar-playing folk singer crooning us to sleep. But the best parts were the ones the kids made up themselves: teaching one another to skip rocks, discovering garfish in a cluster of boulders where we'd stopped for an afternoon swim, organizing an impromptu ultimate Frisbee game on the field next to our makeshift campground. Even better, parents were invited to play.

The sojourns are a pitch-in-and-help sort of experience, but meals are prepared for you, and the gear truck hauls your equipment while you paddle around the river. All you have to do is pitch your tent and find that flashlight you misplaced—and maybe help out with the dishes. You don't even have to have experience on the water: River outfitters are on hand for minimal instruction and safety. And you can take all or part of the week's sojourn.

Contact the Alliance for the Chesapeake Bay, (804) 775-0951, www .acb-online.org/project.cfm?vid=270.

James River Runners (434-286-2338; www.jamesriver.com) is located in the old Hatton Ferry store, built in 1882 by the ferry's original owner and replete with old canal lock stones, pressed tin walls, and heart pine flooring and countertops. The outfit will help you hit the river for an afternoon, a day, or overnight on a trip organized by professionals. Rentals include everything you need (except maybe sunscreen): canoe, kayak, raft, or inner tube; wildlife info; fishing gear; paddles; life vests; parking; transportation; tie-down rope; trip briefing; and maps. Daily 8 a.m. to 6 p.m. in season. Note age restrictions on individual trips.

James River Reeling and Rafting (434-286-4386; www.reelingandrafting .com) will let you choose your float and get out on the water tubing, canoeing, kayaking, or rafting. This family-run outfitter is the closest to Charlottesville, and offers short day trips as well as overnight outings. No children under age 6; must be 10 or older for canoes and kayaks. Apr through Oct 8 a.m. to 6 p.m.

Carter Mountain Orchard (all ages)

Route 53, Thomas Jefferson Parkway, Charlottesville; (434) 977-1833; www.cartermountain
orchard.com. Open daily, July to Thanksgiving, 9 a.m. to 6 p.m.

Enjoy the fruit of the land and pick your own apples, peaches, nectarines, and pumpkins,
or take a hayride around the orchard. You'll also find cider, apple cider doughnuts, pies,
and hand-dipped ice cream as well as handmade crafts and a spectacular view from the
picnic-friendly Apple Barn.

Hatton Ferry (all ages)

Hatton Ferry Road, Cottsville; (434) 296-1492; www.hattonferry.org. Free.

Hitch a free ride across the river on one of only two poled ferries still operating in the
United States. The ferry runs on Fri, Sat, and Sun from 9 a.m. to 5 p.m., mid-Apr to mid-
Oct, as water levels permit. Call for specifics.

Hot-Air Ballooning

Bear Balloon Corporation, (434) 971-1757 or (800) 932-0152, www.2comefly.com; or Monticello Country Ballooning, (434) 996-9008, www.virginiahotairballoon.com.

Catch a scenic balloon flight over the Virginia countryside, morning and evening as
weather permits. Champagne toasts included.

Kluge-Ruhe Aboriginal Art Collection (ages 7 and up)

University of Virginia, 400 Worrell Dr., Peter Jefferson Place, Charlottesville; (434) 244-0234;
www.virginia.edu/kluge-ruhe. Free.

Right here in central Virginia resides one of the most respected collections of Australian
Aboriginal art in the world, holding its own even among those in Australia. Offers a full
program of rotating exhibits, public lectures, research on the collection, and children's
programs like dot painting, bark basket making, and collaborative painting and storytelling. Tues through Sat 9 a.m. to 3 p.m., guided tours Sat at 10:30 a.m.

Free Speech Monument

Across from City Hall on the east end of the downtown pedestrian mall in Charlottesville.

A refreshing change from monumental edifices and statues, check out
this living tribute to freedom of speech. The 54-footlong, two-sided
slate wall is a public chalkboard for free expression of anything from
art to politics. Reminding visitors of the importance of such freedom, the First Amendment is permanently inscribed on one segment. Kids from toddler to teen can reach it, as the slate extends
right from the ground up to 7.5 feet high; it's wiped clean every
two weeks or so. There's also a podium designed to encour-
age speechifying, both planned and impromptu. To see what
other folks have contributed to the slate, see www.tjcenter.org/
monument.

Paramount Theater (ages 5 and up) ♫

On the historic downtown mall, 215 East Main St., Charlottesville; (434) 979-1333 or (434) 979-1922; www.theparamount.net.

Built in 1931, this landmark, once a "movie palace," fell into disrepair, was rescued by community leaders, and was fully restored with a Georgian facade and interior silk painted in colonial scenes. Now the stately building hosts a variety of live performances, from Wynton Marsalis to Wynonna, from modern dance to children's theater. See Web site for current schedule.

Where to Eat

Some of the town's most informal and inexpensive restaurants for families are located in and around University Corner. There are also many on the lively pedestrian mall, where you can sit outdoors and watch the crowds go by.

Bodo's Bagel Bakery, 1609 University Ave.; (434) 293-6021. Classic bagels, soups, and salads at low prices popular among UVA students. $

Crozet Pizza, 12 miles west of town on Highway 240 in Crozet; (434) 823-2132. Crozet's is known for having the best pizza in the state. $

The Ivy Inn, 2244 Old Ivy Rd.; (434) 977-1222. Located one mile from the University of Virginia, this restaurant serves "locally inspired seasonal American cuisine" in a historic house. Stand-out items on the menu include the mountain trout, the pork loin, the mushroom medley. This restaurant is best for 'tweens and teens who like good food. $$$

Michie Tavern, 683 Thomas Jefferson Parkway (Highway 53); (434) 977-1234. The restaurant serves lunch from 11:30 a.m. to 3 p.m. daily. The "ordinary" log cabin serves tasty fried chicken and other lunch fare at a bountiful buffet. Children age 5 and under dine free with a paying adult. $$

The Old Mill Room, in the Boar's Head Inn, 1.5 miles west of Charlottesville on US 250; (434) 972-2230; www.boarsheadinn

.com. Food such as filet mignon, lobster bisque, and rack of lamb in a formal setting, with the tavern next door serving lighter fare. $$$$

Where to Stay

Cavalier Inn, 105 North Emmet; (434) 296-8111 or (888) 882-2129. Across from the University of Virginia, this motel/hotel has 118 rooms, an outdoor pool, and restaurants within walking distance. $$$

Boar's Head Inn, Highway 250; (434) 296-2181 or (800) 476-1988; www.boarsheadinn .com. The inn was built in 1965 but has history surrounding it. An 1834 brick-and-wood waterwheel gristmill was on the inn's property, fieldstones from the mill's foundation were used in the inn's fireplace, and the mill's old pine planks were used as flooring. Simple, but elegant, rooms and suites are furnished with antiques. Indoor and outdoor tennis courts, three pools, a rock climbing wall, a health club, spa, and sprawling grounds with a lake for fishing (gear provided) make this more of a retreat than a hotel. $$–$$$$

Doubletree Hotel Charlottesville, 990 Hilton Heights Rd., (434) 973-2121 or (800) 494-9467; www.charlottesville.doubletree .com. This property is set on a twenty-acre wooded hillside 7 miles north of town. The hotel has 235 rooms, a full-service restaurant, and an indoor pool. $–$$$

English Inn of Charlottesville, 2000 Morton Dr., close to UVA; (434) 971-9900 or (800) 786-5400; www.englishinncharlottesville.com. This Tudor-style inn strives for an English club feel with its wood paneled lobby, wing chairs, and Oriental rugs. The eighty-eight-room inn welcomes children and has a large, heated indoor pool. Eighteen luxury suites have kitchenettes. Full breakfast is complimentary. $–$$$

Guesthouses Bed and Breakfast Reservation Service, P.O. Box 5737, Charlottesville 22905; (434) 979-7264; www.va-guesthouses.com. This service books stays in private houses, guest cottages, and traditional bed-and-breakfast accommodations in Charlottesville and the surrounding area. $–$$$$

Omni Charlottesville Hotel, 235 West Main St.; (434) 971-5500 or (800) THE-OMNI; www.omnihotels.com. This hotel is conveniently located to shopping, theaters, and sightseeing and runs specials during football season. Rooms have mini-refrigerators on request. There are indoor and outdoor pools. Kids get **free** milk and cookies at bedtime and a bag of goodies when they check in. There are also backpacks of activities families can check out at the front desk. $$–$$$$

Annual Events

SPRING

Dogwood Festival, held every spring; (434) 961-9824; www.charlottesvilledogwoodfestival.org. Celebrates the state flower with entertainment, food, crafts, a parade, fireworks, and a carnival.

MARCH

Festival of the Book, late Mar; (434) 924-6890; www.vabook.org. Features readings by international authors, panels, book sales, and special programs for children.

JUNE

Scottsville Batteau Festival, (434) 286-6000 or (434) 528-3950; www.batteaufestival.org. Costumed river enthusiasts bring back the past as they float, paddle, and pole down the river in the flat-bottom batteaux that drove trade in this region in the 18th and 19th centuries. You'll see canvas tents with sticks as poles, linen trousers held up with rope, and a historic village with candle makers, spinners, and weavers. There's also plenty of good music, square dancing and clogging, food, and crafts.

Fridays After Five, Charlottesville Pavilion, all summer; (434) 817-0220; www.fridaysafterfive.com. The pavilion springs to life all summer with **free** live music, from rock and blues to saba and reggae. Food is for sale and proceeds go to local nonprofit organizations. Rain or shine.

AUGUST

Albemarle County Fair, late Aug; (434) 293-6789 or (877) 386-1103; www.albemarlecountyfair.com. Experience the agricultural heritage that continues to occupy much of the population in this rural area. The fair features livestock and other farm exhibits (including, at past fairs, the classic tractor pull, a watermelon-seed-spitting contest, and turkey-calling competitions), as well as crafts, music, amusement rides, food, and historic displays (a Civil War camp and other reenactments have been included in the past).

OCTOBER

Fall Fiber Festival and Montpelier Sheepdog Trials, (434) 296-8533; www.fallfiberfestival.org. A great chance to get your hands on fresh wool and learn to craft it, at the Montpelier Estate. Watch the sheepdogs round up the flock, then you can learn to weave, crochet, and make penny rugs or felted soaps that integrate wool in soap for a colorful scrub. $

Virginia Film Festival, late Oct or early Nov; (800) UVA-FEST; www.VAfilm.com. Features movies, film stars, and directors as well as art exhibits and musical performances.

For More Information

Charlottesville/Albemarle Convention and Visitors Bureau, 610 East Main St., P.O. Box 178, Charlottesville, VA 22902; (434) 293-6789 or (877) 386-1103; www.visitchar lottesville.org. Open daily except Thanksgiving, Christmas, and New Year's Day. Along with providing brochures and information, the convention and visitors bureau can make same-day lodging reservations.

Nelson County

History's great, but don't ignore the spectacular Blue Ridge countryside. Try to combine seeing some of Charlottesville's historic attractions with hiking, bicycling, and exploring the mountains, woods, and valleys of Nelson County, on the "sunrise side of the Blue Ridge Mountains," about 30 miles southwest of Charlottesville. In spring the foothills turn pink with apple blossoms; more than forty varieties of apples are grown in the county. Drive through this scenic countryside in spring when the trees blossom, and come back in fall to buy apples by the bushel.

Apple and Strawberry **Picking**

Apple picking is a serious—but sweet—business in Nelson County, which grows acres upon acres of apples. The county visitor center has a scenic drive mapped out that winds past many of the orchards. This is an appealing drive in spring when the rolling hills seem painted with pink. In fall the following farms offer apples and other produce for sale: Dickie Brothers Orchard, 2552 Dickie Rd., Roseland (434-277-5516; www.dickiebros.com); Drumheller's Orchard, 1130 Drumheller Orchard Lane, off Highway 29, Lovingston (434-263-5036); Silver Creek–Seaman Orchards, Packing Shed, Highway 56 West, Tyro (434-277-5824); and Saunders Orchard, Highway 56 West, Piney River (434-277-5455).

For information on particular types of apples available at individual orchards, click on the Nelson County Web site, www.nelsoncounty.com.

Strawberries can also be picked locally and fresh at Seamans' Orchard Strawberry Patch, 415 Dark Hollow Rd., Roseland (434-277-8130). They can also be picked at the Critzer Family Farm, 9388 Critzer Shop Rd., Afton (540-456-4772).

Wintergreen **Resort**

Forty-three miles southwest of Charlottesville, west on Route 250 to Route 151; (434) 325-2200 or (800) 266-2444; www.wintergreenresort.com. This is a wonderful year-round resort for families. We've been here in all seasons. Although summer and fall are our favorite times to visit; spring brings wildflowers and winter brings skiing. At age 5, my daughter learned to ski in the resort's kids' program.

Wintergreen, an upscale resort sprawled on 10,800 acres in the valley and on a mountain, gives you Blue Ridge Mountains' magic from endless views to varied activities. The resort has 300 units (condos or homes with kitchens; most have fireplaces), in the rental pool, a twenty-acre lake, four pools (one indoor), wading pools, and a playground. You can also enjoy boating, golf, outdoor and indoor tennis, swimming, and horseback riding. For the adventurous, mountain biking, rock climbing, and a skateboarding park are big attractions. Families here also learn about birds, fossils, wildflowers, and stream life on the frequent guided hikes through the resort's own nature preserve.

In summer, on holidays, and on selected weekends, the resort offers a Kids in Action program for ages 2½ to 12. With Kids Night Out (Fri and Sat evenings July through Labor Day), ages 6 to 12 enjoy swimming and movies while parents savor moonlight and romantic dinners.

From Dec to late Mar, guests ski, snowboard, and go tubing. (Wintergreen has a sophisticated and powerful snowmaking system that is able to cover all twenty-four slopes and trails with 2 feet of snow in under three days.) There are also two terrain parks for snowboarders and skiers. Various kids' ski programs are available for ages 3 to 12, like the half-day or full-day Mountain Explorers and Mogul Monkeys, as well as child-care programs for nonskiing tots. There's also a 900-foot megatubing park. Wintergreen has Virginia's only high-speed six-passenger lift. For après-ski, the Wintergarden Spa offers thirteen rooms for massage and wraps, saunas, steam rooms, hot tubs, and a Jacuzzi. Sometimes, because of the warm Virginia weather, the slopes can get fogged in. Nonresort guests are also welcome to ski on Wintergreen's slopes and trails or participate in any of the activities for a daily fee.

Nonresort guests may also enroll their kids in the activity programs. These include a year-round Kids in Action, which introduces 2- to 12-year-olds to the wonders of nature in an action-packed day camp, and a summer Kids Campout, for ages 6 to 14.

In fall Wintergreen is glorious as the mountainsides are covered with brilliant red, orange, and yellow foliage. The chairlifts operate for easy and spectacular mountain views. The resort offers nature hikes and craft workshops.

The Copper Mine serves breakfast and in the evening is the resort's signature restaurant. The Devils Grill Restaurant and Lounge at the Devils Knob Golf Course, is a good place for lunch and dinner (closed in winter). The Edge is an informal family restaurant. All Wintergreen's restaurants have children's menus.

Hiking Opportunities

Twenty-five miles of the **Appalachian Trail** cut through Nelson County. Visit www.nelson county.com for information on a dozen hikes and the Nelson County wilderness area.

Wintergreen Resort maintains 30 miles of nature trails; maps are available at the Wintergreen Nature Foundation (434-325-8169), as are guided hikes. Maps are also available at the main check-in desk at the Mountain Inn, Wintergreen's main lodge (800-266-2444).

Another great area hike for families is the **Crabtree Falls Trail,** which is accessible from Highway 56. The moderately difficult hike, 2.5 miles one-way, follows the Tye River before climbing through the mountains. (When my children were young, we made the first overlook our goal and then headed back down.) Our family has always liked the hike for the reward: the waterfall, the highest cascading waterfall east of the Mississippi River. Crabtree Falls descends 1,200 feet in a series of five cascades. The falls are most dramatic in spring and winter when the water is high. In summer the woods are cool and the waterfall pretty enough to be worth the hike.

Other great hikes are Fortune's Cove Nature Preserve Trail, Piney River Railway Trail (also good for bicycling), and Rockfish River Trail near Nellysford. Children will enjoy these trails as they are flat, so there's no climbing involved.

Bicycling

Nelson County is good biking country. Those people with mountain bikes can find challenging terrain in the Blue Ridge hills, and those who want paved, less challenging roads can follow routes mapped by the Nelson County Tourist Information office (434-263-7015 or 800-282-8223). Some routes include a:

22-mile ride along the Blue Ridge Parkway that begins at milepost 16 in Love and continues south to the Tye River;

31-mile loop from Walton's Mountain Museum that crosses rivers and picnicking spots and returns back to the museum;

24-mile loop that starts at Woodson's Mill convenience store on County Road 778.

Wintergreen Resort has a mountain-biking program, complete with guided tours, that includes 16 miles of single track on a mountain and 114 miles of terrain in adjacent George Washington National Forest.

Bicycling cue sheets and suggestions are available from the Nelson County Visitor Center (see For More Information) and by calling (434) 263-7015 or (800) 282-8223.

Walton's Mountain Museum (ages 5 and up)

6484 Rockfish River Rd., Schuyler, between Charlottesville and Lynchburg on Route 617 in Nelson County; (434) 831-2000; www.waltonmuseum.org. Open daily Mar through Nov; closed Easter and Thanksgiving. $.

The characters from *The Waltons* television show were based on real people in Nelson County, one of whom was the show's creator, Earl Hamner Jr. The community has opened this museum, featuring memorabilia from the television show as well as a re-creation of John-Boy's bedroom, the family kitchen, and the Waltons' living room, complete with piano and Philco radio. There's also an exhibit from the Godsey's general store, from which postcards can be stamped "Walton's Mountain." If your kids are familiar with the show or the movies, they may like this place; otherwise, it's too small to create a great deal of interest.

Where to Eat

Despite the fact that Nellysford is a small village, there are a number of dining options.

Basic Necessities, 2226 Rockfish Valley Hwy. (State Highway 151); (434) 361-1766. Open for lunch Tues through Sat, brunch on Sun, and dinner Wed through Sat. This cafe and wine shop offers light lunches, salads, desserts, fresh homemade bread, and other "basic necessities." $$–$$$

Devil's Backbone Brewing Company, 200 Mosbys Run, crossroads of routes 151 and 664, (434) 361-1001, www.dbbrewing company.com. Lunch and dinner Mon to Sat. Sun brunch. Although the casual eatery, serves ribs, seafood, and wraps, the place gains fame for its pizza as well as for its four to six microbrews on tap. The children's menu has pasta, grilled cheese, burgers, and chicken strips ($6). Reserve ahead for a table at this popular place or call ahead to pick up pizza to go.

Vito's Italian Restaurant, 2842 Rockfish Valley Hwy., Nellysford; (434) 361-9170. Italian-American standards like lasagna, pizza, Stromboli, calzone, cheese steaks. Lunch and dinner daily, year-round. $

Where to Stay

The Acorn Inn Bed & Breakfast, 2256 Adial Rd. (Route 634), 2 miles from Nellysford; (434) 361-9357; www.acorninn.com. The Acorn Inn is as laid-back as a stroll on a backcountry road. This bed-and-breakfast eschews fancy antiques, spacious lodgings, and private baths for serviceable pieces in good enough rooms. Owners Kathy and Martin Versluys wanted to create a bed-and-breakfast in the European tradition: a clean space that is affordable. The inn's style is a mixture of Dutch practicality, tasty health food, and low-cost touring. Ten rooms are in a renovated stable, and they are as big as—you guessed it—a horse stall. Though compact, the rooms are brightened with quilts. Shower rooms, one for men and one for women, are down the hall. There are two guest rooms in the main house open seasonally, plus a cottage with a kitchen, bedroom, and bath. Kids under 12 are **free**. $–$$

Crabtree Falls Campground, 11039 Crabtree Falls Hwy., Tyro; (540) 377-2066. Close to Crabtree Falls, this campground features thirty sites and four camping cabins in a canopy of trees beside the Tye River and Lick Branch Creek. Heated bathhouse, rec room with arcade games and a pool table.

Harmony Hill Bed and Breakfast, 929 Wilson Hill Rd., Arrington; (434) 263-7750. A log cabin with 6 rooms with HDTV, air conditioning, and high-speed Internet.

Meander Inn Bed & Breakfast, 3100 Berry Hill Rd., Nellysford; (434) 361-1121 or (800) 868-6116; www.meanderinn.com. This 80-plus-year-old farmhouse sits on forty acres overlooking the Rockfish River. Sit on the front porch, bird-watch, or admire the

Blue Ridge Mountain views. French Provençal dinners available, wine and hors d'oeuvres as well as breakfast included with room. Well-behaved children 5 years and older are welcome.

Orchard House Bed and Breakfast, 9749 Thomas Nelson Hwy., Lovingston; (434) 262-7747; www.orchardhousebb.com. The 5-room Victorian farmhouse is surrounded by the Blue Ridge Mountains and is one of the area's premier apple orchards. Children over 12 are ok and can spend days in the pool or the hot tub.

For More Information

Nelson County Tourist Information: Visitor Center, 8519 Thomas Nelson Hwy. (Highway 29), Lovingston, VA 22949; (434) 263-7015 or (800) 282-8223; www.nelson county.com or www.virginia.org. Visitor center open 9 a.m. to 5 p.m. daily year-round except some holidays.

Lynchburg

Sixty miles south from Charlottesville along Highway 29, Lynchburg nestles in the foothills of the Blue Ridge Mountains on the James River. The city, with a population of 67,000, is known as the City of Seven Hills and was a supply and communications base for the Confederate Army during the Civil War. Recognizing its importance, General Ulysses S. Grant issued orders to General Hunter to move on Lynchburg, leading to the Battle of Lynchburg in June 1864. Hunter's raid remained primarily on the outskirts of the city, and the Confederate forces prevailed, leaving the supply link to Lee's army intact. Two attractions are now open for both older and younger generations: the National D-Day Memorial and Amazement Square, the Rightmire Children's Museum.

Monument Terrace (ages 9 and up)

In the center of downtown at Ninth and Church Streets.

This terraced monument honors soldiers from all of America's wars. If your family isn't up to climbing the 139 steps leading to the Old Court House and the memorial to Lynchburg's Confederate soldiers, take in the splendid view from the bottom of Court House Hill, at Church and Ninth Streets, where there is a statue honoring World War I doughboys.

Point of Honor (ages 9 and up)

112 Cabell St.; (434) 847-1867; www.pointofhonor.org. Open to the public daily. $.

Once a 900-acre estate, the site was named for the duels fought on its lawns. Situated on Daniel's Hill, one of Lynchburg's seven original neighborhoods, the restored mansion overlooks the James River. Point of Honor was built by Dr. George Cabell Sr., the personal physician of Patrick Henry. Christmas at Point of Honor, held the first Sun in Dec, re-creates a federal-style holiday with plantation party decorations (which remain throughout the month), as well as music and refreshments.

Thomas Jefferson's Poplar Forest (ages 9 and up)

West of Lynchburg 1 mile off US 221; (434) 525-1806; www.poplarforest.org. Open daily Apr through Nov, closed Tues and Thanksgiving. $.

This home, designed by Thomas Jefferson and used as his personal retreat, was where Jefferson found the "solitude of a hermit" away from the constant round of visitors at Monticello. In 1806, during his presidency, Jefferson actually helped the masons lay the foundation for this dwelling, which many consider one of his most original creations. A hands-on history pavilion, available in summer (check for exact months), offers kids a chance to experience activities from Jefferson's era, including brick making, building a bucket, and writing with a quill pen. Or they can try on period clothes, or play hoops or ring-toss. Near the museum shop, children can view artifacts in a window display at the archaeology laboratory. There are special events throughout the year, including an Independence Day celebration featuring living-history reenactors, hands-on activities, children's games from Jefferson's era, and the reading of the Declaration of Independence.

Amazement Square, the Rightmire Children's Museum (all ages)

27 Ninth St.; (434) 845-1888, www.amazementsquare.org. Open daily; closed Mon except major holidays and Memorial Day to Labor Day. $.

With four floors of hands-on activities, plus an Amazement Tower with its tangle of pathways, tunnels, and stairs, kids keep busy at this inventive children's museum. In Kaleidoscope, kids can paint on glass walls, create and act out puppet shows, play musical instruments, and dance. In the Big Red Barn preschoolers can milk a life-size cow or snuggle up with a book. Older children can explore electrical circuits, gravity, and velocity in the Science Gallery. In Your Amazing Body, kids can experience a walk-through heart or

Lynchburg **Travel Tips**

For information about African-American history in the Lynchburg area, ask at the visitor center for the free brochure, *Explore Our Legacy: A Guide to African-American Heritage in Lynchburg and Central Virginia*, which contains a brief history and more than twenty points of interest.

compete on virtual bikes. Budding architects design and construct in Once Upon a Building, while curious archaeologists dig and listen to tales at Indian Island. Check out Family Fun Night every second and fourth Sat of the month for reduced admission and extended hours.

Blackwater Creek Natural Area (all ages)
Blackwater Creek Trail; numerous entrances throughout Lynchburg; (800) 732-5821 (Visitor Center). Free.

Take the kids for a stroll or bike ride through the 300 acres that make up the largest of the city's parks. There are 8 miles of paved biking and earthen hiking trails, several picnic sites, and a number of scenic vistas on the way to Percivals Island, across a foot trestle bridge in the James River.

Community Market
Twelfth and Main Streets; (434) 847-1499. Open Mon through Sat until 2 p.m.

The market, which has operated since 1783, still sells fresh seasonal produce on Fri and Sat. It has, however, added ethnic foods and Virginia crafts and has special events, such as food festivals and music competitions, throughout the year.

The Old City Cemetery
Fourth and Taylor Streets; (434) 847-1465; www.gravegarden.org. Open daily, dawn to dusk.

A registered historic landmark, this cemetery's oldest gravestone dates back to 1807. The Confederate Section contains over 2,000 graves of soldiers from fourteen states. The Pest House Medical Museum, the office of Dr. John Jay Terrell, contains items representative of the house's service as the quarantine hospital for Confederate soldiers during the war. Included here are an 1860s hypodermic needle, a chloroform mask (Dr. Terrell was the first in the area to use one), and a surgical amputation kit. On a more genteel note, the cemetery also has a garden of antique roses, a butterfly garden, and a lotus pond. Stop by the Cemetery Center (open daily) to see the Victorian Mourning Museum and for copies of brochures including *A Kids Guide to the Old City Cemetery,* or peek in the windows of the Pest House, Station House, or Hearse House Caretaker's Museums. Audio available for self-guided tours; guided tours for a fee, by appointment.

Legacy Museum of African American History
403 Monroe St.; (434) 845-3455; www.legacymuseum.org. Open Wed through Sun. $.

Situated in a more-than-one-hundred-year-old Victorian house, this museum has a fine collection of historical artifacts, documents, and memorabilia relating to local African-American history and culture, from the first arrival of the African Americans in central Virginia to the present day. Changing exhibits deal with the lives of early town residents, professions and careers, and the churches.

Appomattox Court House National Historical Park

Twenty miles east of Lynchburg and 3 miles northeast of Appomattox on Highway 24; (434) 352-8987; www.nps.gov/apco. Visitor center open year-round, closed some holidays. $.

This village has been restored to the way it looked on April 9, 1865, when General Robert E. Lee surrendered the Army of Northern Virginia to General Ulysses S. Grant, and the nation was officially reunited after a bitter civil war. Three days later the soldiers of the Army of Northern Virginia marched before the Union Army, stacked their weapons, laid down their flags, and headed home. The roads are closed to automobiles, so it's possible to stroll the quiet streets of the village memorialized forever in American history.

The reconstructed courthouse is the visitor center, where exhibits and slide shows can be viewed. Most of the twenty-seven structures on the site can be entered by the public. The parlor of the reconstructed McClean House is where the terms of surrender were agreed upon. In the Plunket–Meeks store, visitors see the products a general store might have sold during the Civil War.

Outside the village are several spots associated with the surrender, including the site of Lee's headquarters, which is northwest of the village and a five-minute walk from the parking lot on Highway 24. There's also a small cemetery just west of the village with the graves of one Northern and eighteen Southern soldiers killed on April 9. A hiking trail and highway connect the locations, and an official handbook for sale in the park describes the events and the village in detail. Park programs show how the war affected the village and the residents' day-to-day activities. Costumed interpreters answer questions in summer.

The National D-Day Memorial

202 East Main St., Bedford; (540) 586-DDAY or (800) 351-DDAY; www.dday.org. Open year-round except Thanksgiving, Christmas, and New Year's Day. $.

The Normandy invasion of June 6, 1944 (also called D–Day), was the largest air, land, and sea landing ever undertaken and included 5,333 ships, almost 11,000 airplanes, 50,000 military vehicles, and more than 154,000 soldiers. More than 6,000 Americans died there. Bedford, Virginia, with a population of 3,200 in 1944, lost nineteen men in the first fifteen minutes of the invasion—the highest per capita loss of any single community in the United States, which is why Bedford was chosen as the site of this memorial.

The memorial, dedicated on June 6, 2001, by President George W. Bush, currently consists of a 44-foot-high granite arch opening onto Victory Plaza, with statuary and flags and a 16-foot story wall with a series of reflecting pools.

Where to Eat

Shakers Good Food & Drink, 3401 Candlers Mountain Rd. (River Ridge Mall); (434) 847-7425. Lunch and dinner daily. Casual atmosphere with soups, sandwiches, and fresh fish; children's menu. $$

Shoemaker's American Grill, Craddock Terry Hotel at Bluffwalk Center, 1312 Commerce St., (434) 455-1500. Serves steaks as well as hamburgers.

Waterstone Pizza, Craddock Terry Hotel at Bluffwalk Center, 1312 Commerce St., (434) 455-1515, serves thin crust pizza as well as paninis.

Where to Stay

Stop by the Visitors' Bureau for a full list of accommodations.

Craddock Terry Hotel at Bluffwalk Center, 1312 Commerce St., (434) 455-1500.; www.craddockterryhotel.com. This boutique hotel located in the up and coming Bluffwalk area offers 44 rooms, many with memorabilia from the building's former life as a turn-of-the-century shoe factory. Room service breakfast, for example, is served on an old-fashioned shoeshine box tray. Kids also like Buster Brown, the hotel's friendly greeter, a wire-haired terrier. $$–$$$.

Hampton Inn, 5604 Seminole Ave.; (434) 237-2704. A full breakfast is included in the room rate of this moderately priced lodging. Shared pool with the Holiday Inn. **Free** coffee and tea available all day long. $

Annual Events

JUNE

River of Time (Batteau) Festivals, mid-June; (434) 528-3950. Replicas of the flat-bottomed merchant boats follow a trade route more than 200 years old from the waterfront at Lynchburg, stopping at various communities along the way. Festivities include music, entertainment, and storytelling at several stops along the way, much of it about African-American, Native American, and Civil War history.

OCTOBER

Railroad Festival, mid-Oct. Downtown Appomattox; (434) 352-2338; www.appomattox.com. A mix of miniature trains, carnival rides, fireworks, arts and crafts, music, food vendors, and parades.

For More Information

Lynchburg Regional Convention and Visitors Bureau, Twelfth and Church Streets, Lynchburg, VA 24054; (434) 847-1811 or (800) 732-5821; www.discoverlynchburg.org. Open daily.

Petersburg

At Petersburg, only 23 miles south of Richmond, the last decisive engagement of the Civil War occurred in 1864, when an important railway link fell to Union forces. Suffering from hunger and bombardments from cannons, the town was under siege for ten months before the campaign ended. Approximately 28,000 Confederate and 42,000 Union soldiers were killed, wounded, or captured during the Petersburg campaign.

Petersburg National Battlefield Visitor Center (ages 8 and up)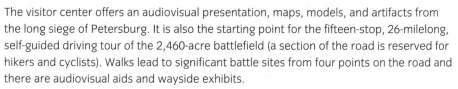
Eastern Front visitor center off Highway 36; (804) 732-3531; www.nps.gov/pete. Open daily except Thanksgiving, Christmas, and New Year's Day. $.

The visitor center offers an audiovisual presentation, maps, models, and artifacts from the long siege of Petersburg. It is also the starting point for the fifteen-stop, 26-milelong, self-guided driving tour of the 2,460-acre battlefield (a section of the road is reserved for hikers and cyclists). Walks lead to significant battle sites from four points on the road and there are audiovisual aids and wayside exhibits.

Probably the most fascinating—and sobering—site is the Crater, a deep depression caused by the explosion that occurred after Union volunteers dug a 500-footlong mine shaft that ended under a Confederate fort and replaced the soil with black powder that they then ignited, killing 278 Confederate soldiers.

At Grant's Headquarters at City Point (804-458-9504), a plantation house has rooms with period furnishings, an introductory video, a diorama, and a bookshop. During the summer, special tours give kids and adults a feel for the battle. At the one-day camp "Earthworks," held in July and Aug, kids dress in uniform, perform marching drills, and create a Civil War camp before turning scientist and performing water tests in a stream and taking part in a geographic scavenger hunt. There's also a National Cemetery and a Visitor Center at Five Forks Battlefield (804-265-8244).

Pamplin Historical Park and the
National Museum of the Civil War Soldier (ages 8 and up)
6125 Boydton Plank Rd.; (804) 861-2408 or (877) PAMPLIN; www.pamplinpark.org. Open daily year-round, closed Thanksgiving, Christmas, and New Year's Day. $$.

This 422-acre historical campus just 30 miles south of downtown Richmond is a combination museum/hands-on experience memorializing an important spot in Petersburg's history: where Union troops commanded by General Ulysses S. Grant broke through the defenses of General Robert E. Lee. The battle that took place on April 2, 1865, led to the evacuation of Petersburg and Richmond and greatly contributed to Lee's surrender at Appomattox Court House one week later, ending the Civil War.

The story of Pamplin Historical Park is an interesting one of strife and Southern redemption. After the war the land passed out of the Boisseau family and was divided into small farms. Robert Pamplin, a Boisseau descendant, was eventually able to buy the land, restore Tudor Hall, and preserve it as a battlefield park.

The park includes four museums, four antebellum homes, costumed living history, and the Breakthrough Battlefield of April 2, 1865. More than 3 miles of interpretive trail winds past well-preserved earthworks (the Fortifications Exhibit), some reaching 8 feet high, and picket posts. Tudor Hall, the Boisseau family plantation, small by manor house standards, has been restored to its mid-19th-century use as a home and military headquarters for South Carolina General Samuel McGowan. The Field Quarter, a depiction of 19th-century slave life, includes two cabins and a collection of outbuildings such as a chicken coop, corn crib, and well house, plus plots where cotton, tobacco, corn, and wheat are grown. One cabin is outfitted as the typical spartan quarters of a field slave; in the other, a video featuring six characters from the late 1850s sharing their opinions on slavery is shown. Included is a planter-class slave-owning woman, a slave, a free black man, a poor Southern farmer who doesn't own slaves, a Connecticut abolitionist, and a Midwestern farmer. This is a very powerful video (the "n" word is used, which may be offensive to some) and it provides an excellent opportunity for families to discuss the issue of slavery and its ramifications in our modern society.

The focal point of the park is the National Museum of the Civil War Soldier, designed to immerse the visitor in the life of an everyday soldier fighting in the Civil War. At the

Amazing
Petersburg Facts

- **Memorial Day.** Local lore credits Petersburg as being the place where Memorial Day got its start. Soon after the Civil War ended, a commander's wife observed schoolgirls placing flowers on graves of defenders of Petersburg at the Old Blanford Church. When she saw them repeat the procedure the following year, she told her husband, and he took measures that subsequently led to Decoration Day, later known as Memorial Day, being observed as a national holiday.

entrance each visitor is given a Soldier Comrade, whose experiences are intertwined with the exhibits. A child's Soldier Comrade is a 13-year-old drummer boy. Both children and adults are given an MP3 player to hear an audio tour of the seven galleries.

Special programs are available for children throughout the historical campus, both in the museum and at Tudor Hall, including impromptu interplay with costumed interpreters, such as the soldiers in the encampment or doctors who practiced Civil War-era medicine (such as it was). There are also supervised day camps throughout the summer, and an overnight Civil War Adventure Camp (http://civilwaradventurecamp.org).

Old Blandford Church and Reception Center (ages 7 and up)
319 South Crater Rd.; (804) 733-2396; www.petersburg-va.org. Open daily year-round except Thanksgiving, Christmas Eve and Day, and New Year's Day. $.

An abandoned church (ca. 1735) used as a hospital during the Civil War, its grounds contain the graves of 30,000 Confederate soldiers. The reception center has exhibits that include Civil War artifacts. The church's Tiffany windows, one of the largest collections in the world, were designed as a memorial to the Confederate dead. Louis Comfort Tiffany's stunning Cross of the Jewels, which he donated to the church (the other fourteen windows were sponsored by the former Confederate states and the local Ladies Memorial Association), is even more awesome when it's illuminated by the setting sun.

Siege Museum (ages 5 and up)
15 West Bank St.; (804) 733-2404. Open daily year-round except Thanksgiving, Christmas Eve and Day, and New Year's Day. $.

It's certainly worth a visit to see the exhibits and an eighteen-minute film of how the citizens of Petersburg lived before and during the ten months they were under siege (the longest any city was under attack in the Civil War). This human side of the war is something that children can particularly understand. (Ask for the printed scavenger hunt for children.) Exhibits show how women hid food, ammunition, and supplies in their hoop skirts. You can also see one of only two revolving cannons ever built.

Where to Eat

Alexander's, 101 West Bank St.; (804) 733-7134. Open Tues through Sat for lunch and dinner. Greek, Italian, and American food. $

Home Place Restaurant, US 1 South in Dinwiddie; (804) 469-9596. Open 7 a.m. to 9 p.m. Southern specialties—chicken, ham, pork, and seafood—are served for dinner in this casual restaurant. Typical breakfast and lunch sandwiches, too. Children's menu available. $

King's Barbeque, 2910 South Crater Rd.; (804) 732-0975. Open 11 a.m. to 8:30 p.m. Closed Mon and Tues. King's has been in business since 1946 offering Southern-style cooking. Locals swear by the barbecue and the fried chicken. $

Steven Kent Family Restaurant, 12205 South Crater Rd. (in the Howard Johnson's); (804) 733-0500. Open daily for breakfast, lunch, and dinner. This casual restaurant serves traditional American fare of burgers, chicken, steak, and pasta. Carryout food is available, too. Children's menu available. $

Where to Stay

Picture Lake Campground, 7818 Boydton Plank Rd. in Dinwiddie; (804) 861-0174. The campground features a thirty-five-acre lake, a swimming pool, and 200 campsites, half of which have full hookups, and six cabins. $

Ramada Plaza, 380 East Washington St.; (804) 733-0000. Outdoor pool, fitness room, full-scale restaurant; continental breakfast included in room rate. $–$$

Roadway Inn, 405 East Washington St. and I-95; (804) 733-1776 or (800) 796-8327. Features 120 rooms, outdoor pool, and continental breakfast included. $

For More Information

Petersburg Visitor Center, 425 Cockade Alley, Petersburg, VA 23803; (804) 733-2400 or (800) 368-3595; TDD (804) 733-8003; www .petersburg-va.org. Open daily. There is also a visitor center at the Carson Rest Area on I-95, open daily. (804) 246-2145.

Richmond

Did you know that George Washington posed for only one statue? You'll find it in Richmond, along with scores of other statues and monuments. The city is, after all, known as the City of Monuments. Once a victim of urban decline, the former Confederate capital, which has been the state capital since 1780, is now restored to its glory days and offers families a wide variety of entertaining and educational possibilities.

Court End (all ages)

Located between Leigh Street or Highway 33 to the north, and Franklin Street to the south.

This is a sightseeing must. Here you'll find seven National Historic Landmarks, three museums, and eleven State Historic Landmarks within an 8-block radius. Obviously, your family may not have the inclination or desire to "see it all." As is always important when traveling with kids, be selective, and allow plenty of time for dallying or unexpected adventures.

Virginia State Capitol (ages 9 and up)
Ninth and Grace Streets, in the heart of the city of Richmond; (804) 698-1788.

The majestic Virginia State Capitol, designed by Thomas Jefferson in 1785, reopened in May 2007 after a $74 million renovation. Guided tours of the grounds reveal myriad statues including the famous life-size statue of Washington by Houdon, said to be a good likeness.

When Jefferson designed the capitol, he was minister to France, and he modeled the building after an ancient Roman temple in Nimes. The historic building houses the oldest law-making body in North America, and the first in the world to function under a written constitution of a free and independent people. Try identifying all eight Virginia-born presidents depicted in sculpture around the rotunda: George Washington, Thomas Jefferson, James Madison, James Monroe, William Henry Harrison, John Tyler, Zachary Taylor, and Woodrow Wilson.

Executive Mansion (ages 10 and up)
Capitol Square; (804) 371-TOUR.

After the capitol, take a stroll of its grounds. On the east, you'll see the oldest continuously occupied governor's mansion in the United States. Visiting hours are limited; call for details.

The Valentine Richmond History Center (ages 7 and up)
1015 East Clay St.; (804) 649-0711; www.richmondhistorycenter.com. Open Tues through Sun year-round. $.

The Valentine Richmond History Center focuses on the life and history of Richmond from the 19th century to the present. See the Settlement to Streetcars exhibit on the history of Richmond, and the 1812 Wickham House on the property. Changing exhibits at the History Center focus on American urban history, using collections of costumes and textiles, prints, and photographs. Driving and walking tours are available.

Virginia Museum of Fine Arts (ages 7 and up)
200 North Blvd.; (804) 340-1400; www.vmfa.state.va.us. Open Wed through Sun year-round. Closed New Year's Day, Fourth of July, Thanksgiving, and Christmas. Donations encouraged. Free.

Currently undergoing a $120-million renovation, it's best to call before your visit, to see which exhibits are open. As the largest art museum in the southeast, the Virginia Museum of Fine Arts is still worth a visit. All ages will be particularly entranced by the jewel-encrusted Fabergé eggs, which were created at the beginning of the 20th century for Russian tsars Alexander III and Nicholas II. Along with Egyptian statues and artifacts and a charming sculpture garden, there's a wide range of art, including colorful contemporary paintings that usually appeal to young children. The museum also has one of the country's best collections of art from South Asia, the Himalayas, and Africa, plus the one-hour Young@Art program on selected Thurs, geared for preschoolers.

Science Museum of Virginia (ages 5 and up)
2500 West Broad St.; (804) 864-1400 or (800) 659-1727; www.smv.org. Open daily except Thanksgiving and Christmas. $.

This is a must for kids. Children are intrigued by the hundreds of permanent and loaned interactive exhibits. Hundreds of exhibits enable kids to bounce as though they are on the moon, test air-pressured hover craft chairs, or explore life science with a five-story DNA strand, a body probe that illuminates the human form, or reel in a giant smallmouth bass. Throughout the year special events such as the Model Railroad Show take place here. Science Saturdays feature hands-on activities in a noon to 4 p.m. session.

The Science Museum also houses the Ethyl IMAX Dome and Planetarium. IMAX films and multimedia planetarium shows are presented in the five-story theater with a tilted-dome screen. Illuminating live theater makes the science even more accessible.

Children's Museum of Richmond (ages 12 and under)
2626 West Broad St.; (804) 474-CMOR or (877) 295-CMOR; www.c-mor.org. Open daily except Thanksgiving, Christmas, New Year's Day, and Easter, and closed Mon Labor Day to Memorial Day except major school holidays. $.

Here kids can crawl under a fish tank, sit in an eagle's nest, wiggle through the human digestive tract, build a dam, turn the gears of a clock tower, tinker in the inventor's lab, experiment with kitchen chemistry, and create a work of art. Focusing on children from birth to 8 years old, this museum gives families a chance to experience things together. Especially fun is the Play House, a child-sized theater with changeable sets, curtains, and costumes for kids to put on their own impromptu performances. The Shadow Play exhibit allows children to have their shadows interact with different screen representations of nature.

Virginia Aviation Museum (ages 7 and up)
5701 Huntsman Rd. in Richmond (exit 47A off I-64), at the Richmond International Airport; (804) 236-3622; www.vam.smv.org. Open daily except Thanksgiving and Christmas. $.

In 1990 the Science Museum of Virginia received this facility as a gift from the Virginia Aeronautical Historical Society. The museum houses vintage aircraft, dioramas on World War II, a special exhibit on Richard E. Byrd, early flight memorabilia, the Virginia Aviation

A Walk along **Monument Avenue . . .**

. . . is a walk into Richmond's past, with statues of Robert E. Lee (at Allen Avenue), J. E. B. Stuart (at Lombardy Street), Jefferson Davis (at Davis Avenue), and Stonewall Jackson (at the Boulevard). What began as homage to the Confederacy was changed forever in 1995 with the addition of a statue honoring Richmond native and tennis star Arthur Ashe (at Roseneath Street).

Richmond and the **Civil War**

As the Confederate capital from 1861 to 1865, Richmond and the surrounding countryside features much Civil War history. Confederate President Jefferson Davis and his family lived in the city during the war at the White House of the Confederacy.

Hall of Fame, and an SR-71 Blackbird. Special events are held here, including Air Fair in June and a Dec celebration of the Wright Brothers' first flight.

Edgar Allan Poe Museum (ages 9 and up)

1914–16 East Main St.; (804) 648-5523 or (888) 21E-APOE; www.poemuseum.org. Open daily Tues through Sun. $.

Older school-age kids familiar with Edgar Allan Poe might enjoy a visit to this museum. Poe, a local boy orphaned at age 2, grew up in Richmond in the home of the Allans. Though he never lived in this 1737 Old Stone House, it is the oldest home in the city, and Poe was surely aware of its existence. Four buildings hold Poe's manuscripts and memorabilia, the largest such collection in the world. The Raven Room features a video of the poem and illustrations by James Carling that were inspired by this chilling tale. The Death Room explores the mystery of Poe's death; it includes a lock of his hair, his walking stick, and the key from his pocket.

Maymont House and Park (all ages)

2201 Shields Lake Dr. (in Byrd Park); (804) 358-7166; www.maymont.org. House, nature center, shop, and cafe open Tues through Sun afternoons. Children's Farm Barn, gardens, and visitor center open daily. Tram rides Tues through Sun; carriage rides Sun, and hayrides June through Aug, Sat and Sun. Suggested donation for Maymont Mansion. Charging for the Nature Center. $.

Although some historic houses leave most kids cold, this will be sure to please because it comes with one hundred acres of grounds dotted with gazebos and planted with a variety of gardens (especially nice are the Japanese and Italian gardens), plus more than 600 animals. At the Nature Center visitors see an otter exhibit and 125 feet of linked aquariums. The visitor center has an indoor cafe, a gift shop, and two Discovery Rooms with computers, microscopes, and wet lab habitats.

Maymont also has a Children's Farm Barn where kids can see (and sometimes feed) piglets, chickens, sheep, donkeys, goats, and cows. Nearby are wilder species, including bison, deer, bobcat, fox, and black bears. An aviary and arboretum complete flora and fauna displays. A Carriage House features late-19th-century horse-drawn vehicles.

This sprawling Victorian estate was purchased by Major James Henry Dooley, a young, self-made millionaire, who built a mansion on the property. An ivory-colored, art nouveau, swan-shaped bed and matching rocker, a grand staircase, and stunning stained-glass windows are just a sampling of the architectural and decorative surprises inside this opulent dwelling. The "Below Stairs" exhibit shows the life of servants who made this lush lifestyle possible.

The American Civil War Center at Historic Tredegar

(ages 7 and up)

490 Tredegar St.; (804) 780-1865. Open daily. $.

During the Civil War, Tredegar, an ironworks factory, manufactured cannons and armored plates for the CSS *Virginia,* the former USS *Merrimack.* The **American Civil War Center,** located on eight acres of the former factory land along the James River, houses a visitor center for the Richmond National Battlefield Park as well as showcases "In the Cause of Liberty." This intriguing exhibit presents the causes and legacies of the Civil War from three perspectives: Unionists, Confederates, and African Americans.

Richmond National Battlefield Park (ages 7 and up)

3215 East Broad St.; (804) 226-1981; www.nps.gov/rich. Open daily dawn to dusk year-round, closed Thanksgiving, Christmas, and New Year's Day. Chimborazo Medical Museum; (804) 226-1981. Civil War visitor center at Tredegar Iron Works, 470 Tredegar St.; (840) 771-2145. Free.

This battlefield park commemorates the four-year struggle for the Confederate capital, the target of seven federal attacks during the Civil War. Richmond's position as a political, medical, and manufacturing hub made it ripe for military takeover; the war that raged here was devastating.

The visitor center offers podcasts (arrange in advance) and sells three-hourlong auto-tape tours that detail the Seven Days Campaign of 1862. The tour covers all 80 miles of the battlefield. Don't, however, do all of this; a little bit goes a long way. Start at the Civil War Visitor Center at Tredegar Iron Works in Richmond on the James River. The center offers exhibits, audiovisual programs, special walking tours, living-history encampments, and other programs throughout the year. At Chimborazo you can see how the wounded and sick were cared for on and off the battlefield. Smaller visitor centers are open at Cold Harbor, where 7,000 of Grant's men were killed or wounded in just thirty minutes, and the Glendale Cemetery Lodge (seasonally). Chickahominy Bluff, Malvern Hill, Fort Harrison, and Drewry's Bluff have interpretive signs and audio stations.

Reconciliation Statue (ages 7 and up)

15th and East Market St., Shockoe Bottom neighborhood.

The Reconciliation Statue, located on Richmond's Slave Trail in the Shockoe Bottom area near the former slave market, depicts two people melded together. The statue, identical to ones in Liverpool, England, and the Republic of Benin, two points of the bustling slave trade, acknowledges the Richmond area's role in the nefarious trade and depicts reconciliation.

The Museum and White House of the Confederacy

(ages 7 and up)

1201 East Clay St.; (804) 649-1861; www.moc.org. $–$$.

The White House of the Confederacy (though it's actually always been painted gray) was home to President Jefferson Davis and his family during the Civil War. After the war all the furnishings were removed and the house was saved from demolition in 1890 by the Confederate Memorial Literary Society. Many of the original furnishings have been returned; the restored mansion is a wonderful example of Victorian style, and not just in decor. It's interesting to note just how close Davis's formal office was to the family's living quarters and how intertwined their political and personal lives were.

Meadow Farm and Crump Park   (all ages)

At Mountain and Courtney Roads in Glen Allen, 12 miles north of downtown Richmond; (804) 501-5520. Open Tues through Sun afternoon; grounds open daily, dawn to dusk. **Free.**

This 150-acre property, a great place to take a break from Civil War history, was donated to the county as a public museum and park in 1975 by the family of the country doctor who practiced and lived here after he inherited the farmhouse and grounds in 1840. Costumed interpreters answer questions, do chores, and cook on open hearths. The house can be toured, too. Don't miss the "floating" balcony attached to a wall on one side only; it's best viewed from the bottom of the stairs. The grounds also include a smokehouse, farrier's shop, barn where tobacco is dried, bird sanctuary, period tool shed, and goose pond.

Pocahontas State Park   (all ages)

Exit 61 off I-95, then go west on Highway 10 to County Road 655, Beach Road; (804) 796-4255. Open daily. Parking fee.

This 7,604-acre park is only 20 miles south of Richmond, but it offers the serenity of Swift Creek and Beaver Lakes and their surrounding forests. Come here to stroll, fish, swim, or hike. The park also offers camping and cabins, along with interpretive programs in the summer, such as guided nature hikes, campfire programs, and children's activities.

Richmond Braves   (ages 5 and up)

3001 North Blvd.; (804) 359-4444 or (800) 849-4627; www.rbraves.com. The baseball season runs from Apr to mid-Sept.

Sports fans can also find something to root for in Richmond. This Triple-A farm team for Atlanta plays at Diamond Stadium. The Richmond Braves have been the top minor-league club in the Atlanta Braves' organization since 1966. Call for schedule and ticket information.

Kings Dominion

Twenty minutes north of Richmond in Doswell (the Doswell/State Highway 30 exit from I-95); (804) 876-5000; www.kingsdominion.com. Open daily from late May until Sept, some weekends in Sept, and for Halloween-themed fun in Oct. $$$.

For pure escapist pleasure, head to movie-themed fun at Kings Dominion, with more than 200 rides, shows, and attractions. Older kids get their kicks on one of fourteen roller coasters with names like Anaconda and Flight of Fear. The newest is Dominator. For more daredevil rides, Hypersonic XLC, the world's first air-launched coaster, throws riders into zero gravity and free-fall sensation, with pneumatic tires and shock absorbers for a smooth ride. A 332-foot replica of the Eiffel Tower provides a panorama of the piedmont.

Younger tots have KidZville, with scaled-down rides perfect for the younger set; and Nickelodeon Central, where they can meet favorite cartoon characters. In the warm weather months, enjoy Water Works, with multiple water slides, a kids' area, and the Lazy River, plus Big Wave Bay, a 650,000-gallon wave pool, and Surf City Splash House, a water-powered fun house.

NIGHTLIFE

Dogwood Dell (all ages)
Byrd Park, Boulevard and Idlewild Avenues; (804) 358-5511.

In summer Richmond hosts its **free** festival of concerts and plays here. Call (804) 646-1437 for the concert schedule.

Theatre IV (ages 3 and up)
114 West Broad St.; (804) 344-8040; www.theatreIVrichmond.org.

Performances run from Oct through May. Reservations recommended. World-class children's entertainment at the Empire Theatre, reputedly the second-largest children's theater in the nation. Theatre IV also owns Barksdale Theatre (1601 Willow Lawn Dr.; 804-282-2620; www.barksdaletheatre.org). Shows here include Broadway, off-Broadway, literary, and new works.

Where to Eat

Bottom's Up Pizza, 1700 Dock St., Shockoe Bottom; (804) 644-4400; www.bottomsuppizza.com. Lunch and dinner daily, music Thurs and Sat nights. Voted best pizza by *Richmond Magazine*. Sourdough crust and all the traditional toppings plus gourmet choices like spinach and portobello. Kids' menu and pizza by the slice, plus sandwiches, salads, and pasta. $

Joe's Inn, 205 North Shield Ave.; (804) 355-2282. Open daily for breakfast, lunch, and dinner. This casual place, in the Fan District, is known for its spaghetti (including a Greek variety, complete with feta cheese) and hearty soups and sandwiches. $

Peking Pavilion, 1302 East Cary St.; Shockoe Slip; (804) 649-8888. Lunch and dinner daily. Try the Hunan chicken, beef and broccoli, sweet and sour chicken, fried rice, or other traditional dishes. $$

Strawberry Street Cafe, 421 North Strawberry St., between Park and Stuart in the Fan District; (804) 353-6860. Open for lunch and dinner Mon through Fri, brunch and dinner on Sat and Sun. Victorian decor, a bathtub turned salad bar, and changing chalk art plus a take-out market next door. Burgers, pasta, crab cakes, quiche, soup, and sandwiches. It's tasty food in an artsy setting at inexpensive prices. $

Where to Stay

Crowne Plaza Hotel River District, 555 East Canal St. near Shockoe; (804) 788-0900; www.crowneplaza.com/RIC-downtown. A 298-room modern hotel overlooking the James River restored Canal Walk and Tredgar Civil War Museum. Indoor pool. $$$–$$$$

Holiday Inn Select, 1021 Koger Center Blvd.; (804) 379-3800 or 800-HOLIDAY. This property has 237 comfortable rooms and an indoor pool. It is located next to Huguenot Park's playground, jogging trails, and tennis courts. $$–$$$$

Omni Richmond Hotel, 100 South Twelfth St.; Shockoe Slip; (804) 344-7000 or (800) THE-OMNI. The Omni is convenient to the Shockoe Slip attractions. Some rooms have great river views and there is an indoor pool. Kids get a goodie bag at check-in and there is a suitcase full of games and books to use. $$–$$$$

Where to Shop

Shops at Carytown, www.carytown.org. A 9-block area along West Cary Street from Thompson Street to the Boulevard with over 200 restaurants, clothing boutiques, bakeries, antiques dealers, bookstores, gift shop, and the historic Byrd Theater that still shows movies at nostalgic discount prices. Restaurants range from French–Vietnamese to New York deli, and there's an annual Watermelon Festival in mid-Aug.

Shockoe Slip, East Cary Street from Twelfth to Fourteenth Streets; www.shockoeslip.org. Kids, especially teens, and adults like walking around the cobblestone streets of this trendy area. Former warehouses now house restaurants, boutiques, and clubs.

Stony Point Fashion Park, 9200 Stony Point Parkway; www.shopstonypoint.com. An open-air mall with a mix of Restaurants include many "firsts" for the Richmond area such as P. F. Chang's China Bistro, Brio Tuscan Grille, and Fleming's Prime Steakhouse and Wine Bar.

Annual Events

MAY–JUNE

Free concerts on Brown's Island at the James River; (804) 788-6466; www.venture richmond.com/events/vrevents.html.

JUNE

Scooper Bowl celebrates the beginning of summer with music, food, children's activities, and entertainment—plus all the ice cream you can eat—at the Science Museum of Virginia; (804) 659-1727.

AUGUST

Down Home Family Reunion; (804) 644-3900. Celebrating African-American folk life.

SEPTEMBER

Annual Rainbow of Arts; (804) 748-1623. Arts and crafts, an Imagination Station for kids, Rockwood Park.

OCTOBER

Second Street Festival; (804) 788-6466; www.venturerichmond.com. Historic Jackson Ward celebrates the heart and soul of Richmond's African-American community with a street festival, including four stages of entertainment, children's activities, dancing, marketplace, and food.

For More Information

You can pick up helpful literature at one of Richmond's two visitor centers, and a wealth of information on the Web site, www.richmond .com/vistors.

Richmond Region Visitor Center, 405 North Third St., Richmond, VA 23219; (804) 783-7450; www.visitrichmondVA.com. Open daily year-round.

Richmond International Airport Visitor Center; (804) 236-3260. Open daily.

Blue Ridge
Highlands

The southwest region of Virginia, from the southwestern tip of the state, stretches in a trianglelike formation from the Cumberland Gap National Historical Park through the George Washington and Jefferson National Forests to Blacksburg and then south to the Virginia–North Carolina border near Galax. This region encompasses some of the prettiest and least-spoiled territory in the state. Although the small towns feature some historical sites and small museums, the outdoors is the big draw for families. Plan to spend most of your time exploring the woods, trails, lakes, and paths of the state parks as well as the George Washington and Jefferson National Forests.

When Daniel Boone arrived here at the end of the 18th century to mark out the Wilderness Road westward to the Appalachian Mountains, the southwest Blue Ridge Highlands was the only frontier known to Americans. Today the Blue Ridge, Allegheny, and Cumberland Mountains still dominate this region. Along with the greenery and spectacular views, you and your family will find the mountain culture alive and well in crafts, country songs, old-time fiddle music, and clog dancing. Summer's interesting festivals, such as the Old Fiddler's Convention (276-236-8541; www.oldfiddlersconvention.com) held in Galax and the Virginia Highlands Festival (800-435-3440; www.vahighlandsfestival.org) held each summer in Abingdon, let you and your kids sample local music and culture.

TopPicks in the Blue Ridge Highlands

1. **Claytor Lake State Park**

2. **George Washington and Jefferson National Forests**

3. **Old Fiddler's Convention,** Galax

4. **Hungry Mother State Park**

5. **Cumberland Gap National Historical Park**

BLUE RIDGE HIGHLANDS

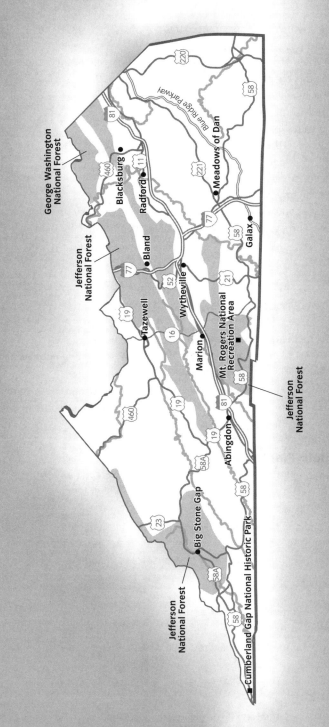

If you're heading southwest or northeast in this region, I-81 provides the shortest route; it's also possible to take the scenic Blue Ridge Parkway south or north to I-77 and proceed until you reach its junction with I-81. The route followed in this chapter is loosely circular, starting at Blacksburg and heading south near Galax and west to Cumberland Gap, then northeast to Breaks and then to Wytheville.

If you're heading south from the Charlottesville area along I-81, you will come to the New River Valley between the towns of Blacksburg and Radford. Although the towns have some historic houses and museums, the real sites are just outside the towns in the scenic countryside. The abundance of state parks and vast expanse of the George Washington and Jefferson National Forests provide great recreational opportunities.

Blacksburg

Located 9 miles off I-81, Blacksburg is a city of 39,000.

Virginia Tech Geosciences Museum (ages 7 and up)
2062 Derring Hall, Virginia Tech Campus; (540) 231-3001; www.geol.vt.edu/outreach/museum .html. Open Mon through Fri 8 a.m. to 4 p.m. Free.

If your kids love looking at minerals, gemstones, or fossils, this museum will entertain them. A working seismograph measures earthquakes, and a life-size skeleton of an allosaur dinosaur towers over the paleontology section.

Historic Smithfield Plantation (ages 7 and up)
1000 Smithfield Plantation Rd.; (540) 231-3947; www.smithfieldplantation.org. Open Thurs through Sun 1 to 5 p.m., Apr through the first week in Dec. Guided tours available. $.

Built in 1775 by Col. William Preston, who named the estate for his wife, Susannah Smith, the plantation, formerly one of the largest west of the Blue Ridge Mountains, was the birthplace of two Virginia governors and the home of another. The manor house features 18th- and 19th-century furniture as well as local items. Tours include a visit to the colonial-style kitchen garden.

Municipal Park (ages 2 to 10)
Located off Patrick Henry Drive; (540) 961-1135.

Highlights here are the Hand in Hand Playground, the Skate Board Park, the Aquatic Center, and an indoor pool.

Bicycling and Hiking
You can pedal or walk along the New River Valley Trail for 39 miles. The former rail bed follows the scenic New River. Call (540) 699-6778. See also the Wytheville section.

Where to Eat

Sub Shack & Pizza, 2767 Market St., Christiansburg; (540) 382-2082. Open daily. Good subs and pizza. $

Zeppoli's Inc., 810 University City Blvd.; (540) 953-2000. Open daily for lunch and dinner. Italian food. $–$$

Where to Stay

Hawthorne Blacksburg, 1007 Plantation Rd.; (540) 552-5636 or (800) 833-1516. All the accommodations are suites with a refrigerator, microwave, and coffeemaker. The property has an indoor pool and serves a complimentary continental breakfast. $$$$

Comfort Inn, 3705 South Main St.; (540) 951-1500 or (800) 228-5150. This motel offers free in-room Internet access and HBO as well as a complimentary continental breakfast. $$$–$$$$

For More Information

Montgomery County Chamber of Commerce, 612 New River Rd., Christianburg, VA 24073; (540) 522-2636; www.montgomerycc.org.

Eastern Divide Ranger District Office, 110 Southpark Dr., Blacksburg, VA 24060; (540) 552-4641. Open Mon through Fri 8 a.m. to 4:30 p.m. While you pick up maps and guidebooks, your kids can grab a pole and fish in the pond or dress up as firefighters, play with puppets, and browse some kid-oriented nature exhibits.

George Washington and Jefferson National Forests

The George Washington and Jefferson National Forests stretch across more than 1.8 million acres from Winchester to Abingdon and also from Breaks Interstate Park running southwest to Pennington. The George Washington National Forest occupies more than one million acres in the northern end, covering the Allegheny, Blue Ridge, and Massanutten mountain ranges. The Jefferson National Forest occupies the southern end of this scenic area.

Don't miss these national forests. The drives and hikes surrounded by thick woods and mountain peaks are good for the soul, especially for work-weary urban dwellers. Kids savor the feel of the woods and the views.

Remember that kids appreciate the unfolding scenic view from the car window; but you need to allow time to get out of the car, even for just a little bit.

Scenic Hikes and Drives in the George Washington National Forest

Here you will find six wilderness areas to explore. With more than 950 miles of trails, you can choose a path that leads to rivers, up mountains, and through dense woods.

Highlands Scenic Tour is a 20-mile-drive on a twisting mountain road.

Amazing
Jefferson National Forest Facts

- **Mount Rogers' Peak:** At 5,729 feet **Mount Rogers** is the highest point in Virginia.
- **Minie Ball Hill** is near Mountain Lake. According to local lore, General George Cook, in his attempt to get by the Confederate troops, was forced to dump a significant amount of ammunition (lead ball bullets) to lighten his load and hasten his flight.

Augusta Springs Wetland Trail, a 0.6-mile, fully accessible, easy loop with a boardwalk, through meadows, forest, and wetlands.

Appalachian Trail cuts through the forest; a portion of the trail leads to Crabtree Falls, a cascading waterfall.

Where to Drive and Hike in the Jefferson National Forest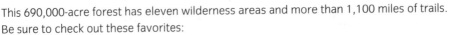

This 690,000-acre forest has eleven wilderness areas and more than 1,100 miles of trails. Be sure to check out these favorites:

Pandapas Pond Trail, located in Montgomery County (540-552-4641), is a 1-milelong loop around an eight-acre pond. Enjoy fishing and canoeing.

Cascades National Recreation Trail is part of the Cascades Recreation area, located in Little Stony Creek Valley (540-552-4641). Four miles long round-trip, this moderate hike offers views of a 66-foot waterfall. This is one of the most popular trails in the forest and can be enjoyed by people of all ages.

John's Creek Mountain Trail, a 4-milelong scenic mountain route.

Two scenic drives are:

Big Walker Mountain Scenic Byway leads 16 miles up the mountain past fishing ponds and old farmsteads to **Big Walker Lookout,** which has a swinging bridge and a lookout tower (open Apr through Oct). (See Wytheville section.)

Mount Rogers Scenic Byway winds through valleys and across ridgetops (see Mount Rogers National Recreation Area).

For More Information

For additional information, call the Forest Supervisor's office, 5162 Valleypointe Parkway, Roanoke; (888) 265-0019 or (540) 265-5100; www.southernregion.fs.fed.us/gwj.

Meadows of Dan

Located off the Blue Ridge Parkway at milepost 177 on US 58, Meadows of Dan is another good point from which to access the surrounding area. From this town, it's also easy to reach Fairy Stone State Park.

Mabry Mill

266 Mabry Mill Rd. Southeast, at milepost 176, where the Blue Ridge Parkway intersects with US 58; (276) 952-2947; www.blueridgeparkway.org. Open from May through Oct.

A primary point of interest in the highlands section of the Blue Ridge Parkway is Mabry Mill, located north of the Meadows of Dan. A restored water-powered gristmill and sawmill that was in operation from 1910 to 1935, the mill now has demonstrations of blacksmithing, tanning, and shoemaking. In the summer on Sun afternoons, there are sometimes bluegrass concerts. Consult the Web site for the schedule.

Fairy Stone State Park

23 miles east of Meadows of Dan. Can be accessed from the Blue Ridge Parkway via US 58 and Highways 8 and 57; 967 Fairy Stone Lake Dr., Stuart; (276) 930-2424; www.dcr.virginia .gov/state_parks/fai.shtml.

The main attraction here is the 168-acre swimming and fishing lake that adjoins Philpott Reservoir. Rowboats, canoes, and paddleboats are available to rent during the summer, and a fishing area is accessible to visitors with physical disabilities. Of course, there are the 14 miles of hiking and biking trails that are open year-round. Kids have fun searching for fairy stones, otherwise known as staurolite stones, a combination of silica, iron, and aluminum. When these minerals crystallize, they create a crosslike structure. Staurolite stones are also found in the mountains of North Carolina and Switzerland, but—supposedly—no place in the world has more staurolite stones shaped so nearly like crosses than Fairy Stone State Park and its vicinity. The visitor center, open weekends throughout the summer, has displays on plant and animal life in the area, as well as on the fairy stone legend. The park has a fairy stone hunt site. Kids are allowed to keep the stones they find. In the summer, guides lead a park treasure hunt for these stones. Guided nature hikes, bluegrass music, and Junior Rangers programs are also available.

The Blue Ridge Parkway (all ages)

This scenic 469-mile parkway (see the chapter on the Shenandoah Valley; 800-228-PARK; www.blueridgeparkway.org) running through the Appalachian Mountains offers scenic views, mountain forests, and pioneer history. Area highlights.

Rocky Knob area, near the intersection of the Blue Ridge Parkway and Highway 8, is a 4,000-acre recreation area with four marked trails. The Rocky Knob Visitor Center, milepost 169, offers information and maps.

The 10-mile Rock Castle Gorge Loop Trail is a strenuous workout that starts out easy with the Hardwood Cove self-guided walking trail, a 0.8-mile easy loop, and with the

The Legend of the **Fairy Stone**

Long, long ago, fairies, naiads, and wood nymphs lived in this forest. One day an elf interrupted the dancing to tell them of Jesus Christ's crucifixion. The news so saddened these sprites that they wept, and when their tears touched the ground, they formed tiny crosses. For many years, these "fairy stones" were considered good luck and protection against witchcraft, sickness, and accidents.

Rocky Knob Picnic Loop, an easy 1-mile walk around the picnic grounds. From there the Gorge Trail goes over Rocky Knob and into the gorge, which is known for its glittering crystalline quartz formations. But be ready—it's an uphill walk back.

Old Fiddler's Convention

Takes place the second weekend in Aug at Felts Park, P.O. Box 655, Galax; (276) 236-8541; www.oldfiddlersconvention.com. All tickets are sold at the gate; no advance tickets. Arrive the weekend before the convention because the park fills up quickly, and book motel reservations many months or even a year in advance. Contact the Galax–Carroll–Grayson Chamber of Commerce or Galax Moose Lodge No. 733 for more information. Galax is located about 43 miles southeast of Meadows of Dan.

Try to attend the Old Fiddler's Convention at least once. This annual festival, billed as the oldest and largest fiddler's convention anywhere, gets you that old-time mountain music. Original tunes and folk songs ring out against the Blue Ridge background. Hear traditional and bluegrass rhythms played on mandolins, banjos, dulcimers, autoharps, and, of course, fiddles. Watch flat-foot dancers (a mountain specialty) stomp in time to the ditties. Half the fun comes from watching the audience. They are down-home and dancing. Fans clog as performers play, and impromptu jam sessions break out in the parking lot and continue until the rooster crows. Musicians and bands compete from all over the world for more than $20,000 in prize money. Since motels book up fast, many of the spectators simply camp in town or at Felts Park. People line up three or four days in advance for these campsites, and it's first come, first served.

Where to Eat

The Squire's Tavern, 155 East Main St., Wytheville; (276) 228-9700. Offers lunch and dinner daily. $$

West Galax Diner, 1011 West Stuart Dr., Galax; (276) 236-0463. Breakfast, lunch, and dinner family style. $

Where to Stay

Doe Run Lodge Resort and Conference Center, Blue Ridge Parkway milepost 189, 10 miles north of Fancy Gap in Patrick County; (276) 398-2212 or (800) 325-6189; www.doerunlodge.com. South of Fairy Stone State Park, Doe Run Lodge offers chalets, a cabin, a small house, and two-bedroom villas equipped with kitchens. A restaurant serves breakfast, lunch, and dinner. There are tennis courts, volleyball, fishing, hiking, an outdoor heated pool, a fully stocked pond, a game room, and a golf course 5 miles away. $$$$

Fairy Stone State Park, off Highway 57; (276) 930-2424. Open Mar through Dec. For cabin or campsite reservations, (800) 933-PARK; www.dcr.virginia.gov/state_parks/fai.shtml. Along with a centrally located bathhouse, there are fifty-one campsites with electrical and water hookups. Eight rustic log cabins with electricity, appliances, basic furniture, kitchenware, and linens are for rent. There are sixteen wood-sided concrete block cabins. All cabins are rented on a weekly basis. $–$$$

Olde Mill Golf Resort, Route 1, Box 84, Laurel Fork, VA 24352; (276) 398-2211 or (800) 753-5005; www.oldemill.net. The focus here is definitely golf. A more relaxed course than those at other more well-known resorts, this could be a good place to teach your kids the game. (Bring your own clubs and call ahead.) Guests stay in two- or four-bedroom cottages equipped with full kitchens or in condominiums. Kids can swim in the indoor pool. Niblicks Restaurant is on the property. $$–$$$$

For More Information

Blue Ridge Travel Association, 468 East Main St., Abingdon, VA 24210; www.virginia blueridge.org.

Radford

About 18 miles southwest of Blacksburg, Radford offers the outdoor activities of Claytor Lake State Park and Bisset Park.

Claytor Lake State Park (all ages)

Take exit 101 from I-81, 4400 State Park Rd. in Dublin; (540) 643-2500; www.dcr.virginia .gov/state_parks/cla.shtml. Open daily year-round.

The lake is the main attraction, and it's big: 4,500 acres, 21 miles long, and 101 miles of shoreline. Boating, swimming, fishing, camping, picnicking, and hiking are some of the activities here. With a valid Virginia fishing license, you can try your luck catching crappie and catfish, walleyes, and largemouth and smallmouth striped bass.

The park stretches over 472 acres and features 3 miles of hiking trails through an oak-hickory forest. The marina rents motor, sail, and rowboats. The visitor center is located in the 1876 Howe House. The center, which is open daily in the summer and fall, has interactive fish and lake ecology exhibits. Park events include a Polar Bear Plunge in early Mar, lake ecology tours in the summer, and an arts and crafts festival in late Aug.

Bisset Park

Off Norwood Street, Radford; (540) 731-3633.

This fifty-two-acre municipal park on the scenic New River sports jogging trails, tennis courts, a swimming pool, playgrounds, and picnic shelters. Available for rent are canoes, kayaks, and tubes.

Where to Eat

BT's, 218 Tyler Ave.; (540) 639-2900. Open daily for lunch and dinner. The eclectic menu features blackened catfish, lemon basil linguine, pork tenderloin, and rib-eye steak. Children's menu available. $–$$

Sal's Italian Restaurant and Pizza, 709 West Main St.; (540) 639-9669. Open daily for lunch and dinner. Specialties are the homemade pasta, especially the spinach ravioli. Children's menu available. $–$$

Spinnaker's, 1501 Tyler Ave., in the Best Western Radford Inn; (540) 639-3000. Open daily for lunch and dinner. Soups, salads, pastas, sandwiches, steak, desserts. Kids' menu. $–$$

Where to Stay

The Best Western Radford Inn, 1501 Tyler Ave.; (540) 639-3000 or (800) 628-1955. The property has seventy-two rooms, an indoor pool, an on-site restaurant (see Spinnaker's), plus a complimentary continental breakfast. $$$$

Claytor Lake State Park, 4400 State Park Rd. in Dublin; (800) 933-PARK; www.dcr.state.va.us/parks. Twelve housekeeping cabins overlook the lake and there are 110 sites in four different campgrounds. Electrical and water hook-ups are available at forty-three sites. $–$$$

Super 8 Motel, 1600 Tyler Ave., Radford; (540) 731-9344. Fifty-eight rooms. $$$–$$$$

Annual Events

JUNE

Family Fishing Tournament and Lake Clean-up Day at Claytor Lake. Kids and parents compete in fishing tournaments and help clean up the lake shore.

AUGUST

Claytor Lake Arts and Crafts Festival, Labor Day weekend; (540) 643-2500. Local and regional craftspeople display jewelry, pottery, woodwork, and other crafts; also offers children's activities.

Radford's Annual Bridge Celebration on the Memorial Bridge over the New River. Food, music, fun, and games.

OCTOBER

Highlanders Festival, mid-Oct. This Scots and Appalachian festival, sponsored by Radford University and the city of Radford, features sheepdog demonstrations, bagpipes, Celtic music, Irish folk tales, crafts, and foods.

For more information about these and other events, call the Radford Chamber of Commerce; (540) 639-2202.

For More Information

Blue Ridge Travel Association, 468 East Main St., Abingdon, VA 24210; www.virginiablueridge.org.

Radford Chamber of Commerce, 1126 Norwood St., Radford, VA 24141; (540) 639-2202; www.radfordchamber.com.

Mount Rogers National Recreation Area

The Jefferson National Forest encompasses some 690,000 acres in western Virginia. Southeast of Abingdon, south of I-81, and west of I-77, the Mount Rogers National Recreation Area is a 114,000-acre section of the forest. The park includes Mount Rogers itself, the state's highest point at 5,729 feet.

Get your bearings as soon as possible because the area covers so much territory. A good start is the visitor center (there is only one in the area). The center dispenses helpful literature and information and the building also serves as a year-round forest ranger headquarters. The bookstore has a good range of nature and children's books.

The recreation area is particularly suitable for families who like to hike. A 60-mile segment of the **Appalachian Trail** runs through the park and is easily accessible from various points, including the visitor center. It's possible to do short segments with young children. Many other well-marked trails wind through the park; ask for literature at the visitor center. Volunteers and park rangers offer interpretive programs on summer weekends at the campsites. Activities might include short walks, slide shows, and environmental education talks.

For More Park Information

The visitor center is at 3714 Highway 16, 7 miles southwest of Marion. Open daily from the end of May to the end of Oct (depending on the weather). Call for information about the recreation area, (276) 783-5196 or (800) 628-7202; or visit the Web site at www .southernregion.fs.fed.us/gwj/mr.

Hikes, Scenic Drives, and Activities

With young children, try the **0.6-mile loop** outside the visitor center, a path that passes small ponds filled with bluegills.

You can't drive to the top of Mount Rogers, but you can hike to the top if your family is reasonably fit and ready for a lengthy outing of moderate difficulty. A 4-milelong trail begins at **Grindstone Campground** (elevation 3,600 feet), on Highway 603, 6 miles west of Troutdale.

Drive to the summit of **Whitetop Mountain** for panoramic views. On a clear day you can see Tennessee and Grandfather Mountain in North Carolina.

Virginia Creeper Fly Shop, 17172 Jeb Stewart Hwy., Abingdon; (276) 628-3826. Open Mon through Sat. This outfitter has guided fly-fishing trips.

Llama treks, Treasure Mountain Farm, Abingdon; (276) 944-4674. These are great ways to hike into the heart of the woods without the burden of carrying gear because the llamas do it for you. Kids love learning to lead these animals.

Grayson Highlands State Park (all ages)

On Highway 58, either 35 miles southeast of Abingdon, or 31 miles south of Marion via Highway 16; 829 Grayson Highland Lane; (276) 579-7092; www.dcr.virginia.gov/state_parks/gra.shtml. The visitor center is 4.5 miles from the entrance off Highway 58. Open daily from Memorial to Labor Day and weekends only until mid-Oct. Reopens weekends May 1.

Adjacent to the Mount Rogers National Recreation Area, Grayson Highlands State Park's 4,935 acres in the Appalachian Mountains afford vistas of rugged alpine scenery.

Along with helpful information, the visitor center (located near the summit of Haw Orchard Mountain) has a number of interesting mountain-life displays, such as arrowheads, farm tools, a weaving loom, and a fiddle belonging to a well-known local mountain musician. Crafts are available for sale at the Mountain Crafts Shop. On summer weekends the center might have a quilting demonstration, an autoharp player, or other mountain cultural activities.

The park appeals to families for a number of reasons, including its manageable size and interpretive programs. The park's nine hiking trails average 1 mile in length, just long enough for young kids to feel accomplished without feeling cranky. Some trails lead to waterfalls, some to vistas, and some to a 200-plus-year-old pioneer cabin. Follow the **Rhododendron Trail,** 0.5-mile from the Massie Gap parking area, and you link up with the **Appalachian Trail,** which stretches from Maine to Georgia. With limited time, hike the one mile Appalachian Spur trail loop. The hearty can hike the Appalachian Trail across Mount Rogers, which at 5,729 feet is the highest point in Virginia.

Take time at the picnic grounds, about 2.5 miles from the visitor center, to view two log cabins, a spring house, and a cane mill. During the summer months check out the interpretive programs held Fri through Sun in the amphitheater at the general campground. Themes might include music, edible plants, or wildflowers. A popular activity here from mid-July to about Sept 1 is picking blueberries (so bring along containers). Also take note that although there are no central swimming areas, there are numerous creeks where you can get wet. There are nearly 10 miles of streams for wild trout fishing. (A Virginia state fishing license is required.) The park also has excellent horse trails, and

Amazing
Grayson Highlands State Park

- **Massie Gap.** Many places in the park are named after pioneers in the region, including Massie Gap, named after Lee Massey, an early settler who lived in the gap in the late 1800s with his wife and five children.

- **Wilburn Ridge.** Wilburn Ridge is named after fearless bear hunter and wolf trapper Wilburn Waters, who triumphed over both creatures in these woods.

horses can be rented from Appalachian Outdoor Adventures (540-579-9431; www.appala chianoutdooradventures.com), which also offers horseback riding tours of the park.

Where to Eat

See restaurants listed for Marion, page 175.

Where to Stay

Grayson Highlands State Park; (276) 579-7092. The park has two campgrounds, one for horseback riders with their own horses (available on a first-come basis) and another for the general public. There are 165 camp-sites. Reserve online, www.dcr.state.va.us/parks, or call (800) 933-PARK. $–$$

Grindstone (on Highway 603, 6 miles west of Troutdale) and **Beartree Campgrounds** (7 miles east of Damascus on Highway 58), in Mount Rogers National Recreation Area, both offer a playground (swings and slides). Beartree has the only swimming facilities, on a fourteen-acre lake complete with a sandy beach (but no lifeguards). Two other camp-sites are in the NRA, Blue Springs and Sunrise Cabins. There are four campgrounds available for horseback riders. Open spring through Dec 1. $–$$$

Comers Rock and Raven Cliff camp-grounds are also family friendly and have several trails nearby such as the **Comers Rock Overlook** and **the Raven Cliff Fur-nace Trail** which takes you to an iron ore furnace from the early 1800s. **Hussy Moun-tain** and **Collins Cove Horse Camps** are also on the "east end" of the park providing camping areas close to the Virginia Highlands Horse Trail.

Annual Events

For information on all of these events, call the Grayson County Tourist Information Center at (276) 773-3711.

MARCH

Whitetop Mountain Maple Festival, held the last weekend in Mar in Whitetop, fea-tures music, crafts, storytelling, and tours of the maple-tapping area and sugar house.

MAY

The highlight of the **Whitetop Mountain Ramp Festival,** the third Sun in May in Whitetop, is a competition to see who can eat the most ramps, which are wild onions that grow in the surrounding mountains. Enjoy music, crafts, games, dancing, and lots of barbecued chicken.

JUNE

Wayne C. Henderson Music Festival, third weekend in June at Grayson Highlands State Park; (276) 579-7712. A guitar competi-tion and bluegrass mountain music concert.

Grayson County Fiddlers Convention takes place on the fourth Sat of the month.

SEPTEMBER

Grayson Highlands Fall Festival, the last full weekend in Sept. Features molasses, apple-butter, and cider making; live mountain music; dancing; a wild pony sale; crafts; and lots of food.

OCTOBER

Mountain Foliage Festival, second Sat in Oct, at the historic 1908 Courthouse Sq. in the town of Independence. Famous for its unique Grand Privy Race, where people race their specially designed outhouses for the coveted Chamber Pot Trophy, plus food, a parade, games, crafts.

Haunted Hayride at Grayson High-lands State Park, Country Store in the

Campground; (276) 579-7092. Hop aboard the tractor-drawn hayride for a scary journey through the park. Hot cider, s'mores, snacks and games are available.

For More Information

Blue Ridge Highlands Regional Information and Visitor Center, 975 Tazewell St., Wytheville, VA 24382; (800) 446-9670; www.virginiablueridge.org.

Grayson County Tourist Information Center, 107 East Main St. in the Historic 1908 Courthouse, Independence, VA 24348; (276) 773-3711.

Marion

Marion, a town of some 7,000 people directly off I-81, is a popular vacation base because of its proximity to Mount Rogers National Recreation Area, Grayson Highlands State Park, and Hungry Mother State Park.

Hungry Mother State Park (ages 2 and up)

Four miles north of Marion on Highway 16, 2854 Park Blvd.; (276) 781-7400 or (800) 933-PARK; www.dcr.virginia.gov/state_parks/hun.shtml. Open year-round. Obtain information at the main office at the park entrance.

Hungry Mother, a 2,215-acre state park, is a particular favorite with families, especially because of its 108-acre lake. In the heart of the mountains, the lake has a sandy beach; a bathhouse; paddleboat, canoe, kayak, and rowboat rentals; and what many people consider to be the best northern pike fishing in the state. Bicycles are also for rent.

The park offers more than 12 miles of trails—it would be a shame not to do at least one hike. For a fairly flat and easy walk, try the **Lake Trail,** which runs for 3 miles along the lakeshore. The 1.1-milelong **Middle Ridge Trail** and the 0.7-mile **Ridge Trail** are more challenging and afford some nice mountain views.

The park's interpretive programs, offered in mid-June through Labor Day, with weekend programs in the fall, are so good that they are one of the reasons this park is popular with families. The offerings might include an interpretive horseback ride; guided nature hikes; a "Critter Crawl," in which kids search for stream creatures such as salamanders and frogs; music, crafts, and local history; and nocturnal programs such as night hikes and star gazing. In addition, there are Junior Naturalist programs for older kids and Wee Naturalist programs for ages 2 to 5. In summer guided canoe tours are offered twice weekly at the lake. (Children at least 3 years old can participate with a parent.) Weekend programs are held in Sept and Oct. Check at the visitor center for schedule, and visit the Discovery Center exhibits while you're there. The park hosts a three-day arts and crafts festival

What's in a **Name?**

How the park got its unusual name is a sad, but interesting, story. The most generally accepted legend is that a young boy named Adam and his mother, Molly, escaped from an Indian raid and wandered through the woods. When hunger set in, they searched for berries, but eventually Molly collapsed next to a small stream. Adam went for help. Hungry and exhausted upon reaching the next settlement, he could only get out the words "hungry mother." When a search party found Molly's body in the creek, they named it Hungry Mother Creek in her honor. Later, when the creek was dammed to make a lake, it was named Hungry Mother Lake. A trail that goes to the highest section in the developed area of the park is called **Molly's Knob.**

on the third weekend of July that features about 125 artisans with wares from toys to stained glass to paintings. The festival attracts about 15,000 people.

Where to Eat

The Apple Tree Restaurant and Gift Shop, Highway 16 South; (276) 782-9977. Open for breakfast, lunch, and dinner. Sandwiches, burgers, and pasta. $

The Restaurant at Hungry Mother State Park; (276) 781-7421. Open for lunch and dinner. Hours vary season to season, so call ahead. This facility has three dining rooms overlooking the lake and a gift shop. $$

Where to Stay

Best Western Marion, 1424 North Main St.; (276) 783-3193 or (800) 528-1234. More than one hundred rooms, an outdoor pool, and a restaurant. $$–$$$

Fox Hill Inn, 8568 Troutdale Hwy.; 20 miles south of Marion via Highway 16, Troutdale; (276) 677-3313 or (800) 874-3313; www .bbonline.com/va/foxhill. Fox Hill sits on a mountaintop with panoramic views. Spread out on seventy acres of woods and pastureland, this lodging offers only six rooms and two suites, so be sure to reserve in advance.

Guests are offered the use of the kitchen to cook their meals. Kids enjoy the farm animals and the easy hiking trails on the property and in nearby Mount Rogers. There are no phones or television in the rooms, but the sitting room has a television. A full breakfast is included in the rates, and a mom-and-pop diner is 2 miles away in Troutdale. Cribs are **free.** $$$–$$$$

Hungry Mother State Park, Highway 16; (800) 933-PARK for reservations; www.dcr .state.va.us/parks. Twenty rental cabins are available from Mar 1 through Nov. During spring and fall, cabins may be rented for a two-night minimum; during summer they are available by the week only. There are four campgrounds within a few miles of the entrance; two have water and electric hookups, one is for tents only, and another has water, electricity, and sewer. All have bathhouses with hot showers. $–$$$$

For More Information

Chamber of Commerce of Smyth County, P.O. Box 924, Marion, VA 24354; (276) 783-3161; www.smythchamber.org.

Abingdon

Abingdon, chartered in 1778, is the oldest town west of the Blue Ridge Mountains and has been designated a Virginia Historic Landmark. Located 133 miles southwest of Roanoke (from I-81, take exit 17 into town), it is a cultural hub and home to some 10,000 residents. Abingdon is well known for its heritage crafts, and even kids who hate shopping might not mind browsing—or buying—here. The simple charm of the handcrafted dolls and toys especially appeals to the younger set.

Barter Theatre, State Theatre of Virginia (all ages)

133 West Main St., P.O. Box 867; (276) 628-3991; www.bartertheatre.com. Performances from Feb through Dec.

One of Abingdon's premier attractions is this theater. Founded in 1933 (when the admission price was "35 cents or the equivalent in produce"), Barter claims fame as one of the oldest professional resident theaters in the United States. Noted for the caliber of both its productions and performers, Barter stars have included Gregory Peck, Hume Cronyn, Patricia Neal, Ernest Borgnine, Barry Corbin, Jerry Hardin, and others. During its season Barter performs on three stages: Barter Theatre Main Stage, Barter Stage II, and the Player Company for young people. Barter also offers workshops for kids. It also has a ghost: Actors have reported seeing the ghost of founder Robert Porterfield on opening nights, sitting in the audience in his white dinner jacket.

Pinnacle Natural Area Preserve

Northeast of Lebanon, near State Routes 640 and 721. For additional information, contact Hungry Mother State Park; (276) 781-7400.

Pinnacle takes its name from the dolomite rock formation that rises 600 feet in this sixty-eight-acre preserve. Trails lead you through fern grottoes and thickets of tall white-cedar trees along the Clinch River's rushing waters. In the clear water you might see the mussels that feed in the river.

If you and your kids are good swimmers, consider snorkeling the **Clinch River.** The river offers a variety of depths and lots to see, including seventy-one species of fish and nineteen species of mussels. The preserve may be closed on occasion for resource protection or management activities, so it's a good idea to call first.

Virginia Creeper National Recreation Trail

Trail begins near the corner of Green Springs Road and A Street. Look for the locomotive that was the last steam engine on the Virginia Creeper Railroad. For more information call the Abingdon Convention and Visitors Bureau, (276) 676-2282 or (800) 435-3440; Mount Rogers National Recreation Area, (276) 783-5196 or (800) 628-7202; www.vacreepertrail .com.

Now a multipurpose recreational trail, the **Virginia Creeper Trail** starts in Abingdon and extends southeast for 34 miles to Whitetop Station at the Virginia–North Carolina border.

A **free** brochure with a map of the trail is available at the Abingdon Convention and Visitors Bureau.

This scenic trail, a former Native American path, was used by pioneers and Daniel Boone. At the end of the 19th century, the trail was a mountain railroad that received its nickname, Virginia Creeper, from the early steam locomotives that struggled slowly up the railroad's steep grades. Now the railroad bed serves as a path for walkers, bikers, hikers, joggers, and equestrians and is off-limits to motorized vehicles. The trail eventually enters Mount Rogers National Recreation Area. You don't have to go too far to enjoy the trail's scenic splendor. Near the trail's beginning, you'll pass farmland and go over a small mountain range and creeks.

Special Tours

With **Abingdon Spirit Tours & Stars in the Sky Storytelling** you can take a spooky walk with the "Mistress of Haints" to learn about Abingdon's ghosts and haunted places or stroll through Abingdon's Civil War history. Reserve ahead. Call (276) 676-0849.

Shuttle Service and Bike Rental 🚲

Blue Blaze Shuttle Service and Bike Rentals, 227 West Laurel Ave.; (276) 475-5095 or (800) 475-5095; www.blueblazebikeandshuttle.com. To fully explore the wilderness, you may want to take a transport service for bikers and hikers that gets you and your gear to high-country trailheads, including the Virginia Creeper. Bikes (including kid-size ones) can be rented by the hour (two-hour minimum) or day, helmets and water bottles included. And you can bring your dog—on a leash. Blue Blaze sponsors night rides to Whitetop Station on the Sat closest to the full moon, May through Sept.

Mount Rogers Outfitters, 110 West Laurel Ave.; (276) 475-5416; www.mtrogersoutfitters .com. Experienced backpacking guides for all parts of Mount Rogers National Recreation Area.

Where to Eat

Alison's, 1220 West Main St.; (276) 628-8002. Famous for their baked potato soup and ribs. $–$$

Gages Restaurant, 309 Falls Dr.; (276) 525-1610; www.fallsplaza.com/gagesrestaurant. A Southwest Virginia eatery serving lunch, dinner, and weekend brunch in Falls Plaza. $

The House on Main, 231 West Main St.; (276) 619-0039; www.houseonmain.com. Open Tues through Sat for lunch and dinner. The restaurant offers casual dining. $$$–$$$$

The Tavern, 222 East Main St.; (276) 628-1118. Built in 1779, the Tavern is Abingdon's oldest building. German and American fare. $$–$$$

Withers Hardware Restaurant, 260 West Main St.; (276) 628-1111. Originally a hardware store, this restaurant offers lunch and dinner at good prices. $–$$

Where to Stay

Abingdon's Martha Washington Inn, A Camberley Hotel, 150 West Main St.; (276) 628-3161 or (888) 888-5252; www.martha washingtoninn.com. A Historic Hotel of America, this inn creates a 19thcentury élan with its antiques and period furnishings. Daily

For More **Accommodation Information**

The **Blue Ridge Bed and Breakfast Reservation Service,** (540) 955-1246 or (800) 296-1246. This service can help you find a bed-and-breakfast inn in the surrounding area that welcomes families.

afternoon tea is served in the lobby or on the veranda; traditional and continental fare for breakfast, lunch, and dinner is available. There are sixty-two rooms and suites. $$$$

Alpine Motel, 882 East Main St.; (276) 628-3178. The motel is set back off the road and has views of the state's two highest mountain peaks, Mount Rogers and Whitetop. $$$$

Four additional motels/hotels offering moderately priced accommodations are:

Comfort Inn, I-81 at exit 14; (800) 221-2222 or (276) 676-2222.

Days Inn, I-81 at exit 19; (276) 628-7131.

Hampton Inn, 340 Commerce Dr.; (276) 619-4600 or (800) 426-7866. The inn has an outdoor pool and gives a complimentary breakfast.

Holiday Inn Express, I-81 at exit 19; (276) 676-2829 or (800) 465-4329. Newly renovated.

Summerfield Inn Bed and Breakfast, 101 West Valley St.; (276) 628-5905 or (800) 668-5905; www.summerfieldinn.com. Located in Abingdon's historic district, Summerfield, a property built in 1921, features a library, wraparound porch, rockers, and private baths. A full breakfast is included in the room rate. $$$

Where to Shop

The Cave House Craft Shop, 279 East Main St.; (276) 628-7721. This nonprofit

130-member cooperative is housed in a landmark Victorian home and features traditional and contemporary crafts.

Abingdon's downtown district, along West Main Street, also has a nice selection of collectibles and antiques shops.

Annual Events
JULY–AUGUST
Virginia Highlands Festival, from the end of July through the first two weeks of Aug; (276) 676-2282 or (800) 435-3440; www.vahighlandsfestival.org. One of the top twenty events in the Southeast, the Virginia Highlands Festival is a showcase of arts and crafts, antiques, music, photography, storytelling, and living-history reenactments.

SEPTEMBER–OCTOBER
Washington County Fair. Call Abingdon Visitors Bureau for information; (276) 676-2282 or (800) 435-3440. You'll find a mix of country music, carnival rides, and displays of prize animals at this county fair/festival.

For More Information
Abingdon Convention and Visitors Bureau, 335 Cummings St., Abingdon, VA 24210; (276) 676-2282 or (800) 435-3440; www.abingdon.com/tourism. The visitors bureau has maps, information, and a brochure outlining a self-guided walking tour of Abingdon's 20-block historic district.

Cumberland Gap

Cumberland Gap National Historical Park

On US 25 East and Highway 58 South; (606) 248-2817; www.nps.gov. The visitor center, located at the US 25 East entrance, is open daily. Closed Christmas and New Year's Day.

An introductory film provides background on Daniel Boone and the pioneers who ventured over the gap. The exhibits, mostly from the pioneer era, include bearskin rugs and rifles. The museum displays a few war items as well.

The **Cumberland Gap National Historical Park** encompasses 20,305 heavily forested acres southeast of Middlesboro, Kentucky. The park, which includes parts of Virginia and Tennessee, traces Daniel Boone's pioneering trail. In 1750 Dr. Thomas Walker discovered an Indian footpath, and in 1769 Boone passed through the gap with a hunting party, eventually blazing what became the Wilderness Road in 1775. Despite the fact that the gap was a horse path until 1796, and no wagons passed, more than 200,000 people came through the gap, venturing into Kentucky and westward. A strategic point during the Civil War, this area changed hands four times, though no major battle was fought.

The park's approximately 70 miles of trails range from easy to strenuous. With younger kids, you needn't venture farther than the visitor center. Park officials call the nearby 2-mile Fitness Trail a "walk through the woods." If tired, you can cut back to the center after 0.75 mile.

One literal high point in the park is **Pinnacle Overlook**, elevation 2,440 feet. Follow the park road for 4 miles (you must walk the last 100 yards). The drive to reach the Pinnacle Overlook is a 4-mile mountain route of hairpin turns. Go slowly and be sure your kids can stomach the twists. Those who can are rewarded (on a clear day) with an impressive view of parts of three states: Kentucky, Tennessee, and Virginia. When park staff is available, shuttles to the overlook can be arranged for a nominal fee.

Another highlight, especially for young grade-school children, is the **Hensley Settlement.** This site is most easily reached by a shuttle service that requires reservations on the weekend. Otherwise, this site is reached by four-wheel-drive vehicle or by a one-day hike. (The road is not passable by regular vehicles.)

The Hensley community existed on this site from 1904 to 1951. The original buildings include log houses, barns, and outbuildings. Although fairly contemporary, the settlement resembles one of the pioneer era. During the summer, park volunteers stay at the settlement to act as guides. Families can visit chestnut-hewn cabins and learn about the self-sufficient lifestyles of the original inhabitants.

Summer also brings some interesting interpretive programs given by a park ranger who dresses in period clothing. Learn about the Civil War and being a long hunter (the correct term for what Daniel Boone did for a living). Programs may include hiking a trail to a beaver dam and campfire activities. Some activities require reservations. Call (606) 248-2817.

Carter Family **Memorial Music Center**

A. P. Carter Highway, P.O. Box 111. Hiltons, VA 24258. Take US 58 West to Hiltons, then turn right onto County Road 614 East for 3 miles; (276) 386-9480; recorded information (276) 386-6054; www.carterfamilyfold.org. Admission. If you're driving to Big Stone Gap from Abingdon, consider timing your trip so you can partake of some down-home evening entertainment. The Carters claim to be country-music pioneers whose family recorded more than 300 songs from 1927 to 1942, one-third of them written by patriarch A. P. Carter. At the music center you and your family will get into the toe-tapping rhythms of the bluegrass and country bands. Often locals head to the small dance floor to do popular mountain dances, such as clogging. Join in if you know how. Tickets are reasonably priced and kids under 6 are admitted **free.** Come the first Sat in Aug for the annual festival, which attracts music groups, artisans, and clog dancers.

Where to Eat

Webb's Country Kitchen, 602 Colwyn Ave., Cumberland Gap, TN; (423) 869-5877. Closed Mon. A short distance northwest of the park, Webb's serves a large variety of fare. Children's menu. $

Where to Stay

The Wilderness Road Campground, located off Highway 58 in Virginia; (606) 248-2817. Available year-round. This facility has 160 campsites on a first-come basis that are available for tent, trailer, and RV campers. There are electrical hookups, as well as hot showers and potable water. Backcountry campsites are located throughout the park and require a backcountry use permit, which must be picked up at the visitor center. $–$$$

For More Information

Blue Ridge Highlands Regional Information and Visitor Center, 975 Tazewell St., Wytheville, VA 24382; (800) 446-9670 or (606) 248-2817; www.virginiablueridge.org.

Big Stone Gap Area

Big Stone Gap (all ages)
Located at the junction of three forks in the Powell River.

Big Stone Gap, northeast of Cumberland Gap on US Highway 23, forms a pass that goes through Stone Mountain. The setting inspired the novel of the early 1900s, *The Trail of the Lonesome Pine,* by John Fox Jr. This tragic love story (based on a true event) details the changes in mountain life after the discovery of coal and is told through the eyes of the young June Tolliver.

June Tolliver House and Folk Art Center (all ages)

Jerome and Clinton Streets; (276) 523-4707 or (800) 362-0149. Open Tues through Sat; closed major holidays. House is free. Fee for drama.

An outdoor musical drama with the same name as the novel (see above), entertaining for families with kids, is held in the summer at the playhouse. At the adjoining folk art center, you can buy such items as coal carvings and hand-made dolls and quilts. The period rooms in the house where the drama's heroine actually lived are open to the public.

John Fox Jr. Museum (ages 9 and up)

117 Shawnee Ave.; (276) 523-2747 or (800) 362-0149. Open the Wed following Memorial Day through the Sun before Labor Day, Wed through Sun. $.

If you see the play about June Tolliver, it may pique your family's interest into visiting the author's rambling, two-story home which now houses this museum. The property is furnished as it was during the time of the Fox family.

Harry W. Meador Jr. Coal Museum (ages 9 and up)

East Third Street and Shawnee Avenue; (276) 523-9209. Open year-round Wed through Sun. Free.

Located in a historic building, this museum details the history of the region's coal mining—past and present—using artifacts such as a shuttle car, crank calculator, and hundreds of old photos.

Southwest Virginia Museum Historical State Park (ages 7 and up)

Downtown on West First Street and Wood Avenue; (276) 523-1322; www.dcr.virginia.gov/state_parks/sou.shtml. Open from Mar through Dec; Memorial Day through Labor Day open daily; after Labor Day through Dec, open Tues through Sun. $.

The museum, located in the former home of a state attorney general, was built during the 1880s. It's dedicated to the area's early settlers and the coal boom period of the 1890s and features four rotating exhibits per year. Displayed items (from a collection of 20,000) include Indian artifacts and handmade quilts, a century-old gun collection, and mining memorabilia. The museum staff also conducts a variety of programs to educate the public about the area's heritage. In Oct there's Appalachian Ghost Storytelling. A Festival of Trees, with seventy-five decorated Christmas trees, is featured mid-Nov through late Dec.

Natural Tunnel State Park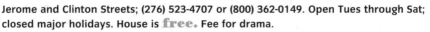

18 miles southeast of Big Stone Gap on US 23. At Duffield travel 4 miles west on Route 871; (276) 940-2674; www.dcr.virginia.gov/state_parks/nat.shtml. The chair lift is open daily Memorial Day through Labor Day; in May, Sept, and Oct on weekends only; closed Nov through Apr. Picnic facilities and the swimming pool are open from Memorial Day through Labor Day. Tunnel tours start at the visitor center and lead to the mouth of the tunnel. $$.

As the name suggests, this state park is centered around an enormous natural tunnel. The tunnel's formation began more than a million years ago in the early glacial period, when groundwater containing carbonic acid crept through crevices, gradually dissolving the surrounding bedrock of limestone. Then, geologists believe, what's now Stock Creek was diverted underground to continue the carving process over many centuries. In 1890 the South Atlantic and Ohio Railroad arrived and laid tracks through the tunnel. The railroad still passes through today. Later acquired by the Commonwealth of Virginia, the tunnel, which is about 850 feet long and 100 feet in diameter, along with 850 acres now make up the focal point of this popular park.

Take a chair lift (located right next to the visitor center) to see the sights or opt for one of the many hiking trails. Within a mile or two of the visitor center, there are picnic facilities (shelters can be reserved in advance), an Olympic-size swimming pool, a large bathhouse, and a concession building. Seven walking trails—the longest is only 1.1 miles—allow for short strolls. The most popular trail follows the rim of the cliff from the visitor center to **Lover's Leap,** 0.3 mile away.

Interpretive programs, generally held at the campground on summer weekends, emphasize local culture, with presentations on basket-weaving, blacksmithing, and environmental science. Evening campfire talks feature local folklore and, sometimes, night hikes. The Cove Ridge Center has eight dormitory rooms, an auditorium, and a library with computers designed to accommodate groups and classes. Ask about the park's cave tours and geology workshops.

Breaks Interstate Park

Located on State Highway 80 off I-460; (276) 865-4413 or (800) 982-5122; www.breakspark
.com. Open Apr 1 to Dec 21.

Pick up brochures as well as information on special events at the entrance gate. Less than a 0.5-mile away is the visitor center, where you can get maps of the park's thirteen trails. You'll also see exhibits on the surrounding area's culture and natural habitats. The park is jointly administered by Kentucky and Virginia.

Amazing
Natural Tunnel State Park Facts

- **Daniel Boone** was probably the first white man to see the tunnel.
- **Lt. Col. Stephen H. Long.** The first written account of the tunnel was by Lt. Col. Stephen H. Long in a geology journal in 1832.
- **Wonder of the World.** William Jennings Bryan dubbed the tunnel "The Eighth Wonder of the World."

This park occupies 4,600 acres on the Kentucky–Virginia border at the eastern edge of the Cumberland Mountain Plateau. Visitors come here to see what some have dubbed the "Grand Canyon of the South." At this site the Russell Fork of the Big Sandy River has cut a 1,600-foot-deep gorge through Pine Mountain.

Breaks Canyon is the park's highlight. A paved road leads through a forest of evergreens to the rim of this beautiful canyon. Here, from four different overlooks, you'll be treated to superb views of the gorge, springs, caves, and rock formations—such as the **Towers Overlook,** a 0.5-mile pyramid of rocks—as well as a blossoming array of colorful rhododendron. A recreational area just a short distance from the entrance sports an Olympic-size swimming pool (open Memorial Day through Labor Day), a playground, and a concession stand for snacking.

Laurel Lake is not suitable for swimming. But there are paddleboats, and fishing is allowed. Bluegills and bass are what anglers hope to catch. Obtain a fishing license at the visitor center. Horseback trail rides are available (weekends only after Labor Day) and pony rides for the little ones, plus there are 2 miles of bike trails. Among the annual special events that stand out are a summer arts and crafts fair and the Autumn Gospel Song Festival on Labor Day weekend, which is the region's biggest song festival.

Where to Eat

Rhododendron Restaurant, Breaks Interstate Park, Highway 80; (276) 865-4413 or (800) 982-5122. Open from Apr 1 through Dec 21, serving breakfast, lunch, and dinner. The restaurant serves basic fare such as steak, pasta, salads, and hamburgers. Children's menu available. $–$$

Where to Stay

Breaks Interstate Park Campground, (276) 865-4413 or (800) 982-5122. Open daily Apr through Oct. There are 122 tent, camper, and RV sites. Electrical hookups, water, and sewer. No reservations taken. $

The Country Inn Motel, 627 Giles Ave., Big Stone Gap; (276) 523-0374. The motel has forty-two rooms. $$$–$$$$

Natural Tunnel State Park, (800) 933-PARK. Twenty-three campsites are available

on a drop-in or reservation basis. Electric and water hookups are available. $

Rhododendron Lodge, Breaks Interstate Park, Highway 80; (276) 865-4413 or (800) 982-5122; www.breakspark.com. Open from Apr 1 to the Sun before Christmas. This eighty-two-room lodge overlooks Breaks Canyon. Four housekeeping cottages are also available and can be rented by the week or month. $$–$$$

For More Information

Heart of Appalachia Tourism Authority, P.O. Box 207, Cloverleaf Square, Suite G3, Big Stone Gap, VA 24219; (888) SWVA–FUN, (276) 523-2005; www.heartofappalachia.com.

Blue Ridge Highlands Regional Information and Visitor Center, 975 Tazewell St., Wytheville, VA 24382; (800) 446-9670; www.virginiablueridge.org.

Tazewell County and Bland County

Pocahontas Exhibition Mine and Museum (ages 5 and up)
At the junction of County Roads 644 and 759 in Pocahontas; (276) 945-2134; http://wvweb .com/www/pocahontas_mine. Open daily from Apr through Oct. Joint tickets for the mine and the museum available at a discount at either entrance. $.

The area's coal-mining history is brought to life through exhibits of mining equipment and demonstrations of coal cutting, blasting, and loading. It's cool inside—a constant 52 degrees—so bring a jacket.

Wolf Creek Indian Village & Museum (ages 3 to 9)
US 52, off I-77, exit 58, Bastian; (276) 688-3438; www.indianvillage.org. Open daily, but hours vary in the winter, depending on the weather. $.

This one-hundred-acre site, part of an archaeological dig, was once a Shawnee and Chero-kee hunting ground. The re-created Native American village is based on the excavations of the 600-year-old site. Some of the recovered tools and arrowheads are on display. The life of European settlers is portrayed through 19th-century weapons, horse-drawn equip-ment, tools, furniture, and the eight log and two stone buildings on the premises. Hands-on activities include learning basket weaving, cordage (making rope), and working with clay. Although Wolf Creek is not as large as some of the better-known living-history muse-ums, younger children may find the size just right for them. Kids will enjoy the opportunity to interact with the museum interpreters to learn about how to tan hides, make pottery, and work with flint.

Llama Trekking: Virginia Highland Llamas
Route 42 East, Bland; (540) 688-4464. The treks operate from Apr through Nov and stop during deer-hunting seasons. $$–$$$.

In Bland families can find a way to hike the southwest Virginia mountains with ease. You do the walking while a beast of burden (not your spouse) carries your gear. Llama trek-king with Virginia Highland Llamas takes the work out of walking. On these scenic day trips, you lead your llama for 3 miles to the top of Big Walker Mountain. Both of you take a break for lunch and enjoy the expansive views. The llama grazes while you munch a Southern picnic of fried chicken, potato salad, lemonade, and homemade pecan tarts. For those who prefer, there's also a shorter, less strenuous trek to a beautiful spring called Walker Creek.

The mountain is sweetest in spring when wildflowers dot your path, and in fall, when the hills turn russet and yellow.

Historic Crab Orchard Museum and Pioneer Park (ages 5 and up)

Crab Orchard Road at US 19 and 460, Tazewell; (276) 988-6755; www.craborchardmuseum .com. Open Memorial Day through Labor Day, Mon through Fri, except major holidays; Sat except Christmas through Mar. Family rates.

This historical museum and five-acre pioneer settlement is the region's cultural museum. It tells the story of the area's earliest Native American inhabitants and those who came after them, through the periods of the Revolutionary and Civil Wars. Costumed interpreters interact with visitors and provide information about the pioneer lifestyle. Included among the exhibits in the museum are rare maps from the colonial period, the 400-million-year-old remains of a woolly mammoth, and beadwork and weapons of the Native Americans who first settled the region. Special living-history events are held in the spring and on Appalachian Independence Day (July 4). Pioneer Park has fifteen original buildings dating back to 1802.

Bicycling

The Heart of Appalachia Bike Route and Scenic Drive winds for 128 miles through Tazewell, Russell, and Wise Counties in southwest Virginia. Pedal past creeks, along riverbeds, and in mountain foothills.

Where to Eat/Where to Stay

Cuz's Restaurant and Cabins, Highway 460, 30 miles south of Bluefield; (276) 964-9014. The restaurant is open Mar through Dec, Wed through Sat. Cuz's is a country combination of restaurant and lodge. Cuz's Uptown Barbecue, the restaurant, serves ample portions of steak and fish. On weekends bluegrass bands and country singers entertain. The cabins are simple; kids like the tepees in which they can camp. The property has an outdoor pool and tennis courts. $$–$$$.

The Laurel Inn Bed and Breakfast, 386–7 West Water St. in Pocahontas, located within walking distance of the coal mine; (276) 945-2787. The Laurel Inn Bed and Breakfast consists of two adjacent brick colonial buildings. Guests have the use of a communal living room and kitchen as well as a pool. A continental breakfast is served. $$–$$$.

For More Information

Blue Ridge Highlands Regional Information and Visitor Center, 975 Tazewell St., Wytheville, VA 24382; (800) 446-9670; www.virginiablueridge.org.

Wytheville–Wythe–Bland Chamber of Commerce, 150 East Monroe St., Wytheville, VA 24382; (276) 223-3365 or (877) 347-8307; www.chamber.wytheville.com.

Wytheville

As you drive south on I-77, the next major stop is Wytheville (pronounced *With*-ville), a town of 8,000 and a popular vacation hub nestled between the Blue Ridge and Allegheny

The Big **Pencil**

While in Wytheville, don't miss the Big Pencil above Main Street's Wytheville Office Supply. The late owner, John Campbell Findlay, had this 30-footlong, metal advertisement made more than fifty years ago, and it still draws customers to the store.

Mountains. Wytheville was a prime Union target during the Civil War because it possessed both valuable lead mines and the only salt mine in the South. Here's an interesting tale to tell your kids, one especially appreciated by daughters. A Union attempt to take the town was thwarted by Molly Tynes, who rode 40 miles over the mountains to inform the home guard to come to the town's defense. If you've been in the woods for any extended time, you may appreciate Wytheville's shopping, which includes outlet and antiques malls.

New River Trail State Park and Shot Tower Historical Park

At Jackson's Ferry, 6 miles east of Wytheville on I-81, then 7 miles south on Highway 52; or take the Poplar Camp exit off I-77 South. Foster Falls Visitor Center (276-236-8889) and Cliffview Visitor Center (276-699-6778) serve these parks; www.dcr.virginia.gov/state_parks/new.shtml. Admission to Shot Tower.

New River Trail State Park is a 57-mile greenway that follows an abandoned rail bed. Paralleling the New River for 39 miles, the trail slopes gently, making it ideal for young children. There are bicycle paths (bikes can be rented), trails for horseback riding (no horse rentals), and canoes for rent. Tubing this stretch of the river is also popular.

Shot Tower Historical Park serves as one of the entrances to New River Trail Park. This is something different. Built in 1807, the tower, which looks like a fortress, sits on a bluff over the New River, 75 feet above the ground, with a water tank sitting 75 feet below ground. The tower was used to make ammunition. First the lead was brought to the top room, where it was melted, then poured through sieves with various size openings. The lead became round during its 15-foot descent (it was thought necessary to drop it this far to change shape) before hitting the water. The pellets were then sorted by rolling them down an incline, with faulty ones sorted out and remelted. There's a historian on-site to answer questions.

Other entrances to New River Trail are at Galax, Cliffview, Gambetta and Chestnut Yard, Byllesby Dam, Draper, Foster Falls (where the visitor center is located), Pulaski/Xaloy, Fries, and Ivanhoe. The park can also be accessed at Hiwasee, Allisonia, Austinville, and Lone Ash, but there are no developed parking areas at these entrances.

Big Walker Lookout

12 miles north of Wytheville on Highway 52, on the Big Walker Scenic Byway; (276) 228-4401; www.scenicbeauty-va.com. Open June through Oct 31.

Don't miss a visit to this great view of the heart of the Appalachians. On a clear day you can see five states from the 100-foot observation tower at an elevation of 3,405 feet; there's also an observation deck across the street. The kids will like the walk over an old-fashioned wood-and-steel-wire swinging bridge that leads from the souvenir shop and cafe to the observation tower.

Where to Eat

Log House Restaurant, 520 East Main St.; (276) 228-4139. Open daily for lunch and dinner. Kids like the log house's pioneerlike exterior, interior with fireplaces, and back-yard with rabbits to pet. The menu features chicken, ham, and other country staples. $$

Skeeter's E. N. Umberger Store, 165 Main St.; (276) 228-2611. Breakfast, lunch, and dinner daily. This old-fashioned eatery offers counter food complete with red swivel stools and old signs. The locals swear by the cheese hot dogs and chili. $

Waffle House, 1975 East Main St.; (276) 228-7767. Breakfast, lunch, and dinner in a casual setting. $

Where to Stay

Best Western Wytheville Inn, 355 Nye Rd., I-77 North, exit 41; (276) 228-7300 or (800) 224-9172. This lodging has a pool, ninety-nine rooms, and a restaurant. $$$–$$$$

Comfort Inn, 315 Holsten Rd.; (276) 228-4488 or (800) 228-5150. Outdoor pool and a restaurant. $$$–$$$$

Hampton Inn Wytheville, 1090 Pepper's Ferry Rd.; (276) 228-6090 or (800) 426-7866. Outdoor pool, restaurant, and complimentary breakfast. $$$–$$$$

Quality Inn and Suites, 2015 East Main St., Wytheville; (276) 228-4241 or (800) 228-5151; www.qualityinn.com. Rates include continental breakfast. The property has an indoor pool. $$$–$$$$

For More Information

Wytheville Convention and Visitors Bureau, 150 East Monroe St., Wytheville, VA 24382; (276) 223-3355 or (877) 347-8307; www.visitwytheville.com.

Index